Final Resting Place

THE LIVES
AND DEATHS OF
FAMOUS ST. LOUISANS

BY KEVIN AMSLER

Printed in the United States of America.

First Edition.
ISBN 0-9631448-8-X
Library of Congress number: pending

Other books on St. Louis history by Virginia Publishing Company:

The Days and Nights of the Central West End
St. Louis Lost
The Streets of St. Louis
Lost Caves of St. Louis

Virginia Publishing Co.
4814 Washington Blvd., Ste. 120
St. Louis, MO 63108
(314) 367-6612

TABLE OF CONTENTS

Dedicated to
Jane Catherine Andres

She told me near the end,
"Don't cry when I'm gone."

That was an impossible request.

AUTHOR'S NOTE

Thomas Jefferson once called death, "that great adventure, untried by the living, unreported by the dead." And indeed, Jefferson and other famous people who have gone before us, have always been intriguing. We grew up reading about their deeds and accomplishments in school and in the newspapers. However, as Jefferson himself noted, what we know of these people is incomplete. We do not always know what living aspirations or thoughts they took with them to the grave. St. Louis' rich biographic history, as captured in the cemeteries and burial grounds, offers us a glimpse into their lives. In examining this history, this book celebrates the lives of many well-known St. Louisans.

I made several visits to Bellefontaine, Calvary, and the other burial grounds in preparation of this book. Visiting these places can be both a moving and humbling experience. A walk through these hallowed grounds also reveals some of the unique monumental architecture of the time. The monuments themselves evoke memories of St. Louisans' achievements — real people who were giants in their day. For some, there is immediate name recognition; streets, schools and even towns have been named after them. Others have statues erected in their honor. It is thrilling to discover a specific grave, whether it's a simple stone pressed flat to the ground or a grand mausoleum honoring the entombed. Each marker affords an opportunity to pause and consider a person and the life they led.

Reading the names and dates on the various markers gives visitors a sense of a person's era. Were they a witness to the Civil War or did they die before it? Could they have visited the St. Louis World's Fair? It is easy to imagine what it may have been like to see them or talk to them, to listen to William Clark describe the western expedition with Meriwether Lewis, to see Dred Scott's trial at the Old Courthouse as he sued for his freedom from bondage, or even to ask George Sisler what it was like to play against legends Ty Cobb and Babe Ruth.

Determining which individuals were to be included in this book was an interesting and difficult task. The prominent citizens that have called St. Louis home are innumerable. The challenge lay in deciding who among them was to be included. The original list was changed and updated many times. The individuals profiled must have been either born in St. Louis or are buried here, preferably both. Some individuals who have had connections to St. Louis, such as Charles Lindbergh, do not fit the criteria and for that reason are not profiled in the book.

For me, this book was a therapeutic exercise. When I first began writing, my mother had been ill with cancer for some time. Several operations helped her beat the odds but during the summer of 1996, the cancer once again enforced its will. She passed away in October, two days after I first met the publisher to discuss this book. If she were here today, she would be more excited about the book than perhaps even I.

I have received a great deal of help from many people in preparing this book. Cemetery personnel at Bellefontaine, Calvary, Resurrection, St. Peter's, St. Lucas, Sunset Memorial Park, Bellerive Heritage Gardens, and Oak Grove were helpful in locating graves. The library staffs at the University of Missouri-St. Louis, Webster University, the Missouri Historical Society, and the St. Louis County Libraries aided in the research for reference materials. Though most were nameless faces, I want to collectively thank them for their assistance. Thanks also goes to Jeffrey Fister and the staff at Virginia Publishing. Without Jeffrey's interest in the subject matter for this book, it would have never been possible; his commitment to the material was strong throughout.

I want to thank my brother Jerry and his wife Janice for their constant support and help in proofreading the manuscript and giving comments and criticisms. And to little Jerry, my one-year-old nephew, who has made the time away from the book enjoyable.

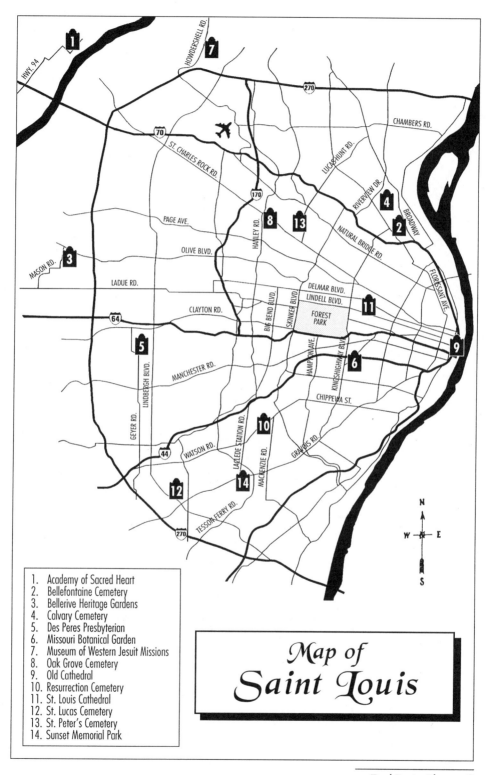

1. Academy of Sacred Heart
2. Bellefontaine Cemetery
3. Bellerive Heritage Gardens
4. Calvary Cemetery
5. Des Peres Presbyterian
6. Missouri Botanical Garden
7. Museum of Western Jesuit Missions
8. Oak Grove Cemetery
9. Old Cathedral
10. Resurrection Cemetery
11. St. Louis Cathedral
12. St. Lucas Cemetery
13. St. Peter's Cemetery
14. Sunset Memorial Park

Map of
Saint Louis

Bellefontaine Cemetery

Bellefontaine Cemetery

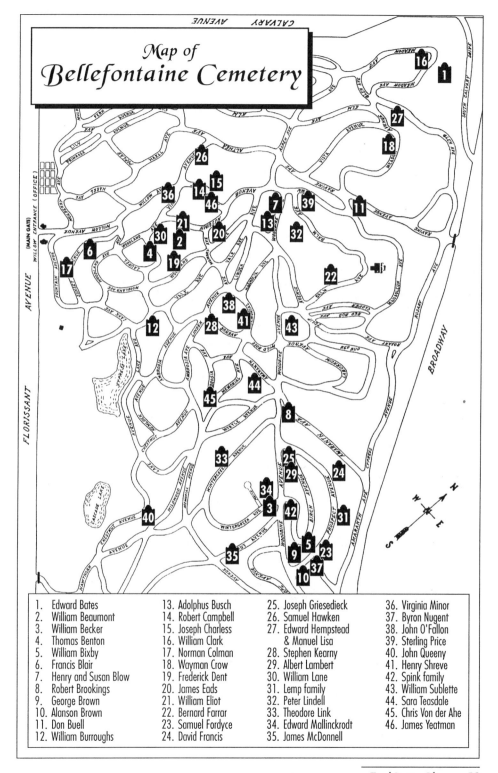

Map of
Bellefontaine Cemetery

1. Edward Bates	13. Adolphus Busch	25. Joseph Griesedieck	36. Virginia Minor
2. William Beaumont	14. Robert Campbell	26. Samuel Hawken	37. Byron Nugent
3. William Becker	15. Joseph Charless	27. Edward Hempstead	38. John O'Fallon
4. Thomas Benton	16. William Clark	& Manuel Lisa	39. Sterling Price
5. William Bixby	17. Norman Colman	28. Stephen Kearny	40. John Queeny
6. Francis Blair	18. Wayman Crow	29. Albert Lambert	41. Henry Shreve
7. Henry and Susan Blow	19. Frederick Dent	30. William Lane	42. Spink family
8. Robert Brookings	20. James Eads	31. Lemp family	43. William Sublette
9. George Brown	21. William Eliot	32. Peter Lindell	44. Sara Teasdale
10. Alanson Brown	22. Bernard Farrar	33. Theodore Link	45. Chris Von der Ahe
11. Don Buell	23. Samuel Fordyce	34. Edward Mallinckrodt	46. James Yeatman
12. William Burroughs	24. David Francis	35. James McDonnell	

On March 7, 1849, a group organized by William McPherson, a banker, and John Darby, a lawyer and Mayor of St. Louis, incorporated a new burial ground under the name "Rural Cemetery Association." That spring, the State of Missouri issued a charter to the group for the 138 acres of land on Bellefontaine Road and a short time later, the cemetery's name was changed from "Rural" to "Bellefontaine." Almerin Hotchkiss, a well-known landscape architect and the superintendent of Greenwood Cemetery in Brooklyn, was hired to develop the new grounds. He was superintendent of the cemetery for 46 years.

In July of that year, the *Missouri Republican* commented:

> We look forward with confidence to the day, not distant, when the people of St. Louis will point to this cemetery with the same satisfaction that Boston does to Mount Auburn.

In 1849, people did turn to Bellefontaine but it was not with tremendous satisfaction for the worst cholera epidemic in St. Louis history had hit the city in June. At the height of this epidemic there were more than thirty funerals each day. When a law went into effect requiring burial grounds to be located outside the city limits for reasons of public health, Bellefontaine began to receive interments from Christ Church Cemetery and other cemeteries.

Its original 138 acres have been expanded to over 330 acres.

Today, Bellefontaine Cemetery is one of St. Louis' most renowned cemeteries. It has become the final resting place of governors, mayors, war heroes, and business leaders. Fourteen miles of road wind through the cemetery's beautiful environs, over 100 varieties of trees mark the landscape. The rolling hills contain over 82,400 gravesites.

Bellefontaine Cemetery is located in North St. Louis near the Broadway exit of I-70. The main entrance is located at 4947 West Florissant Avenue. The cemetery is open 8:00 a.m. to 5:00 p.m. daily, including Sundays and holidays. Office hours are Monday-Friday 8:00 a.m. to 4:30 p.m., weekends and holidays by appointment only. Information regarding the cemetery is provided at the office.

WILLIAM CLARK

(August 1, 1770 - September 1, 1838)

William Clark's grave.

On September 23, 1806, Meriwether Lewis and William Clark returned to St. Louis from their two-year expedition across the Upper Louisiana Territory to the Pacific coast and staked their place in American history. Their detailed journals and maps were the first documented materials on the untamed west.

William Clark was a native of Caroline County, Virginia. He grew up on a large estate on the eastern slopes of the Alleghenies with nine brothers and sisters. Five of his brothers fought in the Revolutionary War; his older brother, George Rogers Clark, became a hero and was awarded a gold medal by General George Washington.

When William was thirteen, his family moved to Kentucky and settled in the wilderness south of Louisville. Following his brother's lead, he signed on with the army in 1789 and was involved in military campaigns to thwart the attacks of Native Americans. It was during this time that Clark became good friends with a man who would one day help to make him famous, Meriwether Lewis.

In 1803, when Thomas Jefferson chose Lewis, his private secretary, to lead an exploration of the far western territories, Lewis selected his own friend William to share in the leadership of the expedition. On May 14, 1804, Lewis and Clark, and 45 men started their journey. The 8,000 mile trip lasted two years, four months, and nine days. The group explored the uncharted wilderness in a journey which took them up the Missouri River, across the Continental Divide and down the Columbia River to the sea. They kept detailed journals on the rivers, mountain ranges, animals, plants, and most importantly the western Native Americans. These journals later were published in 1814.

When Lewis and Clark officially presented their findings to Thomas Jefferson, they each received $1,228 and sixteen hundred acres of land. They were also appointed to government positions; Lewis became the Governor of the Louisiana Territory and Clark was named Superintendent of Indian Affairs and brigadier general of militia for the Louisiana Territory. Clark established his headquarters in St. Louis.

In October 1809, Meriwether Lewis was enroute to Washington D.C. along the Natchez Trace in Tennessee. In the early morning hours of the 11th, he was found shot to death. He was 35. The circumstances of his death, murder or suicide, are still unknown. William Clark was devastated when he received the news of his friend's death. He would never speak of it to anyone.

Clark settled permanently in St. Louis and became one of the city's most accomplished citizens. He accumulated a vast amount of land in Missouri and Kentucky and, due to his position as Superintendent of Indian Affairs, he developed close relationships with the Native Americans, often welcoming them to his home. Clark also was involved in St. Louis' emerging business community and the city's politics. He was a founding member of the St. Louis Missouri Fur Company along with Auguste and Pierre Chouteau, and Manuel Lisa. Clark also served as chairman for the St. Louis Schools board of trustees, whose other members included Thomas Hart Benton, Alexander McNair, and the Chouteaus. In June 1813, President James Madison appointed Clark Governor of the Missouri Territory.

Despite such successes, William had his share of tragedy and upset. Politically, he lost the Missouri gubernatorial election of 1820 to his close friend Alexander McNair. That same year, his wife of 12 years, Julia, died after an illness induced by child birth. Two of their children also died. One year after his wife's death, William married Harriet Radford but their infant son passed away in 1827.

William Clark was staying at the home of his eldest son, Meriwether Lewis Clark, when he died on September 1, 1838. The Monday, September 3 issue of the *Missouri Republican* said of Clark:

> Through a long, eventful and useful life, he has filled the various stations of a citizen and officer with such strict integrity and in so affable and mild a manner, that, at that day of his death, malice nor detraction had not a blot to fix upon the fair scroll which the history of his well-spent life leaves as a rich and inestimable legacy to his children, and the numerous friends who now mourn his death.

Clark was buried with full military honors. His funeral procession on September 3 was the largest in St. Louis history up to that time. Thousands lined the streets leading to the farm of Clark's nephew, Colonel John O'Fallon (now O'Fallon Park) where Clark was buried initially. As the procession approached the cemetery, minute guns were fired. When Bellefontaine Cemetery was opened 11 years later, Clark's body and several other family members were moved to a roadside lot in the northern corner of the cemetery. The impressive granite obelisk and bust of William Clark centered in the lot was dedicated in October 1904 during the World's Fair. When his youngest son Jefferson died in 1900, he left behind $25,000 to construct the monument.

William Clark faces the confluence of the Mississippi and Missouri Rivers where he and Meriwether Lewis set out to discover the west. The inscription beneath the bust reads:

William Clark
Born in Virginia
August 1, 1770
Entered into Life Eternal
September 1, 1838
Soldier, Explorer,
Statesman and Patriot
His Life is Written
in the History of His Country

JOSEPH CHARLESS

(July 16, 1772 - July 28, 1834)

Joseph Charless was one of early St. Louis' most enterprising businessmen. During his lifetime, he would prosper as the editor and publisher of his own newspaper, a bookseller, a pharmacy owner, and a hosteler. Born with the surname Charles, Joseph grew up in Westmeath, Ireland on a large, family farm. In 1794, he moved to Dublin and became a printer. One year later, he left for America to establish his own bookstore and printing press in Lewistown, Pennsylvania. He realized his true dream to publish a newspaper just

Joseph Charless.

months after arriving in the States. The first issue was called the *Mifflin Gazette*. It was during this time that Joseph changed the spelling of his last name by adding an "s" in the hopes that this unique spelling might preserve the Irish pronunciation and differentiate him from the countless other "Charles" in America.

In 1798, Joseph moved to Philadelphia and there he married a widow, Sarah Jordan McCloud. This was Joseph's second marriage and the couple would have five children, three sons and two daughters of their own. While in Philadelphia, Joseph worked on *The Aurora*, an influential newspaper run by Benjamin Franklin Bache.

In 1808, Meriwether Lewis, by then the Territorial Governor of Missouri, contacted Charless with an offer to come west and start a paper in a news-starved St. Louis. Joseph agreed and arrived in St. Louis by July. Not wasting any time, he edited and published the first issue of the *Missouri Gazette* on July 12. It was the first newspaper printed west of the Mississippi.

For a short time, Joseph explored another business opportunity outside of publishing. In 1812, he and another gentleman, Doctor Bernard Farrar, opened an apothecary shop or pharmacy. They sold a variety of medicines and drugs but in less than a year the two men discontinued the partnership to run their own shops. Before the year was out, Joseph quit the pharmaceutical business entirely.

Real estate was his next venture. Joseph amassed a large amount of property and, in 1819, he built a two-story brick house on his property just southwest of the city on Fifth and Main. The area was known later as "The Hill."

During his years in St. Louis, Joseph became good friends with the Lucases, a prominent family in the city. When Charles Lucas was killed by senator-to-be Colonel Thomas Hart Benton in their famous duel on Bloody Island, Joseph vented his bitter feelings about Benton in his paper. He continued to attack Benton during the next year. In 1818, Benton became the editor of the *St. Louis Enquirer*, an opposing newspaper. The two men traded words until Benton left St. Louis to serve in the U.S. Senate.

Joseph eventually sold the paper in 1820 and retired from

publishing, sending his regards to the people of St. Louis in his final issue:

> Fellow Citizens and Patrons, my interests, although I leave this establishment, is still connected with yours. For 12 years I have lived among you. My family has been educated and brought up among you. My little property is in this state. Here are the tombs of my children, and here I expect to rest myself, when the cares and vexations of life are over. You must therefore believe me, when I say that nothing is, nothing can be so dear to me as your prosperity, and your welfare.

Joseph's first-born son, Edward, took over the newspaper in 1822. He renamed it the *Missouri Republican* and ran it successfully for 15 years.

Joseph was a strong presence in St. Louis. He served as president of the board of alderman in 1825 and 1826 and involved himself in several business pursuits including a revival of the pharmaceutical business he had once enjoyed. The company was called "Jos. Charless & Son" after his son Joseph joined him. But in November 1859, Joseph Jr. was murdered on the streets of St. Louis by a Joseph Thornton against whom young Charless had testified in court. He was married to Charlotte Blow, daughter of Peter Blow, brother of Henry Blow. His headstone at Bellefontaine reads, "Here Rest Beloved Till Christ Shall Bid Thee Rise."

In one of his final ventures, Joseph Charless Sr. opened a boardinghouse on one of his properties. His charge for one night's lodging was 25 cents, which he later reduced to 12 1/2 cents.

Joseph Charless died in his home on July 28, 1834; he was 62 years old. He was praised for his kind Irish manner and was dubbed the Father of St. Louis journalism. He was buried at Bellefontaine Cemetery near his son, Joseph Jr. The weather-beaten, unreadable monument stands across Lawn Avenue.

Members of the Blow family also are buried in the Charless lot. They include Peter Blow, the original owner of Dred Scott and his son, Taylor, who gave Scott his freedom in 1857.

MANUEL LISA

(September 8, 1772 - August 12, 1820)

Fur trader and explorer Manuel Lisa was born in New Orleans. Upon his arrival in St. Louis, Lisa immediately became active in the city's booming fur trade. At the time, the Chouteau family dominated the fur market and Lisa was determined to break their monopoly. Serving as an explorer and a fighter, he led expeditions into Native American territory and, in 1807, he established a trading post at the Bighorn River in Montana. One year later, Lisa built a fort at the

Manuel Lisa.

post. It was the first American fort located in the upper Missouri River region. He also built Fort Lisa in what is now Omaha, Nebraska. His spirit and enthusiasm brought him to the attention of the Chouteaus, who along with William Clark and others, formed the Missouri Fur Company in 1808.

In September of that same year, Lisa and George Drouillard, his employee and a member of the Lewis and Clark Expedition, were on trial for the murder of Antoine Bissonette. In May 1807 during a fur trading expedition, Bissonette deserted after signing a contract to work for Lisa. Bissonette was captured by Drouillard but he sustained a bullet wound during his flight. Bissonette was placed in a canoe and sent back to St. Charles for medical treatment but died before his arrival. Edward Hempstead served as Lisa's attorney and argued the case to Judge John B.C. Lucas. Bissonette's desertion and broken contract guaranteed Lisa and Drouillard a not-guilty verdict.

Lisa married three times. His first wife, Mitain, an Omaha Native American, bore him two children, Rosalie and Christopher. His second wife, Polly, had three children, all of whom died before adulthood. In 1818, six months after Polly died, he married Mary Hempstead Keeney, widowed sister of his lawyer, Edward

Hempstead. William Clark and Pierre Chouteau were among his wedding guests.

Two short years later, Lisa returned to St. Louis from another fruitful expedition in ill health. Feeling weak and fatigued, he went to a sulphur springs near St. Louis in hopes that the waters would ease his pain. Bernard Farrar attended to Lisa day and night but could do nothing. On August 12 of 1820, Lisa passed away. Lisa dominated the fur trading industry for twenty years and was among the group that established the Bank of St. Louis in 1813. An active St. Louisan, his death was a notable loss for the whole city.

Lisa was buried in the churchyard at Walnut and Second streets but his grave was later moved to the Hempstead Farm near the grave of his confidant, Edward Hempstead. Lisa's obelisk was erected by his wife Mary in the Hempstead family lot. The weather has taken its toll on the stone and granite marker.

EDWARD HEMPSTEAD

(June 3, 1780 - August 10, 1817)

Edward Hempstead developed one of the most successful law practices in St. Louis and became the first delegate to Congress from the Missouri Territory. In early August 1817, he was returning to St. Louis from St. Charles on horseback when he was thrown from his horse and injured his head. Though he was dazed, Edward thought the injury minor and continued his journey back to St. Louis. On the morning of August 8, he was back in court arguing a case for a client. During the proceedings he suffered a brain hemorrhage and collapsed to the floor. Upon hearing of Edward's collapse, Stephen Hempstead, a Presbyterian minister, went to his son. Later that day he wrote in his diary, "Went into St. Louis this afternoon and found my son Edward in a fit of apoplexy and not able to speak. Every medical aid was used to restore his system again, but to no purpose. He...expired in the bloom of life, at the age of thirty-seven years and three months."

Edward Hempstead was a native of New London, Connecticut. His father, Stephen, fought for the colonies in the Battle of Lexington and throughout the Revolutionary War. Edward was educated by prominent Connecticut lawyers. In 1801, he became a licensed lawyer and spent the next two years in Newport, Rhode Island practicing law before coming west.

Edward arrived in St. Louis a few months after the United States officially took possession of the Louisiana Territory. He was accompanied by William Henry Harrison, the Governor of the Indiana Territory and future ninth President of the United States.

Edward spent a year in St. Charles practicing law before moving to St. Louis in the fall of 1805. Over the next several years, Hempstead built a reputation as a fair and honest man and a lawyer of high moral standards. Due to the respect he inspired among St. Louisans, he was elected the first delegate to Congress from the Missouri Territory in November 1812. Two years later, he declined reelection and returned to St. Louis. Edward founded the Board of Education and helped St. Louis public schools obtain property and revenue to meet the demands of the city's burgeoning population.

When news of Edward's untimely death spread, citizens were moved; a young man of great promise was lost. Edward Hempstead's obituary appeared in the August 16 issue of the *Missouri Gazette*:

> Died on Sunday night last, after a short illness, Edward Hempstead, Esq., counselor and attorney-at-law, and formerly a delegate from this Territory to Congress. In the dear relation of husband, son, and brother, the deceased is believed to have fully acted up to his duty. The sorrow of his widow and relations offered the most eloquent expression of his worth.

Thomas Hart Benton, a longtime friend of Hempstead, wrote, "The lives of useful and eminent man should be written, not for the dead, but for the living. They should display not a vain panegyric, but a detail of circumstance which would lead the living to the same line of conduct and the same honorable result." One day later, Benton was to fight Charles Lucas in the first of their two duels on Bloody Island.

The funeral and burial were held at his father's farm, now part of Bellefontaine cemetery. The Hempstead lot now lies off of Meadow Avenue in the oldest section of Bellefontaine Cemetery.

THOMAS HART BENTON

(March 14, 1782 - April 10, 1858)

Thomas Hart Benton is one of Missouri's most renowned statesmen. He was a soldier, lawyer, editor, and politician; he excelled in each role with the drive of a man possessed. His political career spanned from Thomas Jefferson to Abraham Lincoln and his powerful influence matched that of his Senate rivals, Daniel Webster, John C. Calhoun and Henry Clay. Among his friends were Presidents Van Buren, Polk, and Buchanan. Benton's very physical presence underlined his stature. He was a strong-featured, muscular man whose moods were volatile.

Benton was born in the hills of North Carolina near Hillsborough in March, 1782. Four days later, his future political rival John Calhoun was born. In 1798, Benton left home to attend the University of North Carolina at Chapel Hill but in less than a year he was expelled from the univer-

Thomas Hart Benton.

sity for petty theft. The family later moved to Tennessee where he was admitted to the bar in 1806. Six years later, Benton served as a colonel of volunteers under General Andrew Jackson in the War of 1812.

Benton's grave.

During this period, Benton made negative remarks about Andrew Jackson's integrity and judgement. Ironically, Benton's criticism arose from a duel in which his brother, Jesse, was seriously wounded by a loyal friend of Jackson. On September 4, while Thomas and Jesse Benton were in Nashville on business, the dispute exploded into violence. As the story is told, Jackson appeared in Benton's hotel and drew his pistol on Benton in the hallway. Jesse Benton, in turn, fired at Jackson from across the room and his brother was able to fire at the general twice. Jackson hit the floor with a wound in the left arm. Thomas was only grazed by Jackson's shot. Others joined in a vicious fight with guns and daggers. Thomas sustained five knife wounds and his brother likewise was stabbed several times. Jackson, though bleeding profusely, was saved by the quick response of his physicians.

After the war, in 1815, Benton moved to St. Louis, still a small town with a population just over two thousand people. Benton started his law practice and later was editor of the *Missouri Enquirer* which competed directly with Joseph Charless' *Missouri Gazette*.

One of Thomas's earliest friends in St. Louis, Edward Hempstead, played an important role in shaping Benton's interest in politics. Benton's first public position was as a member of the Board of Trustees for Schools. He was appointed by Governor William Clark; Auguste Chouteau was also on the Board of Trustees for Schools.

The summer of 1817 was a bitter season for Benton. His sister

Mary died at 37, she was the last of his sisters, three others having previously died. Edward Hempstead, Benton's good friend and mentor, died of a head injury a week after he was thrown from his horse. And on August 12, the day after Hempstead's funeral, Benton fought Charles Lucas in their famous duel on Bloody Island.

In 1820, Benton was elected the first Senator from Missouri. The election took place at the famous Missouri Hotel. He beat out Judge John B.C. Lucas, the father of Charles Lucas among other candidates for the position. Three years later, Senator Benton and Senator Andrew Jackson made peace and became friends. During his thirty years in the Senate, Benton opposed the annexation of Texas and was against the rechartering of the Bank of the United States. The latter earned him the nickname "Old Bullion."

In 1824, Thomas spent Christmas Eve in Charlottesville, Virginia with Thomas Jefferson. He was struck by Jefferson's wisdom and in a speech he delivered later to the United States Senate, Benton said "the individual must manage badly who can find himself in the presence of [Jefferson] and retire from it without bringing off some fact or some maxim of eminent utility to the human race."

Benton's final session in Congress was a difficult one. In 1848, his son-in-law, Lieutenant Colonel John Fremont, was found guilty of insubordination and faced court-martial. His chief accuser was General Stephen Watts Kearny. Benton was relentless in his persecution of Kearny. In the end, President Polk upheld the Kearny's verdict but allowed Fremont to return to duty. One month later, Benton's good friend and former president, John Quincy Adams collapsed in the House chamber while watching a debate. Adams died at the Capitol two days later. Benton delivered Adams' eulogy in the Senate.

Thomas retired from the Senate in 1850. At that time, cholera was still a vital threat and in 1852 his son Randolph succumbed to the disease. Thomas and his wife Elizabeth were overcome by the death of their only remaining son; their son McDowell died years earlier. In a speech relating to the reinterment of family members in new Bellefontaine Cemetery, Benton said, "What is my occupation? Ask the undertaker, that good Mr. Lynch, whose face, present on so many mournful occasions, has become pleasant to me. He knew what occupies my thoughts and cares; gathering the bones of the dead—a mother, sister, two sons, a grandchild— planting the cypress over assembled graves, and marking the spot where I and those who are dear to me are soon to be laid." A short two years later in September 1854, Elizabeth died suddenly in Washington D.C., while Benton was in St. Louis. The senator was disconsolate.

In retirement, Thomas stayed in Washington D.C. and wrote his autobiography entitled <u>Thirty Years' View.</u> He also wrote an extensive examination of the Dred Scott case. He ran for Governor of Missouri in 1856 but lost the election. One year later, in May 1857, he was injured in a railroad accident and was confined to home for three weeks. That September, he took ill while working on the Scott manuscript. His physician diagnosed cancer but within two months he improved enough to resume working.

The illness returned in March 1858 and by April his condition declined quickly. Thomas was nearly incapable of any movement and could only speak at a whisper. He told his son-in-law John Fremont of his remorse over the death of Charles Lucas in 1817 and asked Senator Sam Houston upon his visit that no notice of his death be recognized in Congress. When President James Buchanan visited him, Benton spoke only three words, "Preserve the Union!"

Later that evening Thomas told his daughters, "I am comfortable and content." They were his last words. Thomas Hart Benton died at 7:30 the next morning. Two days later, McDowell Jones, one of Thomas' favorite grandsons, also died in the house.

The Monday, April 12, funeral was conducted in his Washington D.C. home. Benton rested in a black coffin in the parlor. A smaller casket with his grandson McDowell rested beside him. President Buchanan, his cabinet, foreign ministers, and members of congress attended the ceremony. Afterwards, the coffins were taken to the train station in a driving rain.

The train arrived on the east side of the Mississippi River on April 14. The coffins were taken by ferry across to St. Louis. (Eads

Bridge, the first to cross the river, wouldn't be built for another 16 years.) A hearse with two black horses took the bodies to Joshua Brant's home at Fourth and Washington; Brant was married to Benton's niece Sarah. The next morning, Benton's body was taken to the Mercantile Library Hall at Locust and Fifth streets where he lay in state. Thousands paid their respect to the senator.

Homes and buildings around the city were draped in black and flags were at half-mast the day of the funeral. On Friday afternoon, Benton's body was carried from the Mercantile Library to the Second Presbyterian Church at Walnut and Fifth. McDowell's coffin was brought to the church from Joshua Brant's home. A large crowd gathered outside the church. When the service ended at 2:30 p.m., the procession marched toward Bellefontaine. Family, friends, military personnel, members of the bar, and city dignitaries made up a two-mile cortege. An estimated 40,000 people clogged the sidewalks, windows, and rooftops to watch the procession.

A short prayer service was held at the gravesite. Thomas Hart Benton was then placed into the earth next to his wife Elizabeth: he was 76 years old. His red granite obelisk recognizes his service to the State of Missouri. A public school, a park, and three streets in St. Louis are named in his honor.

HENRY MILLER SHREVE

(October 21, 1785 - March 6, 1851)

Many historians have called Henry Miller Shreve the "Master of the Mississippi," others refer to him as the "Father of the Mississippi Steamboat." Shreve was a native of Burlington County, New Jersey and grew up in Fayette County, Pennsylvania. From an early age, he loved the river. Its rippling waters offered the most natural, rapid form of transport. Henry began his career on the river working on keelboats in the Ohio and Mississippi valley. By his mid-twenties, he was captaining his own vessel and transporting goods between New Orleans and various other Midwestern cities along the river.

In 1807, Shreve made his first trip to St. Louis and landed his boat at the foot of Market Street. Shreve unloaded his goods at a warehouse operated by Auguste Chouteau, the city's most important business and civic leader. He was impressed by Chouteau, who was well-known throughout the Midwestern territories. By the time Shreve set off he knew he would return to St. Louis and, for the next three years, he operated a St. Louis-to-Pittsburgh fur trading business.

During the War of 1812, he carried military supplies in support of Andrew Jackson's forces. His steamship *Washington* revolutionized transportation on inland rivers. Though many predicted the new steamship would fail, its shallow hull and deck-mounted engine allowed for easier navigation. Within a few years, he had a fleet of steamships. In 1838, Shreve also patented the snagboat, a boat used to clear fallen trees and other debris that often clogged the rivers.

Shreve's success on the river led to his 1827 appointment by President John Quincy Adams to Superintendent of Western River Improvements. He held that position for 14 years through both the Jackson and Van Buren administrations. His biggest accomplishment during this period was the removal driftwood that blocked 160 miles of the Red River in Louisiana.

In 1835, Henry helped establish a port in Louisiana and four years later, the town adopted the name Shreveport. The next year, he purchased 300 acres of land four miles

Shreve's grave.

northwest of St. Louis, between what is now Euclid and Taylor avenues near Bellefontaine Cemetery. He retired there in his new home, Gallatin Place. He spent his time supervising his farm and he often returned the riverfront to visit old acquaintances.

In 1844, a great flood hit the area and the Mississippi River widened to six miles in some places. Steamboat traffic slowed to a crawl, much of the riverfront was underwater, and businesses that counted on the river suffered badly. Warehouses were flooded; merchandise was ruined. Shreve personally felt the effects of the flood as well as much of his farmland at Gallatin Place was flooded and he could not plant the spring crop.

During this time, Henry's wife Mary became ill and died February 25, at the age of 54. And though Henry initially was devastated by the loss, a new housekeeper, by the name of Lydia Rodgers, brought a youthful vigor into the household and lifted the spirits of Shreve. The two were married within a year; she was 30 years his junior. They had a daughter, Mary, named after his first wife.

With a new found purpose in life, Captain Shreve became more involved in civic leadership with his friend John O'Fallon. He was the leading authority on the steamship business and the river and his expertise was often called on to settle problems. He later took part in the expansion of the railroads into Missouri. In 1847, St. Louis became the first city west of the Mississippi to have a direct connection to the eastern cities via the telegraph. In the ceremony to open the telegraph service Shreve was chosen to send the first message, a greeting from St. Louisans to President James Polk in Washington D.C.

Two years later, the city's morale was greatly undermined by the disasters of 1849. Flooding hurt businesses on the riverfront and the Great Fire destroyed warehouses in the central business district, including those in which Shreve had a financial interest.

Henry's granddaughter, Virginia, died of cholera on the same day the "Great Fire" began. That day also marked the beginning of the decline in Shreve's physical and mental health. He had his second and last child with Lydia later that year who brought him one of the final joys in his life. They named her Florence. Another wave of cholera hit St. Louis in 1850 and took two more of Shreve's grandchildren. The final blow came in January with the death of his daughter Florence. By March, weakened by his life's hardships, he was ready to die.

From his home he could hear the faint sound of the steamboat whistles on the river. He is said to have remarked, "When it reaches you from somewhere in the distance, a steamboat whistle is the sweetest music in the world."

Henry Shreve died peacefully on March 6, 1851 and was buried the same day. The *Missouri Republican* paid tribute to him the next day:

> He was for nearly forty years closely identified with the commerce of the West, either in flat-boat or steamboat navigation. His name has become historically connected with western river navigation, and will be cherished by his numerous friends throughout this valley.

Shreve was buried at Bellefontaine Cemetery quite near his Gallatin Place estate. His first wife, Mary, was reinterred on his left. Lydia, who outlived him by 41 years, is buried on his right. Also beside him is a small monument inscribed, "Our Little Florie." The monument of his friend, John O'Fallon, towers behind him. His monument faces the river.

WILLIAM BEAUMONT

(November 21, 1785 - April 25, 1853)

In 1822, Doctor William Beaumont was a military physician stationed at Fort Mackinac, Michigan. While stationed there, he was called in to treat a French Canadian by the name of Alexis St. Martin who accidently had been shot in the stomach at a close range. St. Martin eventually recovered from his wound but was left with a permanent hole in his stomach. For the next three years, Dr. Beaumont cared for St. Martin and in the process he performed some of the first comprehensive studies on the digestive system.

William Beaumont was born at the turn of the 18th century in Lebanon, Connecticut. In 1807, William left Lebanon to join his older brother Samuel who had opened a dry goods store in Champlain, New York. There, Beaumont worked as a schoolteacher and put in hours at his brother's store. When he decided that medicine was his true calling, William stopped teaching and began studying under the direction of Dr. Benjamin Moore.

After the United States declared war on Great Britain in 1812, Beaumont enlisted in the army and was assigned to the Sixth Infantry Regiment as a medical officer. One year later, he received word that his brother, Samuel had died suddenly of pleurisy. To overcome his loss, William buried himself in his studies and experiments on digestion while serving at various forts after the war. Eventually, William married Deborah Platt in August 1821 and had two daughters and two sons.

William's book, <u>Experiments and Observations on the Gastric Juice and the Physiology of Digestion</u>, was published in 1833. The book detailed his study of the digestive system on his patient, Alexis St. Martin. His study established that food was digested by stomach fluids. Beaumont's work was praised by doctors around the country and William became the leading expert on digestion.

Beaumont's grave.

Doctor Beaumont was posted to St. Louis in July of 1834. He arrived at Jefferson Barracks to take over as surgeon and medical officer. Beaumont was impressed by the barracks' hospital and considered it one of the best on the frontier. Two years later, William was notified by Reverend William Greenleaf Eliot, grandfather of poet T.S. Eliot, that he had been elected chairman of surgery for the new medical school at St. Louis University. The two men became close friends.

In 1837, the Beaumont family moved to a new home in a building owned by the explorer William Clark. They lived in the second floor apartments and shared meals with the Clarks until William Clark and his family moved in early 1838. William's book had gained him fame throughout St. Louis and he associated with other prominent St. Louisans. The Beaumonts often entertained friends including a young army lieutenant, Robert E. Lee, who had been sent to St. Louis to improve the navigation of the Mississippi River by removing obstructive sand bars, such as Bloody Island.

During this period, William gradually was becoming deaf and he resigned from the army to run his private practice in St. Louis. The family purchased property located on the outskirts of the city and called it Beaumont Place. The street where it stood later was named Beaumont Street. In 1846, William was appointed as a consulting physician in the new St. Louis City Hospital, the first public hospital in the city. That same year he began work on a second edition to Experiments and Observations.

In 1849, Doctor Beaumont treated hundreds of patients who had contracted cholera, many of whom ultimately died. To William's joy, none of his children were affected by the disease. In March 1853, William slipped on a step at a patient's home and hit his head. The doctor was dazed for some time. For a time, Beaumont believed he was recovering until his own doctor noticed a carbuncle, an inflammation of the skin and tissues, at the back of the neck. The carbuncle was painful and Beaumont, who by now was almost completely deaf, came down with a severe fever. He told his concerned family, "Don't say a word about my health or strength; both will hold out as long as I shall need them."

William Greenleaf Eliot spent much of his time with Beaumont before he died; he helped him write his will and gave him communion. Eliot described his friend as a strong, faithful and passionate man.

Beaumont High School is named after Doctor William Beaumont.

BERNARD FARRAR

(July 4, 1785 - July 1, 1849)

Bernard Farrar.

Doctor Bernard Farrar was born in Goochland County, Virginia and later settled with his family near Lexington, Kentucky. He began studying medicine at the age of 15 and graduated from medical school at Transylvania University. Farrar's first wife, Sarah Christy, bore him a daughter and two sons, who both died in their infancy. After Sarah's own death in 1817, Bernard married Ann Thruston, the niece of Governor William Clark. Bernard came to St. Louis in 1807 and was the first American physician to practice west of the Mississippi. His medical practice was listed in the May 24, 1809 issue of the *Missouri Gazette*:

> Dr. Farrar will practice medicine and surgery in St. Louis and its vicinity. He keeps his shop in Mr. Robidoux's house, Second Street.

Farrar's first surgery took place the first year he arrived in St. Louis. A man by the name of Shannon, who had accompanied Lewis and Clark on their expedition, was shot in the knee by hostile Native Americans during another expedition. By the time he was brought back to St. Louis, Shannon's wound was infected and Dr. Farrar successfully amputated the leg. Shannon's future success was not impeded by the loss of his limb and he went on to become a judge in Kentucky.

Bernard entered the U.S. Army during the War of 1812 and served as a surgeon. After his service, he built a large practice and was often called in to assist other physicians with their treatment of extremely ill patients. Farrar was well respected among his peers and fellow citizens for his impeccable professionalism and his personal charm.

The Farrar family lot.

In 1810, Farrar was a participant in a duel on Bloody Island. He challenged a lawyer named James Graham after an insult had been exchanged. Both men were wounded in the duel; Farrar's injury was minor, Graham would ultimately die from his wound. Farrar was back on the island in August 1817 serving as the surgeon for Thomas Hart Benton in his duel against Charles Lucas.

Farrar continued to practice medicine successfully in St. Louis. By 1849, the cholera epidemic demanded a tremendous amount of the city's doctors. By mid-June, Doctor Farrar himself was infected with the disease. He fought the illness for ten days with all his strength. He even welcomed friends into his home on Church Street, now Second, and tried to conduct himself in his usual manner. On the evening of June 30, about 10 o'clock, Bernard complained of having the chills. In the early morning hours, he passed away at the age of sixty-four.

Farrar Street in north St. Louis is named for the Doctor. The Farrar family lot is located on Balm Avenue. A yellow columned monument is centered in the lot.

WILLIAM CARR LANE

(December 1, 1789 - January 6, 1863)

On April 5, 1823, William Carr Lane was elected the first Mayor of St. Louis, after defeating Auguste Chouteau by a margin of 52 votes. His starting salary was $300 a year. Lane came to St. Louis from Fayette County, Pennsylvania. He was the third son of eleven children by his parents Presley Carr and Sarah Lane. In Pennsylvania, he studied medicine at Dickinson College and he later apprenticed under a doctor in Louisville, Kentucky. Like many doctors in his day, Lane volunteered for the War of 1812 and served as a surgeon's assistant at Fort Harrison where he helped soldiers suffering from malaria and bilious.

Eventually, William Lane resigned from the army and enrolled in the University of Pennsylvania to continue his medical training. He returned to the army in April 1816 when President James Madison appointed him post surgeon. While on furlough in February 1818, William married Mary Ewing. One year later, William again left the army and moved to St. Louis where his wife gave birth to four children.

In St. Louis, William formed a partnership with Dr. Samuel Merry and developed a reputation as an excellent and popular practitioner. Lane had a commanding, handsome appearance, and much like Senator Benton, his moods were volatile; he could be ill-tempered one moment and genial the next. Lane's success as a doctor eventually gained him an appointment as aide-de-camp to Governor Alexander McNair. He was later named quartermaster-general of Missouri. After only

William Carr Lane

four short years in the city, he was elected Mayor of St. Louis, an achievement which testified to his stature and appeal.

As mayor, Lane expanded the city government, improved the riverfront and improved overall health conditions. He and U.S. Senator Thomas Hart Benton also established the first Episcopal church in St. Louis. The people reelected him five times for one year terms. Ten years later, he returned as mayor to finish an unexpired term and the voters elected him for two more times. William finished his political career as Governor of the New Mexico Territory. He was appointed to the position in 1852 by President Millard Fillmore.

Bellefontaine records reveal that Lane died of "congestion of the brain." His funeral was celebrated in his home at Fourth and Walnut. He is buried near Laurel Avenue between his wife Mary and daughter Anne.

JOHN O'FALLON

(November 17, 1791 - December 17, 1865)

John O'Fallon's father, James, emigrated to America from Athlone in central Ireland. He was a physician who served in George Washington's Army during the Revolutionary War and settled in Louisville, Kentucky. Here he made the acquaintance of his future wife Frances Clark, sister of the explorer William Clark.

John was born in Kentucky and raised by his mother after his father died. As John was fatherless from an early age, his uncle, William, played a large role in his young life. John followed in his father's footsteps, joined the military and fought as an army captain during the War of 1812. He was severely wounded in the famous Battle of Tippecanoe and, near the end of the war, O'Fallon was appointed commandant of Fort Malden.

After the war, O'Fallon resigned from the army and came to live in St. Louis. By then, William Clark had concluded his expedition and was working in St. Louis as an Indian Agent. O'Fallon joined his uncle as an assistant agent.

In 1821, John married Harriet Stokes. Unfortunately, Harriet passed away and the marriage was short lived. His Uncle William then introduced him to Caroline Sheets and the two instantly fell in love and married in 1827. Through his many army connections, O'Fallon started a successful military supplies business and made a substantial fortune. He also served the State of Missouri as a member of both the Senate and House of Representatives.

A few years earlier, in August of 1817, during the election between John Scott and Rufus Easton for the territorial delegate to Congress, O'Fallon was nearly killed. Supporters of the two candidates clashed and violence ensued. O'Fallon, a Scott supporter, stabbed one man and baited another man, Dr. Robert Simpson. Two days later, O'Fallon again provoked Simpson who this time pulled a pistol from his vest and fired a shot straight into O'Fallon's chest. The gun, however, had misfired and O'Fallon emerged shaken but unharmed.

John was known for his keen business sense. He had a natural knack for investing in profitable enterprises. During his career, he served as President of the Branch Bank of the United States and first President of the Missouri Pacific Railroad, the Baltimore and Ohio Railroad, and the Wabash Railroad. His real estate investments included numerous tracts of land in downtown St. Louis and over 600 acres of land north of the city. On this northern property, John built his country estate, a brick mansion called "Athlone," after his father's Irish hometown. The 40-room mansion was a massive structure with huge columns supporting the portico. The house was partially destroyed by fire in 1875 and later demolished. The acreage is now O'Fallon Park.

O'Fallon gave generously to charitable and educational

O'Fallon's Athlone house.

institutions. Much of his philanthropy benefited Washington University, St. Louis University, and the O'Fallon Polytechnic Institute. He also contributed to the building of a Methodist Church at Fourth and Washington Avenues and donated the land for Fairgrounds Park.

When O'Fallon's health began to decline in December 1865, he moved into a house at 1125 Washington Avenue to reduce the amount of travel required to conduct his businesses in the city; only occasionally did he visit "Athlone."

John O'Fallon.

The Monday, December 18, 1865 issue of the *Daily Missouri Democrat* said of O'Fallon:

> No man has been more thoroughly identified with the growth and history of St. Louis, than Col. O'Fallon, and so familiar is his countenance to all of our people, that its absence will be most painfully marked. In his departure, one of the landmarks of our community is gone.

O'Fallon died of lung congestion. As news spread of his death, the citizens mourned the passing of the great soldier. St. George's Episcopal Church hosted the funeral. Hundreds were turned away when the church filled to capacity. Mayor James Thomas and other city officials attended as did the directors of the Polytechnic Institute. Robert Campbell and Henry Shaw were among the pallbearers.

John O'Fallon's will read in part, "I, John O'Fallon, of Athlone in the County of St. Louis, do make and declare this, my last will and testament in manner and form following. First, I resign my soul into the hands of Almighty God, and my body I commit to my vault or earth in my lot, in the Belle Fontaine Cemetery. This lot and its magnificent monument in the form of a tall pedestal surmounted by the figure of 'Hope,' is one of the most beautiful in that cemetery."

His burial lot is the largest in Bellefontaine Cemetery; his monument the tallest. It reads, "In peace and in war he fulfilled every duty of a citizen and soldier and lived and died without a blemish on his name."

EDWARD BATES

(September 4, 1793 - March 25, 1869)

In 1813, Edward Bates left his birthplace in Goochland, Virginia and followed his older brother, Frederick, to the territory of Missouri. Once in St. Louis, Edward studied law and started his own practice. He was working as a circuit attorney when Governor William Clark appointed him attorney for the Northern District of Missouri. From this position, he went on to become the state's attorney general and served one term in the state House of Representatives before moving on to the U.S. Congress. While in Congress, Bates was instrumental in the formation of Missouri's Whig party and gained national attention as president of the River and Harbor Improvement Convention in Chicago in 1847.

Bates was very outspoken in his opposition to slavery. He freed his own slaves and pushed for emancipation nationally. He strongly opposed the admission of Kansas as a slave state. At the 1860 Republican Convention in Chicago, Frank Blair nominated Bates for president. He received little support and the nomination went instead to a Springfield lawyer, Abraham Lincoln. When Lincoln offered Bates a position in his cabinet, Edward chose attorney general. He was the first cabinet member from west of the Mississippi.

One month after he took office, the Civil War erupted with the Confederate attack on Fort Sumter. The following four years were frustrating for Bates. In a cabinet dominated by Edwin Stanton and William Seward, Bates struggled to be effective. Though he respected Lincoln, Bates opposed many of the president's military policies and was against West Virginia's admission to the Union. In

1864, Bates resigned and returned to St. Louis where he wrote a column called "Letters to the People of Missouri" for the *Missouri Democrat.*

When Edward learned of Lincoln's assassination, he was deeply saddened. He wrote of the president, "I appreciated that character, in its beautiful simplicity of truth and kindness, and in its strength and goodness."

For most of his life in St. Louis, Bates and his family lived in the three-story house at 16th and Chestnut. He called the house "Grape Hill." Bates' personal life was not an easy one. His brother Frederick, whom Edward had followed West, died after a brief year in office as Governor of Missouri in 1824. A second brother, Tarleton, was killed in the duel. Edward and his wife, Julia Coalter, had seventeen children; only five lived to maturity.

Bates also had financial troubles near the end of his life and was forced to sell much of his property around St. Louis to pay his debts. The family eventually moved into a new house at Morgan Street, now Delmar, and Leffingwell Avenue. In July 1865, Edward became ill with a troubling lung condition. His wife, Julia contacted a doctor as his shortness of breath grew worse. But Bates' condition improved enough within a few days to allow him to sit up in bed. Weeks later, he once again was receiving visitors. In September, he planned a reception in honor of President Andrew Johnson and welcomed the president and former cabinet colleagues William Seward and Gideon Welles to his home.

Edward Bates spent the remainder of his time with his grandchildren and entertaining friends, including Father Peter De Smet, the famous Jesuit missionary to the Native Americans. He also served as a vice-president for an organization he co-founded, the Missouri Historical Society.

In early December 1868, Bates' health steadily declined again. In March, he suffered from a severe pain in his chest and later slipped into unconsciousness. Edward rallied briefly but died peacefully on March 25, 1869. He was 75. Friends and relatives were at his bedside when the end came. In his lifetime, Edward Bates established himself as one of St. Louis' finest leading citizens. He took his place among the likes of Thomas Hart Benton and Auguste and Pierre Chouteau.

A simple service was conducted at the Bates' home on Morgan Street. Edward Bates rests with his in-laws in the Coalter family lot in Bellefontaine. Today, a monument honoring Edward Bates stands in Forest Park.

STEPHEN WATTS KEARNY

(August 30, 1794 - October 31, 1848)

Stephen Kearny was born the youngest of fourteen children on his family's estate in Newark, New Jersey. He joined the military and rose through the ranks to become a major by 1825. The next year, he received orders to move his command to Fort Bellefontaine near St. Louis. His troops stayed at Bellefontaine for two months before moving a short distance down the Mississippi to begin construction on a new army post, Jefferson Barracks. Named in honor of Thomas Jefferson, Jefferson Barracks was to become one of the most famous army posts in America. Its central location in the Mississippi Valley made it ideal for the army's regional depot and infantry training school. The barracks would be home for many of the leading figures of the Civil War including, Ulysses Grant, Robert E. Lee, James Longstreet, Philip Sheridan, and Jefferson Davis. Kearny was Jefferson Barracks first commander and went on to supervise the construction of several forts and barracks throughout the Midwest and the west.

In the early nineteenth century, St. Louis was developing an influential society. The town was known for its hospitality and its close-knit community. During his post at the Barracks, Kearny made acquaintances with some of St. Louis' prominent citizens including, William Clark and Senator Thomas Hart Benton, who would become a bitter enemy in later years.

In 1828, Kearny was assigned commander of Fort Crawford in Wisconsin. It was there that he met a new medical officer named William Beaumont. By 1830, Stephen was back at Jefferson Barracks and in early September, he married William Clark's stepdaughter, Mary Radford at the Clark's country home. The couple had eleven children, though a daughter died in infancy one year into the marriage.

Stephen Watts Kearny.

In March 1833, Stephen was appointed lieutenant colonel of the First Dragoons, the first cavalry unit of the United States Army. The post earned Kearny the nickname, "Father of the U.S. Cavalry." Eventually appointed as a general, Kearny took part in the Mexican War and spent several years in California building military posts and training soldiers. He was said to be firm yet fair with his soldiers. One of his aides was a young lieutenant named William Tecumseh Sherman. Another lieutenant, Ulysses S. Grant, who was stationed at Jefferson Barracks in the early 1840's, described his first impression of Kearny:

> "…one of the ablest officers of the day…under him discipline was kept at a high standard but without vexatious rules or regulations. Every drill and roll call had to be attended but in the intervals officers were permitted to enjoy themselves."

Kearny's health deteriorated after he contracted a fever on an assignment in Veracruz, Mexico in 1847. Disease was widespread throughout Mexico and hundreds of soldiers died of yellow fever and dysentery. Before returning to Jefferson Barracks, he was made military governor of Mexico City though his fever had taken much of his strength. Kearny's condition did not improve greatly upon his return to St. Louis but his spirits were raised by the news that President James Polk had nominated him to the rank of major general. On September 7, 1848, Kearny received his commission. By this time, he was dangerously ill; doctors could not do much to help him. Stephen spent his remaining days at the home of Meriwether Lewis Clark, son of William Clark.

On October 15, his wife Mary gave birth to a boy at Jefferson

Barracks. Stephen smiled proudly when told of the news and died peacefully October 31, never having seen his child.

On Thursday morning, two steamboats brought Kearny's body up the Mississippi to St. George's Episcopal Church on Locust Street. A large crowd was awaiting the General outside the church, the funeral was one of the largest the city had witnessed up to that time. After the service, the 7th and 8th Infantry Regiments and a regiment of First Dragoons from Jefferson Barracks led Kearny's procession. A full military band played. Following the hearse was the General's favorite horse with boots reversed in the stirrups to symbolize a soldier's death.

The procession, which stretched for one mile, moved down Olive Street and turned on Broadway toward the private cemetery on the estate of Colonel John O'Fallon. Reverend Hawks performed a short service at the grave after which an honor guard fired a military salute. Kearny's body was placed in O'Fallon's family vault.

On November 6, the War Department officially announced his death to the country, stating, "His character and bearing as an accomplished officer were unsurpassed, and challenge the admiration of his fellow citizens and the emulation of his professional brethren." It ordered flags at half-mast and thirteen-minute guns were fired at twelve noon.

Kearny's body was buried in O'Fallon's family vault but in 1861, the remains were reinterred in Bellefontaine Cemetery. Kearny and his family are buried in a circular roadside lot across the road from the monument of his friend John O'Fallon.

ROBERT CAMPBELL & WILLIAM SUBLETTE

Campbell in Colorado
Robert Campbell was one of St. Louis' wealthiest citizens when he died in 1879. Upon his passing, the *St. Louis Globe Democrat* wrote:

No man, who has been twenty years a citizen of St. Louis, need be told to-day who and what Robt. Campbell was. The man wrote his name with his deeds while he was yet alive.

Robert was born in Tyrone, Ireland on February 12, 1804. He arrived in St. Louis when he was just 20 years old. In 1825, one year after his arrival, Robert set out for the Rocky Mountains to treat a bronchial affliction he had suffered since childhood. The trip was recommended by his doctor, Bernard Farrar. During this Colorado sojourn, Robert met General William Ashley, a renowned fur trader in the West. Ashley took Robert on expeditions and taught him all about the fur business. When Ashley retired in 1830, Robert formed a partnership with one of Ashley's associates, William Sublette. The two became friends and founded the Rocky Mountain Fur Company. They established their fur trading headquarters in St. Louis. When they retired from the fur trading business in 1835 and returned to St. Louis, they both were wealthy men. Together they opened Sublette & Campbell and sold military and Native American goods. The original store was destroyed in the Great Fire of 1849.

William Sublette

William Sublette was a native of Lincoln County, Kentucky. His family settled in St. Charles in 1818 before moving to St. Louis. As a young man he headed west with his brothers, Milton and Andrew, to enter the fur trading business. William, a frontiersman, was tough and courageous and had an engaging personality. These combined traits eased his trading and negotiations with Native Americans. While in Colorado, William became an associate of General Ashley and through the General made Robert Campbell's acquaintance.

Sublette set up trading posts along the Upper Missouri River and helped pave the way for the Oregon Trail by discovering a westward shortcut called "Sublette's Cutoff."

After returning to St. Louis, Sublette married Frances Hereford in March 1844; he was 23 years her senior. The couple lived on the large Sublette Farm, called Sulphur Springs, on the River des

Robert Campbell.

Peres. The property was bounded by the current streets of Manchester, Kingshighway, Southwest Avenue and Tamm Avenue.

Based on a recommendation from Senator Thomas Hart Benton, President Polk appointed Sublette the new superintendent of Indian Affairs. In July 1845, both William and his wife fell ill. Their family physician, Dr. William Beaumont, recommended a trip East to improve their health. On July 14, Sublette and his wife, left St. Louis by steamboat with her sister Mary and Robert Campbell. As they reached Pittsburgh, Sublette came down with tuberculosis. He was taken to the Exchange Hotel to recover but he passed away a few days later on the 23rd of July. His body was brought back to St. Louis and he was buried near his house on the Sublette Farm.

Sublette's will, which was written in Pittsburgh just before his death, stipulated that if his wife remarried and changed her name, she would lose her inheritance. Robert Campbell was one of the executors of Sublette's will. In the end, William's widow, Frances, did remarry but to Solomon Sublette, William's brother, whereby keeping the family name and her inheritance.

In October 1868, after the Sublette Farm was sold, 17 members of the Sublette family were reinterred at Bellefontaine Cemetery. Two St. Louis avenues are named for William and Solomon.

Campbell in St. Louis

After William's death, Robert continued running Sublette & Campbell. He was known for his congenial and hospitable manner. In 1854, he and his wife, Virginia Kyle, whom he had met during a trip to North Carolina, moved to a Victorian mansion at 1508 Lucas Place. They built a summer house next door.

Campbell invested large sums of money in St. Louis real estate, including ownership of the Southern Hotel in the 1860's which burned down in 1877. Campbell was also president of the Missouri State Bank and the Merchants' National Bank. In 1870, President Ulysses Grant appointed him Indian Commissioner.

In early spring 1879, Campbell's childhood bronchial illness returned. In an attempt to improve his health, Robert took another trip but this time he went east to the resort spa in Saratoga, New York. When he returned to his home on Lucas Place in September, Robert was no better and he declined rapidly. When Campbell died on the evening of October 19, his wife Virginia and three surviving sons, Hugh, James and Hazlett, were present as well as his friend James Yeatman. He was forty-six.

Campbell's funeral took place at his home. The mansion was crowded with mourners from all walks of life, and businessman Wayman Crow was among those paying respects. Both Crow and Yeatman were named as pallbearers. Reverend Dr. Samuel Niccolis gave a half an hour sermon in which he praised Campbell saying, "A prince and true man among his followers has fallen." More than sixty carriages escorted Robert to Bellefontaine.

Campbell house.

The large square-shaped family lot is located roadside on Lawn Avenue.

Robert Campbell's house at 1508 Lucas Place is now a museum.

W̲A̲Y̲M̲A̲N̲ ̲C̲R̲O̲W̲

(March 7, 1808 - May 10, 1885)

Wayman Crow grew up in Hopkinsville, Kentucky. When he was 12, Wayman quit working on his family farm and began an apprenticeship in a dry goods business. The experience taught him a tremendous amount about conducting a successful business and the knowledge he acquired became the basis for his own career. Years later when the company expanded, Wayman was given control and interest in a new branch store in Cadiz, Kentucky. He built a respected reputation in the community and was appointed Postmaster of Cadiz at the young age of 19.

In November 1829, he married a woman by the name of Isabella Conn and fathered nine children, though four died in childhood. In 1835, Wayman was in St. Louis. He fell ill for a time and, as he recovered his health, he noticed the prosperity of the city's business owners. Wayman determined to set up his own shop in the city. In November of that year, he established Crow & Tevis with his cousin Joshua Tevis. The business later was known as Crow, Hargadine & Company. The wholesale dry goods business proved quite profitable for its owners.

In 1840, Wayman served the city and state first as president of the St. Louis Chamber of Commerce and then as a State Senator and a member of the Whig Party. While in the Senate, Wayman helped organize the Hannibal, St. Joseph and Missouri Pacific Railroads. He was also a member of William Greenleaf Eliot's Church of the Messiah and contributed to the construction of two other churches of that denomination. Wayman's biggest accomplishment, however, was drafting the charter to establish Washington University in 1853. He appointed the university's board members and conducted the first meeting of university business in his home. William Eliot was named the university's president.

On November 1, 1855, Wayman nearly lost his life on an ill-fated inaugural, train ride across the new Gasconade Bridge. For the first time, the bridge opened railroad traffic between St. Louis and Jefferson City. There were many luminaries aboard the Missouri Pacific train, including Mayor Washington King and the city counsel. Shortly after the locomotive began crossing the span, the new bridge gave way, hurling the train thirty feet into the river below. Thirty-one people were killed. Wayman was injured but alive. Mayor Washington also survived the crash.

Wayman was to lead a long life. He was 77 years old when the effects of paralysis eventually confined him to his bed at home at 603 Garrison Avenue. For three weeks his health sank though his spirits were strong. On May 10 at 3:30 p.m., Wayman died among family and friends. President of Washington University, William Greenleaf Eliot said of his good friend, "For all these years, from early manhood to a ripe of age, he was one of my dearest and closest friends...His death is to me like the loss of a right hand— nay, more than that, for a part of the directing power by which the hands work is also taken away."

Two days later, in honor of Crow, operators of dry goods establishments throughout the city closed their businesses during his funeral at the Church of the Messiah. Mayor David Francis closed City Hall and was in attendance. A large number of faculty and students from Washington University were also present. William Greenleaf Eliot delivered the eulogy and his honorary pallbearers including General William Sherman, James Yeatman, and Henry Shaw.

Wayman Crow's grave on Meadow Avenue is marked by a tall granite obelisk with his name in large letters near the base.

STERLING PRICE

(September 20, 1809 - September 29, 1867)

When Sterling Price was born, his family lived in Prince Edward County, Virginia where they raised tobacco on a sizable piece of property. Sterling went to college at Hampden-Sidney and later studied law. In 1831, he moved to Missouri, purchased a farm in Chariton County, near Columbia and, two years later, he married Martha Head. The couple had six children and, for a time, Sterling both farmed and practiced law.

Sterling developed a reputation as a hard worker and in 1844, he was elected as a Democrat to the U.S. Congress. Two years later, during the Mexican War, he left his congressional seat to join the Second Missouri Infantry under the command of General Stephen Watts Kearny. He later was appointed to brigadier general of forces in New Mexico by President Polk at the end of the war.

Sterling returned to Missouri and in 1852 he was elected Governor. He was widely respected for his diligence in making tough decisions and improving the living standards of his constituents. During his term, public schools were improved and railroad construction increased dramatically. On the brink of the Civil War, Sterling determined to train his soldiers for the Confederacy. This fateful decision left him an outcast in a state that would reluctantly pledge its allegiance to the Union.

Price was true to the Confederate cause and helped defeat the Union army at Wilson's Creek, Missouri in August 1861. And as the war neared its close and Confederate defeat was certain, Sterling refused to surrender and relocated to Mexico.

While in Mexico, Sterling's health suffered due to a stomach disorder and in April 1866, Sterling's family boarded a ship in New York to join him in Vera Cruz. A short time into the voyage the ship ran aground and sank. The family was safely returned to New York but they lost all their possessions. When the family finally arrived in May, Sterling's health had improved.

The Sterlings took up temporary residence in Cordoba while their new home was being built in Carlota. Sterling worked on the house himself and the laborious activity left him weak. Both he and his son Hebert came down with typhoid fever. Though he had bitter feelings about his homeland and the war, Sterling and his family returned to Missouri in January 1867.

They arrived in St. Louis and stayed at the Southern Hotel. Sterling recovered by March and opened a tobacco business with his son Celsus. "Sterling Price & Company" was located on the corner of Commercial and Chestnut streets. The business thrived under his leadership. Meanwhile, supporters of Price had collected money to help the family purchase a house on 16th Street.

By the summer of 1867, Sterling was sick again. This time he was diagnosed with early signs of cholera. Sterling died a few days later.

On October 3, his body lay in state in the First Methodist Episcopal Church at Eighth and Washington. Sterling rested in a silver-trimmed mahogany casket. The plate of the coffin was inscribed, "Major General Sterling Price, died Sept. 29, 1867, aged

58 years. After life's fitful fever, he sleeps well." Hundreds viewed the general before the two o'clock funeral. A great many soldiers who had served under Price were in attendance.

The procession to Bellefontaine Cemetery was the largest in the city to that time. The hearse was pulled by six black horses and driven by Jesse Arnot, the same man who lead the funeral hearse for Abraham Lincoln. Six gray horses pulled a second hearse with the remains of his daughter-in-law, son Thomas' wife. She died shortly before the general. Sixty to seventy carriages followed in procession. At the burial site, the reverend preached his final words before dirt anointed the general to the earth.

A tall granite obelisk marks the Balm Avenue roadside grave of Sterling Price. The monument is inscribed,

Farmer, Legislator, Governor,
Brigadier General during the Mexican War,
Major General in the Confederate States Army,
His purity of character was equaled
only by his exalted patriotism.

WILLIAM GREENLEAF ELIOT

(August 5, 1811 - January 23, 1887)

Born in New Bedford, Massachusetts, William came from an educated and established family. His father was a merchant and shipowner and his mother, Margaret Dawes, was a descendant of William Dawes who made the famous midnight ride with Paul Revere. William, one of eight children, graduated from Georgetown in 1831 and three years later finished his education at Harvard University's Divinity School.

After graduation, William settled in St. Louis and established the First Congregational Church at Garrison and Locust, later called the Church of the Messiah. He was ordained pastor of the church and held the position until 1871. William married Abigail

Cranch and the couple lived at 2660 Washington Avenue. They had 14 children though most of them died before their parents. The most tragic of these deaths was their daughter's, Mary, who fell through a patch of ice and drowned while skating on a pond in 1873.

During the Civil War, William was appointed a member of the Western Sanitary Commission under its president James Yeatman. The commission worked to aid civilians and soldiers by organizing medical facilities and distributing supplies. He was a large benefactor of educational institutions in the city and co-founded Washington University with his good friend, Wayman Crow

On February 22, 1853, the University's charter was signed by Missouri Governor, Sterling Price. William was named president of the board of trustees. The university's original name, Eliot Seminary, was eventually changed to Washington Institute and finally Washington University. Eliot became chancellor in 1871 and was associated with the university for the rest of his life. Education was one of Eliot's primary interests. He also laid the ground work for Mary Institute and was an incorporator of the Missouri Historical Society.

In 1887, Eliot left St. Louis for Pass Christian, Mississippi in hopes of recovering from a pulmonary condition. The trip was

short-lived, however, and William died while away. His body was returned to St. Louis by train on the 27th. A short service was conducted in his home by two of his sons, Reverend Thomas Eliot and Reverend Christopher Eliot. A mass also was celebrated at the Church of the Messiah. Alumni and directors of Washington University were present.

William Greenleaf Eliot was buried in Bellefontaine beside

The gravesite of William Greenleaf Eliot.

his wife Abby in the family lot. His headstone reads, "Looking Unto Jesus."

Don Carlos Buell

(March 23, 1818 - November 19, 1898)

The Civil War general, Don Carlos Buell, was born near Marietta, Ohio and grew up in Indiana. He graduated thirty-second in his class from West Point in 1841 and fought in the Mexican War under the command of Zachary Taylor. Buell later served as commander of Jefferson Barracks in St. Louis. At the outbreak of the Civil War, he was promoted to brigadier general. In this new role, he helped organize the Army of the Potomac and by November 1861, he was again promoted to major general. Buell was given command of the Army of the Ohio. His first major Civil War engagement took place in Tennessee at the Battle of Shiloh. His reinforcements arrived on the second day of battle and helped General Ulysses Grant gain Tennessee.

In October 1862, Buell and his army met the Confederates under General Braxton Bragg at Perryville, Kentucky. Neither army secured a decisive victory and when Bragg's forces retreated, Buell did not pursue. This inaction came at a cost, however, and Buell was removed from active duty. In defense of his failure to pursue Bragg's retreating forces, Buell argued that he lacked both the men and supplies to continue. A military commission investigated his conduct and delivered a formal report in April 1863 but did not make a recommendation as to the future of Buell's command. It was later thought that Buell's allegiance to General George McClellan, who was running against Abraham Lincoln for president, precluded his receiving another command. Buell ultimately resigned from the military on June 1, 1864.

He returned to Kentucky and was president of the Green River Iron Company from 1865 to 1870. While in the mining business, President Grover Cleveland appointed him Pension Agent for Kentucky, a position he held for four years before retiring to his country home in Rockport. During the warm weather months of 1898, Buell weakened and on the 19th of November, he passed away.

Buell's body arrived in St. Louis from Louisville for his funeral at St. Francis Xavier's Church on Grand and Lindell boulevards. Military men who had known Buell for half a century were in attendance as were soldiers from Jefferson Barracks.

Buell was laid to rest beside his wife Margaret. His wife was first married to Brigadier General Richard Mason who died of cholera in 1850 at Jefferson Barracks while serving as its commander. Mason was born in Stafford County, Virginia and began his career in 1817. He was at Jefferson Barracks in March 1833 where he served as a major under Stephen Watts Kearny in the First Dragoons. In 1857, during the Mexican War, Mason was appointed the first military governor of California.

Buell, Mason and their wife Margaret are all buried in the same wedge-shaped roadside lot. Two large memorials mark the graves, one for Buell and Margaret, the other for Richard Mason. Mason's monument resembles a dismantled cannon.

JAMES YEATMAN

(August 27, 1818 - July 7, 1901)

Thomas Yeatman was a prosperous banker and manufacturer. His son, James was the second of his six children, born near Wartrace, Tennessee. James attended the New Haven Commercial School before becoming an apprentice in his father's business. In 1842, James came to St. Louis as his father's representative. His mild manner won him a significant amount of business

James Yeatman.

and many friends. James regularly entertained St. Louis socialites in his house, the "Belmont."

In September 1838, James married Angelica Thompson. The marriage ended with Angelica's death in May of 1849. He later married Cynthia Ann Pope but she also passed away three years after their marriage. Between these two marriages, Yeatman had five children.

James was one of the founders of the Missouri Pacific Railroad and the Merchants' Bank. A decade later he became Merchants' president and, after

The gravesite of James Yeatman.

some reorganization, he changed its name to Merchants' National Bank. Yeatman oversaw the bank for the next 35 years.

He was a renowned civic leader in St. Louis and sat on several boards including Bellefontaine Cemetery's. He was the first president of the Mercantile Library and an original trustee of Henry Shaw's Missouri Botanical Garden. His philanthropy supported regional charities and education, most notably the Missouri School for the Blind.

Yeatman was best known for his role as president of the Western Sanitary Commission. The commission, started in 1861, aided military and civilian victims of the Civil War. They organized hospitals, recruited medical personnel, and distributed sanitary supplies. The commission also established one of the first railroad hospital cars and a hospital boat on the Mississippi River. Soldiers affectionately referred to Yeatman as "Old Sanitary."

On Sunday, July 7, 1901, James Yeatman died of exhaustion in St. Louis (Mullanphy) Hospital. His funeral took place at the home of his relative, Isaac Sturgeon, and among the attendants were former St. Louis Mayor and Missouri Governor David Francis and the surviving daughters of William Clark; more than 100 carriages followed the hearse in procession.

The gates of Bellefontaine Cemetery were draped in black in honor of the former president of its board.

The Yeatman family lot is located next to James' friend, Robert Campbell, on Lawn Avenue. His monument is adorned by ornate, angel-like carvings on each corner.

JAMES EADS

(May 23, 1820 - March 8, 1887)

On the first morning James Eads and his family stepped onto the levee in St. Louis in 1833, their steamboat was engulfed in a sudden burst of flames. In that instant, they lost all of their possessions and the family was left penniless. In order to recoup some of their loss, James' mother opened a boardinghouse and James began working for a dry goods store. The young boy also sold apples and newspapers on the streets.

Some time later, when James was 18, he started working on the Mississippi River. During that period, James worked on a steamboat called the *Knickerbocker* which wrecked on a snag of trees that lay beneath the river's murky waterline. On that day, James was struck with a novel idea: he would develop a ship to salvage wrecks from the bottom of the Mississippi. The success of this venture was rooted in James' lifelong fascination with mechanics.

Born in Lawrenceburg, Indiana in 1820, James Buchanan Eads was named after his second cousin who would later become the fifteenth President of the United States. At an early age, he began to explore the way things worked and frequently experimented with machinery. When he was just 13, Eads constructed his own miniature steam engine.

Years later, when Eads formed a salvaging business with his friend Bill Nelson, this interest would serve him well. The partners developed a unique, double-hulled ship with derricks, pumps, and a diving bell. In a brief time, their boat, dubbed the *Submarine*, proved a tremendous success. The partners salvaged countless wrecks from the Mississippi River, all the way from St. Louis to New Orleans, and their business prospered. Eads personally made over 500 trips to the bottom of the Mississippi in his diving bell. Insurance companies paid Eads and Nelson handsomely for recovered cargo and they were allowed to keep anything that had remained under water for over five years. Before long, James and his partner established a whole fleet of ships. By the age of 25, Eads was a wealthy, married man living on Compton Hill in the company of other prominent St. Louisans.

In 1852, James lost his wife to cholera. His own health also declined during this period. Hundreds of underwater trips in the diving bell left James suffering from tuberculosis, he never clearly understood the effects of decompression. His doctor recommended retirement. But Eads, 32 at the time, obliged for only a short while. He married a second wife, Eunice, with whom he had five daughters, and went back to his work on the river.

In 1861, the Civil War erupted and Eads proposed to build a fleet of ironclad gunboats for the Union army. Edward Bates, Lincoln's attorney general, submitted this proposal to the President and Lincoln agreed. Upon the President's approval, Eads and Nelson employed 4,000 workers at the Union Marine Works in Carondelet to build the fleet. With the recent invention of gas lighting, the shipyard ran around the clock. Eads' ships were integral to the Union's capture at Vicksburg and other

James Eads.

Confederate strongholds.

After the war, Eads' doctor again suggested retirement. But instead, James took on the ambitious project of building the first steel bridge across the Mississippi River. Eads had never built a bridge nor did he have any formal education in engineering but he was not to be deterred and, in August 1867, construction began. Workers used the newly invented cofferdams, or caissons, to build the bridge's underwater supports. In those days, techniques for using the caissons safely were still ill-defined and fourteen workers died of the "bends" due to improper decompression.

On July 4, 1874, thousands celebrated when the Eads Bridge officially opened. General William Tecumseh Sherman hammered in the last spike and a 100-gun salute was fired. Eads ran 14 locomotives across the bridge to proof its strength. Today, Eads Bridge is one of St. Louis' most famous, historic landmarks and one of the city's finest examples of innovative engineering and architecture.

Despite his age, Eads was always busy developing new projects. One of these plans was to build a canal across Panama. The canal would serve as a marine railway, moving ships from the Gulf of Mexico to the Pacific Ocean. Eads wanted the U.S. government to grant him exclusive rights to the project but instead his doctors sent him to Nassau in the Bahamas to regain his strength. One of his daughters escorted him on the trip and he told the girl, "I shall not die until I accomplish this work, and see with my own eyes great ships pass from ocean to ocean over the land." The government however, refused Eads' proposal for the Panama project.

While away, Eads came down with a cold which turned into pneumonia; he never recovered. "I cannot die." he said to his daughter, "I have not finished my work." Sadly, Eads was not able to complete his projects and he died in the spring of 1887.

Eads' funeral took place at Christ Church. As Eads would have wanted, the service was simple. There was no mourning drapery and only a small bouquet rested on the steps in front of his casket. The church was filled to capacity including many of the construction workers from Eads Bridge. Mayor David Francis and businessman James Yeatman were also in attendance. Eads is buried with his family in Bellefontaine.

FRANCIS BLAIR

(February 19, 1821 - July 9, 1875)

Francis Blair was born in Lexington, Kentucky and spent his early years in Washington D.C. where his father was the editor of the *Washington Globe*. Blair attended Princeton and went to law school at Transylvania University in Kentucky. In 1842, he came to St. Louis to practice law with his brother Montgomery, who would later serve as one of Dred Scott's lawyers.

When the Mexican War broke out, Francis joined the army and after America's successful capture of New Mexico, he was appointed attorney general of the territory. During this time, Blair was embroiled in a controversy with Sterling Price, who was then serving as the military governor of New Mexico. When Price had Blair arrested for insubordination, Blair resigned from his position and made public his hatred for Price.

In 1847, Francis returned to the midwest to marry Appoline Alexander and once again resumed his practice of law. By this time the slavery issue had become a divisive issue throughout the country. Blair ardently opposed slavery and expressed his views in his paper, the *Barnburner*. Blair later organized the Free Soil Party and further politicized the slavery issue. He spent four years in the Missouri legislature and a term in the U.S. Congress where he was well respected by his colleagues for his political brilliance and his honest, personal approach. Blair's forthright and spontaneous style of speaking made him one of the best orators of his time.

In March 1849, Blair was involved in an unusual fight which came about as a result of some articles he had written in the *Missouri Republican*. Some of Blair's stories had criticized a man named L. Pickering, the editor of the *Republican's* rival newspaper, *The Union*. For a time, the two men traded editorial barbs until one morning they unexpectedly encountered each other on Second Street. After exchanging a few words, they began dueling with their umbrellas. The two were separated when Pickering pulled a knife. Neither was injured.

At the 1860 Chicago Republican Convention, Francis supported his friend and fellow Missourian Edward Bates for the presidency. When Bates' defeat looked inevitable, Francis placed his support behind Abraham Lincoln. Blair himself was again elected to Congress in 1860. Within a year, the Civil War erupted and Blair returned to St. Louis to organize men to fight for the Union; his efforts in St. Louis ensured Missouri's support of the Union.

In early 1862, when the Union army had suffered several, major defeats at the hands of the Confederates, Blair raised seven regiments of soldiers with his own finances and received an appointment as brigadier general. He was considered a soldier's soldier and was popular among his men. In May 1863, he fought in his first battle, the Battle of Vicksburg. He was promoted to major general and was a member of General Sherman's March to the Sea.

Francis was back on the political scene after the war. He received the 1868 Democratic nomination for vice-president. The Democrats lost the election by a wide margin to former Union commander Ulysses S. Grant. Blair, however, was elected to the U.S. Senate. He lost his re-election bid in 1873.

Francis Blair.

General Blair's health began to decline in 1871 with an attack of paralysis. In retirement he suffered a second, more severe attack. He recovered only slightly and was confined to bed. Doctor Franklin, his physician, attempted various remedies with little success; a blood transfusion only gave him temporary relief. On July 9, 1875, while walking about his bedroom, Francis fell and struck his head and he died soon after of a brain hemorrhage.

In Blair's death, the city of St. Louis lost a great statesman and the country lost a strong defender of the Union. Sherman said, "Frank Blair was a noble, honorable, and magnanimous man. He was brave, open, and unselfish. His virtues will always be recognized and never forgotten, while his faults will be buried with him, as they hurt no one but himself." His funeral was held at First Congregational Church at Tenth and Locust. The church was filled to capacity.

Blair's grave sits atop a hill near the entrance to Bellefontaine. A large Celtic granite cross with the inscription "Blair-Graham" marks the spot.

A monument of Francis Blair stands in the northeast corner of Forest Park.

HENRY AND SUSAN BLOW

Henry Blow was born in Southampton County, Virginia on July 15, 1817. Henry Taylor Blow and his daughter Susan played unique and distinctive roles in St. Louis as leaders who helped bring about change in their respective fields.

Henry came to St. Louis when he was 13 at the time and attended St. Louis University for two years. Eventually, Henry entered a partnership with Charless and the two manufactured and sold drugs, oils, and paints. The partnership dissolved within a few years and Henry kept the manufacturing side.

He expanded his business and incorporated "The Collier White Lead and Oil Company." After the Civil War, Henry began to explore other business opportunities. He and his older brother Peter formed "The Granby Mining and Smelting

Henry Blow.

Company" in southwestern Missouri and they became pioneers in lead mining. The mining business made Henry and the Blow family a vast fortune. Henry was later president of the Iron Mountain Railroad and, in this role, he oversaw the construction of new rail lines.

In 1840, Henry married Minerva Grimsley. The two were very fond of each other and were inseparable for the next 35 years. Henry was in good health his entire life, seldom did he face a day of illness. He was said to be kind, sociable, and ambitious but never arrogant. His gentle manner and affluence eventually earned him a seat in the Missouri State Senate in 1854 as a member of the Whig party.

When the Whig party collapsed, Henry worked with Francis Blair and Edward Bates to establish the Republican Party in Missouri. Henry was a delegate to the Chicago Convention that elected Lincoln in 1860 and he himself was propelled to the U.S. House of Representatives two years later by his party's success. He served two terms and wrestled with the divisive issues surrounding a country torn by war. Henry returned to his mining business for a brief time before serving as Ulysses Grant's ambassador to Brazil.

Henry returned to St. Louis in 1871 hoping to retire. Instead, Henry served his country one final time as a member of the Board of Commissioners for the District of Columbia. Henry's wife Minerva died in June 1875. Soon after her death, Henry went to Saratoga, New York for rest and relaxation and was strickened with a cerebral hemorrhage while away. He died on the 11th of September. The next day the *St. Louis Globe Democrat* wrote:

> No death among the many whose names are intimately linked with the social and material history and progress of this community could occasion a more profound sorrow than that of Hon. Henry T. Blow, which occurred at Saratoga yesterday.

Henry's body was returned to St. Louis for the funeral which took place at his home in Carondelet. His pallbearers included

James Yeatman, James Eads, and Robert Campbell.

Henry's large monument at Bellefontaine stands just off the road on Woodbine Avenue. The inscription on his monument reads, "Be still and know that I am God."

Susan Blow: The Development Of The Public Kindergarten

During their life together, Henry and Minerva had four daughters and two sons. Their most distinguished child was his daughter Susan. Born in St. Louis on June 7, 1843, Susan and her brothers and sisters were given the best education St. Louis had to offer. In May 1849, when Susan was five years old, the family's home burned down during the Great St. Louis Fire. Henry had another house built in Carondelet. Susan left St. Louis to study with some of the finest educators in New York and Germany. Under their guidance, she developed a strong interest in education and, in September of 1873, with the support of superintendent of schools, Dr. William Harris, Susan opened the first public kindergarten in America at the Des Peres School in Carondelet. One year later, she opened another school to train kindergarten teachers. Susan's work was vocational; she never sought financial gain and she was never a paid employee of the St. Louis school system.

In 1884, Susan was forced to semi-retire due to illness. But for ten years, she continued training teachers and often lectured on the importance of education. Susan eventually moved to New York where she worked at the New York Kindergarten Association. She published six books between 1894 to 1900. Susan died on Sunday evening, March 26, 1916 at The Berkeley on Fifth Avenue in New York. She never married.

Susan's funeral was held

The gravesite of Susan Blow.

at Christ Church Cathedral. Over 80 kindergarten teachers from around the country attended. Susan was buried beside her father at Bellefontaine.

NORMAN COLMAN

(May 16, 1827 - November 3, 1911)

Norman Jay Colman was born in Richfield Springs, New York. He graduated from Louisville Law University in 1849 and married Clara Porter two years later. Colman practiced law in Albany, Indiana for twelve years before coming to St. Louis. His wife Clara died in 1863 and he remarried three years later to Catherine Wright of St. Louis. They lived at 5499 Delmar Boulevard in a home he would own for the next 50 years.

Colman had a lifelong passion for agriculture. Upon relocating to St. Louis he established an agricultural journal called, *Colman's Rural World*. A Democrat, Colman served on the Board of Alderman for two years and spent another two years in the Missouri State Legislature. In 1873, he was elected lieutenant governor. When, President Grover Cleveland was looking for a commissioner of agriculture in 1885, he selected Colman for the job. Four years later, the position became a cabinet post and Cleveland officially appointed Colman the first Secretary of Agriculture.

Colman continued to serve St. Louis and Missouri by holding positions on the Board of Curators at the University of Missouri, the State Board of Agriculture, the board of the St. Louis World's

Norman Colman.

Fair. He was also the first president of the Missouri State Fair and founded the Missouri State Horticultural Society.

In early November 1911, while Colman was enroute by train to Plattsburg, Missouri, to purchase a horse for his farm near Creve Coeur Lake, he suffered a severe stroke. The next morning, November 2, his son-in-law, Dr. C.M. Nicholson went to Lexington to bring him back to St. Louis. He died the next day when the train was in Moberly. His body was returned to St. Louis the morning of November 6. He was survived by three children.

Colman's funeral was held at St. John's Methodist Episcopal Church. Respects were paid by Missouri Governor Herbert Hadley and members of the numerous organizations to which he belonged. A huge list of honorary pallbearers included David Francis (then Secretary of the Interior), William Marion Reedy, and Charles Lemp. Colman was eulogized as, "…an idealist, but unlike artists, who worked their visions out on canvas, or in music, he sought to convert his ideals into better homes for the people's shelter and into better food for the people's hunger." Norman Colman is buried in a roadside grave on Fountain Avenue.

ADOLPHUS BUSCH

(July 10, 1839 - October 10, 1913)

Eberhard Anheuser was the wealthy owner of a soap factory when he purchased the Bavarian Brewery in 1860. The German-born Anheuser came to America in 1843 and settled in St. Louis two years later. In 1861, on the eve of the Civil War, his daughter Lilly married Adolphus Busch, the owner of a brewery supply business. It was a double wedding as Anheuser's other daughter, Anna, married Adolphus' brother Ulrich.

Adolphus and Ulrich Busch were born in the German wine country near the city of Bad Schwalbach. Their father Ulrich was a wealthy merchant and the father of 22 children. In 1857, at the age of 18, Adolphus came to St. Louis and began working as a shipping clerk in a malt and hop storage house. This was his first taste of the brewing business. Two years later, he established a brewery supply business of his own.

During the Civil War, Adolphus served in the Union Army. After the war, he joined his father-in-law at Eberhard Anheuser and Company. In 1876, the brewery introduced its trademark brand Budweiser and three years later, the brewery was renamed Anheuser-Busch. The brewery employed 5,000 at its St. Louis headquarters and various branches around the country. Adolphus was named president after Eberhard Anheuser died in 1880. Anheuser was buried at Bellefontaine.

After Eberhard's death, Adolphus started complimentary businesses to support the brewery, including the Manufacturers' Railroad and the Adolphus Busch Glass Manufacturing Company which became the largest bottling manufacturer in the world. Adolphus was also president of Busch-Sulzer Brothers Diesel Engine Company and Geyser Ice Company.

Adolphus and his wife, Lilly, had 13 children though three of their daughters died at birth. Tragically, their oldest son, Edward died of peritonitis while serving at Kemper Military School in Boonville, Missouri on December 24, 1879. The boy was 15. Another son Adolphus Jr., a vice-president at the brewery, died in August 1898 of a perforated appendix. Adolphus' second son, August Busch, would eventually become his successor.

Adolphus Busch.

Adolphus' philanthropy was well-known nationally. He donated large sums to Washington University, Harvard University, and University of Missouri-Columbia. He was also an active promoter of the St. Louis World's Fair and supported victims displaced by floods and earthquakes at the turn of the century.

On Christmas Eve 1907,

Adolphus suffered a severe attack of pneumonia which developed into dropsy. By May 1913, his physical health deteriorated further and he suffered from a heart condition. He could not walk without assistance and often used a wheelchair. On June 9, he traveled with the family back to Germany. It would be his last trip to the Villa Lilly, his German estate near the Rhine. He relaxed by entertaining guests and hunting deer in his private forest. He continued to run the business by sending telegrams back to St. Louis.

By October, Adolphus was seriously ill. His son August Busch sailed from New York to Germany and arrived on October 8. He rallied temporarily when doctors removed fluid from his lungs. By the 10th, he was relaxed and was even able to enjoy a cigar. His son later recalled, "Just after noon he became weak but was in no pain whatever. He spoke to all of us and was quite clear of mind on all subjects. I don't think father thought he was dying." At 8:15 that evening, Adolphus died peacefully. He was 74; the same age his father-in-law Eberhard Anheuser reached upon his death. His wife Lilly, son August, and three daughters were at his bedside. His good friend Carl Conrad, who developed the Budweiser brand for Adolphus, was also present. Adolphus' estimated worth at the time of death was $40 to $50 million.

According to the October 11 *St. Louis Post Dispatch*:

"The news of Busch's death was received over the private telegraph wires at the brewery at 5 p.m. Friday, just as 5000 employees were being dismissed for the day. It was flashed from department to department, but many of the employees did not hear of it until they were on the streets and saw the flags from the buildings dropped to half-mast."

The town of Bad Schwalbach mourned their native son. The body was transported to Bremen on a private rail car and transferred to the steamer *Kronprinz Wilhelm* for the trip back to America. The ship pulled into New York harbor on October 21. Busch's son-in-law, Edward Faust, and longtime friend, Charles Nagel, met the body which was placed in the rail car Adolphus on a private train.

The Busch mausoleum.

The train pulled into St. Louis at 9:20 in the evening. Amid a heavy rainstorm, the casket was taken into Number One Busch Place as hundreds of people looked on. Adolphus was finally home, resting in the house where he had entertained the likes of Teddy Roosevelt and William Taft. The day before the funeral, Adolphus laid in state in the main drawing room of the mansion. As many as 30,000 people came to pay their respects to the beer baron.

Members of the St. Louis Symphony Orchestra played at the mansion the morning of the funeral. When the funeral began at two o'clock, all business in St. Louis came to a stop for five minutes. In attendance were U.S. Congressman Richard Bartholdt, and the presidents of Harvard and the University of Missouri. Also among the honored guests was Baron von Lesner, a representative of German Kaiser Wilhelm II, a longtime friend of Adolphus. Reverend John Day celebrated the service. Charles Nagel gave the funeral oratory, calling Adolphus, "a giant among men. Like a descendant of one of the great and vigorous and ancient gods, he rested among us and with his optimism, his far seeing vision, his undaunted courage and his energy shaped the affairs of men."

A 250-piece band led the cortege to the cemetery. The Busch mausoleum is located on Woodbine Avenue. Eberhard Anheuser is buried just behind the mausoleum.

Samuel Fordyce

(February 7, 1840 - August 3, 1919)

The multimillionaire capitalist, Samuel Fordyce, was a native of Guernsey, Ohio. He was publicly educated in Guernsey and attended Madison College in Pennsylvania and North Illinois University. When the Civil War started, Fordyce volunteered for the First Ohio Cavalry and, after the war, Samuel established the bank, Fordyce & Rison in Huntsville, Alabama. It was there that he met Susan Chadwick, his future wife. The couple were married in 1866 and had three sons and a daughter.

A decade later, the family moved to Arkansas and Fordyce got involved with the railroads. He helped reorganize the St. Louis Southwestern Railway Company in 1885 and subsequently was named its president. He is credited with constructing over 24,000 miles of railroad tracks throughout Missouri and Arkansas. Samuel quickly built a reputation for himself. He was known as a straightforward and fearless man. His life's philosophy, "reward your friends and punish your enemies," was simple if not a bit harsh. Fordyce served as vice president or director of numerous other railway lines and corporations. Eventually, Fordyce moved his railroad's headquarters to St. Louis. He later became director of the St. Louis Union Trust Company and founded one of the largest health resorts in Hot Springs, Arkansas.

Given Fordyce's success, he moved with a fairly prominent crowd. In time, he became good friends with both Presidents McKinley and Grant. Fordyce had fought as a lieutenant for General Grant during the Civil War. At Shiloh, he assisted the General when he had been thrown from his

Samuel Fordyce.

horse. After Fordyce's first visit with Grant in the White House, he wrote:

> "Grant reached out his hand and shook hands with me. I said: 'General, you don't know me.' Whereupon he said, 'I don't know your name, but you were one of my old soldiers.' I said, 'General, where did you ever see me.' He said, 'You were the young officer who caught my horse when he fell with me at Pittsburg Landing.' The event happened nearly 15 years before this."

Near the end of his life, Samuel Fordyce spent little time in St. Louis. Instead, he stayed and at his large country home in Garland County, Arkansas. He was prominent in Democratic politics in Alabama and Arkansas.

On July 19, 1919, Samuel went to Atlantic City for an extended vacation to improve his health. By August 1, his health declined quickly. He died of pneumonia soon after and his body was returned to St. Louis for a funeral in his home at 21 Washington Terrace.

On August 6, when friends and family gathered to say goodbye to the railroad magnate, many of St. Louis' most prominent citizens turned out for the service. The casket was draped in an American flag denoting his military service. Reverend William Black of the Missouri Valley Presbyterian College recited the prayers. He was assisted by Reverend C.F. Swift, Fordyce's brother-in-law.

EDWARD MALLINCKRODT

(January 21, 1845 - February 1, 1928)

Edward Mallinckrodt was born in 1845 on his family farm in North St. Louis. His father Emil was an immigrant from Germany and Edward grew up working on the family farm. When he was 18, at the height of the Civil War, he grew interested in agricultural chemistry. Edward began to read books on the subject and soon discovered his calling.

Emil Mallinckrodt agreed to send his sons Edward and Otto back to Germany to study chemistry. The brothers arrived in Germany in 1864 and for the next three years they studied at the Fresenius' laboratory in Wiesbaden and the De Haen Chemical Works near Hanover. In 1867, the brothers sailed back to the United States and opened a chemical manufacturing company with their elder brother Gustav. The company was called G. Mallinckrodt & Company and its first office was in a small building on the Mallinckrodt family farm.

During the first decade of business, there were many hardships for the Mallinckrodts. In the span of a single year, both Otto and Gustav died. Later that year, Edward temporarily lost his eyesight after an explosion in his laboratory. The one bright light during this time was his marriage in June 1876 to Jennie Anderson of St. Louis.

When the business was incorporated in 1882 as the Mallinckrodt Chemical Works, Edward became its president. The company prospered for the next 40 years and expanded rapidly. Mallinckrodt Chemical Works produced 1,500 different chemical products and operated branch offices in New York, New Jersey, Toronto, and Montreal. The plant at 3600 North Second Street was located on a portion of the farm where Edward was born. Edward also established the National Ammonia Company in 1889.

Mallinckrodt accumulated vast holdings of real estate in St. Louis, including the Arcade Building. He used his substantial wealth to give back something to his community and his philanthropy benefitted Harvard University, Washington University, and the St.

Edward Mallinckrodt.

The Mallinckrodt mausoleum.

Louis College of Pharmacy. He gave an endowment to St. Louis Children's Hospital to establish the Jennie Mallinckrodt Ward in memory of his wife who died in 1913. Edward also gave generously to St. Luke's Hospital of which he was head of the board of trustees. Edward held positions as director of the Missouri Botanical Garden, president of the Mercantile Library, and he served on the board of Washington University.

In 1928, a few days after his 83rd birthday, Edward suffered a heart attack in his home at 16 Westmoreland Place. A severe bout of pneumonia following the heart attack further weakened Mallinckrodt. He died on Wednesday, February 1. Two days later, on the same day St. Louis Mayor Victor Miller laid the cornerstone for the new city courthouse, mourners filled Christ Church Cathedral to pay their respects to the philanthropist.

After the service, Edward Mallinckrodt was buried at Bellefontaine. He rests in a white granite mausoleum on Wintergreen Avenue. Above the gated-door is his name and the biblical quote,

"Yea though I walk through the valley of the shadow of death I will fear no evil."

ROBERT BROOKINGS

(January 22, 1850 - November 15, 1932)

Robert Brookings was a native of Cecil County, Maryland. He came to St. Louis where his elder brother worked as a "drummer" or traveling salesman for Cupples & Marston, a wood products manufacturing company. With the help of his brother, Robert worked as a receiving clerk at Cupples; his monthly salary was $25. Later, he became a traveling salesman. In 1871, his hard work and persistence was rewarded and he was offered a partnership in the business. Robert was only 21 years old.

For the next 25 years, he turned Cupples into a leader in its industry. He expanded the company's product line and, in process, accumulated a personal fortune. Brookings retired at the age of 46.

In retirement, Brookings turned his attention to Washington University. He was made president of the Washington University Corporation in 1897. He purchased new properties for the University and constructed new buildings. He also convinced the Board of Directors to establish a medical school and financed its development himself. Washington University medical school was to become one of the finest in the country, on par with the medical programs of well-established schools on the East coast.

Brookings' dedication to the University was boundless and he donated his own home at 6510 Ellenwood Avenue as a residence for the chancellor. In 1929, Brookings was given honorary degrees of doctor of laws and doctor of medicine. He had previously received honorary degrees from Harvard University, Yale University, and the University of Missouri.

In 1917, President Woodrow Wilson appointed Brookings chairman of the Price Fixing Committee of the War Industries Board. His primary responsibility was fixing prices on commodities. After World War I, he moved permanently to Washington DC. where he was commissioned by President William Taft to do a study of the president's budget plan. In 1923, he established the Robert Brookings Graduate School in Economics and Government, later called the Brookings Institute. He was also the author of several books on economic theory and government. In June 1927, at the age of 77, Robert married his longtime friend Isabel Valle January; she was 26 years his junior.

Robert had problems with his eyesight in his later years. He completely lost sight in one eye and underwent a series of operations at the Wilmer Eye Institute in Baltimore. Feeling weak from age, Robert spent the summer of 1932 at Gloucester, Massachu-setts and Saratoga Springs, New York. He returned to Washington D.C. but within a short time he came down with the chills and a fever. The illness developed into an acute kidney infection and Robert passed away on November 15.

Senator Harry Hawes, an alumnus of Washington University, said of Brookings, "He had been my friend for thirty years, and, through personal contact and correspondence, I had grown to greatly admire him for his sturdy qualities. He was a very patriotic man, a man of unusual intelligence and stamina and a benefactor to the nation."

A funeral service was held at Washington Cathedral and on Saturday, November 19, another funeral service took place at Graham Chapel on the campus of Washington University. Classes at the university were canceled for the day. The chapel was filled with civic and business leaders, the faculty and students of the university were well represented.

His ashes were buried in a roadside grave on Amaranth Avenue.

THEODORE LINK

(March 17, 1850 - November 12, 1923)

Renown architect Theodore Link was born near Heidelberg, Germany and educated in England and France. He attended the Ecole Centrale in Paris to study architecture and engineering. In 1870, he came to the United States and practiced architecture in New York and Philadelphia. Three years later, Theodore moved to St. Louis to work as a technical representative for the Atlantic & Pacific Railroad Company. In September 1875, he married Annie Fuller, and they had four sons and a daughter. The family resided at 628 North Spring Avenue.

Link eventually left the railroad company for a position as an assistant chief engineer at Forest Park. Later, he became the super-intendent of public parks for St. Louis. In 1883, Link opened his own architectural office in the Chemical Building where he designed numerous churches, libraries, and other public facilities. He also designed the buildings for the Washington University Medical School including Barnes Hospital and constructed his share of residences, many in Clayton and the Central West End. He served as one of the

Link's grave.

architects for the 1904 World's Fair and designed the Mississippi State House and Metallurgy buildings.

Theodore was one of only ten architects, selected from around the country, invited to submit designs for a train station in St. Louis. He won the commission in 1891 and set about building one of St. Louis' grandest buildings and perhaps his greatest architectural achievement.

He designed Union Station's main building which was 750 feet long with a ten-acre train shed and 19 miles of track. Romanesque in style, the station is constructed in limestone and brick with a red-tile roof. The station was completed in 1894. Its grand opening was held on September 1 and the event was attended by 20,000 people. In its heyday, more than 100,000 passengers a day would move through the station's terminal.

In November 1923, Link came down with a severe cold while working in Baton Rouge, Louisiana. He had been supervising construction of Louisiana State University and the Greater Agricultural College. The architect passed away on November 12. He was 73. His funeral took place in the chapel at Wagner Undertaking on Olive Street and he was buried in front of his parents, on Wintergreen Avenue.

Theodore was a fellow of the American Institute of Architects and member of the Missouri State Society of Architects. At one time he served as president of the St. Louis Artists' Guild.

DAVID FRANCIS

October 1, 1850 - January 15, 1927)

David Francis.

David Francis was born in Richmond, Kentucky and educated at the Richmond Academy. In 1866, he moved to St. Louis and was one of the first graduates of Washington University. After graduation, he worked with his uncle at Shryock & Rowland, a wholesale grocery house. He went on to establish his own business, D.R. Francis & Brother, in 1884 which exported grain. During that time, David also became vice-president of the St. Louis Merchant's Exchange.

Francis, a lifelong Democrat, won the election for Mayor of St. Louis in 1885 when he was only 35. He was extremely popular during his tenure and he worked hard to improve the city's economic base. Three years later, after his mayoral success, Francis became Governor of Missouri. As Governor, he was a strong proponent of public education both at the elementary and university level. Francis would be a powerful figure in Missouri politics for the rest of his life. For one year, 1896 to 1897, David served at a national level as Secretary of the Interior for the final year of President Grover Cleveland's term.

Francis built a large home on Newstead Avenue when his governorship ended. The house was often the center of social activities in the St. Louis area. While in St. Louis for dedication ceremonies of the World's Fair, President Theodore Roosevelt and former President Grover Cleveland were guests at the Francis home. In 1920, David leased the house to the Junior Chamber of Commerce and the Boy Scouts. He also donated the acreage on Eichelberger Street to the city. It is now Francis Park.

David returned to private business after his term in Jefferson City. He owned the *St. Louis Republic* newspaper which later merged with the *Globe-Democrat*. Francis' greatest contribution to St. Louis was perhaps his work on the St. Louis World's Fair. He was chairman of the executive committee and president of the exposition company. On April 30, 1904, Francis conducted the opening ceremonies. Secretary of War, William Howard Taft stood in for President Roosevelt. Francis Field at Washington University, built during the fair and used as an Olympic site, was named in David Francis' honor.

The 'shrouded angel' at the Francis grave.

In 1916, Francis served as Ambassador to Russia under President Wilson. He left his post at the outbreak of the Russian Revolution. He later wrote of his experiences in his book, <u>Russia from the American Embassy</u>, published in 1921.

David had been ill for many months by January 1927. He spent most of his time at his Ellenwood Avenue home which he purchased after his wife's death. Five of his six sons were at his bedside when he died on January 15. The *St. Louis Globe Democrat*

House on Newstead where funeral was held.

announced the passing of one of Missouri's most distinguished citizens on the morning of January 16, 1927:

> David Rowland Francis, 76, former Mayor of St. Louis, former Governor of Missouri, former Ambassador to Russia and former Secretary of the Interior in the Cabinet of President Cleveland, died at 6:10 o'clock last night of infirmities of age.

Francis' funeral was held in his former residence on Newstead Avenue. Former St. Louis mayors Edward Noonan, Rolla Wells and Henry Kiel were present. Following the service, he was taken to Bellefontaine. A shrouded angel now watches over Francis and his family on Prospect Avenue.

CHRIS VON DER AHE

(October 7, 1851 - June 5, 1913)

Chris Von der Ahe was the flamboyant, hard-drinking owner of the St. Louis Browns baseball club. As it is told, Chris knew very little about the game; for a time, he boasted that he had the largest baseball diamond in the league until his manager quietly informed him that, in fact, all baseball diamonds were the same size. What Von der Ahe did know was there was money to be made in the sport. For Von der Ahe, baseball was much more about entertainment than athletics. He himself craved the spotlight and he was once referred to as the P.T. Barnum of baseball for his tireless showmanship. Von der Ahe went so far as to erect a life-sized statue of himself at the front gate of his ballpark. With a thick, German accent he called himself "der poss bresident."

Von der Ahe was quirky man. After baseball games, the gate receipts would be thrown into a wheelbarrow and gallantly pushed down the street to his office. He would walk alongside with an armed guard and a smug air of satisfaction.

Von der Ahe was born in Hille, Germany. He came to America and settled in St. Louis in 1870. He opened a grocery with a small saloon at Sullivan and Spring avenues on the city's north side. But it was not until Sportsman's Park was built across the street that Van der Ahe would make his fortune. Before and after games, fans would fill his saloon and buy up his groceries. In 1880, he organized the Sportsman's Park Association with John Peckington and Al Spink of the *Sporting News*. Eventually, the organization gained control of Sportsman's Park. Van der Ahe expanded and moved his

Von Der Ahe's monument.

saloon to a more prominent location at Grand and St. Louis avenues. One year later, though he knew little about the game of baseball, he sponsored a professional team in St. Louis. He called his team the Browns.

Von der Ahe was married three times and had only one son, Edward. He was very fashionable and often frequented saloons with other women on his arm. In 1882, a year after his Browns were playing, Von der Ahe organized the American Baseball Association and was named its first president. His St. Louis Browns won pennants from 1885 to 1888 under the leadership of manager Charles Comiskey. In 1886, they took the championship from the Chicago White Stockings. Von der Ahe was not known for his generosity. He paid his players minimal salaries and fined them heavily for insubordination. To his credit, Von der Ahe was an innovator. He was the first owner to use a tarpaulin to cover the field on rainy days and the first to sell souvenirs of his team.

The Browns played poorly during the 1890's for Von der Ahe had lost several of his best players to a new league called Players Brotherhood. The departure of Charles Comiskey in 1892 brought the team to near collapse. Von der Ahe moved his team to a park at Natural Bridge and Vandeventer. When attendance declined, he attempted to draw crowds by staging Wild West shows, fireworks displays, boxing matches, and even hired an all-female brass band to play between innings.

Von der Ahe was a free-spender and faced financial problems which would ultimately liquidate his fortune. In 1888, he purchased some apartment buildings in St. Louis. When the buildings were proved unprofitable, he was forced to sell some of his players to offset the loss. The Browns still won the pennant and Von der Ahe spent $20,000 for a special train to take the team to New York to play the Giants in the World Series. The Browns lost the series.

On April 16, 1898, a fire broke out in the grandstand during a game. About 100 spectators of the 6,000 in attendance were injured. The ensuing lawsuits all but undid Von der Ahe. He had already accumulated massive debts and was forced to sell his players and finally the team itself for $33,000. He had also been ousted by the other owners as president of the American Baseball Association.

After the collapse of his baseball empire, Von der Ahe opened a saloon on Market Street across from the Municipal Courts Building but the saloon closed after a short time. The once wealthy, prominent baseball man was now in financial ruin and fell into obscurity. In the spring of 1908, the St. Louis Browns and St. Louis Cardinals played a preseason series at Sportsman's Park in which the gate receipts for the third game went to Van der Ahe; about $5,000 was collected.

By spring 1913, Von der Ahe's health was declining. He was confined to his St. Louis Avenue home suffering from dropsy and cirrhosis of the liver from his years of hard drinking. Chris Von der Ahe died at 3:15 p.m. on June 6. The funeral took place in the front parlor of his home. The pallbearers included former Browns manager Charles Comiskey, by then the owner of the Chicago

White Sox, and Ban Johnson, president of the American League. Al Spink and his brother Charles were also in attendance.

Von der Ahe built his monument at Bellefontaine when he was at the top of his financial game. His life-sized statue, which once stood at his ballpark, now caps his monument at Bellefontaine. In a prophetic moment, Von der Ahe had the accurate year of his death inscribed on the monument before he died.

THE BROWN BROTHERS

George Warren Brown, born March 21, 1853, was chairman of the board of Brown Shoe Company, the pioneering shoe manufacturing company. He founded the company in November of 1878 and served as its president for the next 38 years. In April 1873, Brown came to St. Louis to work as a shipping clerk at Hamilton-Brown Shoe Company, where his older brother Alanson was president and partner. During those days, shoes were imported from the East Coast and custom shoemaking was only done for the wealthy. When George left the company five years later, he established St. Louis' first successful shoe manufacturing company.

George and Alanson Brown were born and raised in Granville, New York. Alanson, born on March 21, 1847, was eight years George's senior. He worked for a drug and grocery store before coming to St. Louis in 1872. Here, he met James Hamilton and together they formed the Hamilton-Brown Shoe Company with offices at 12th and Washington. Alanson married Ella Bills in 1877 and his family resided at 4616 Lindell Boulevard.

George Brown set out on his own in 1878. Along with two other partners, George organized Bryan, Brown, and Company. Two years later, he married Betty Bofinger. The business started meagerly with only five shoemakers and little capital. Gradually, its business grew and in 1893 the company's name was changed to the Brown Shoe Company. The business was located at 17th and

George Brown.

Washington. Its Buster Brown label became a trademark for children's shoes. At the time of George's death, the company employed 6,000 workers.

George married Betty Bofinger in 1885, the couple lived with their adopted son Wilbur at 40 Portland Place.

Near the end of April 1913, Alanson came down with leucaemia, a rare and incurable disease. He and his family went to San Antonio, Texas in an attempt to improve his health. On May 10 Alanson died. His body was returned to St. Louis for a funeral in his home. Directors of the 1904 World's Fair, of which he was a member, attended the services as a group. All the Hamilton-Brown Shoe factories were closed the day of the funeral.

Eight years later on December 13, 1921, George Brown passed away during a recuperative stay at a spa in Tucson, Arizona. He had been ill for 18 months suffering from a bronchial infection. His body was also taken to his home in St. Louis for the funeral. On December 19, St. Louis employees of Brown Shoe Company were given the day off.

George is now buried in a hexagonal mausoleum at the corner at Woodbine and Prospect avenues. Inscribed above the iron-gated doors are the words, "God Hath Given Us Eternal Life." His brother, Alanson, was buried in a domed mausoleum across Prospect.

Alanson Brown mausoleum.

JOHN QUEENY

(August 17, 1859 - March 19, 1933)

John Queeny was born in Chicago in 1859. He was eleven years old in October 1871 when the Great Chicago Fire destroyed thousands of buildings and took hundreds of lives. His father John lost his own property to the fire. Queeny's first job was with Tolman and King, a wholesale drug company. In 1891, he took a position as buyer for Meyer Brothers Drug Company in St. Louis.

Although many chemical companies used saccharin as a sweetener, no company in the United States produced it. Instead, saccharin had to be imported from Germany. In 1901, John established his own small chemical company and began producing saccharin locally. He called his firm Monsanto in honor of his wife, Olga Monsanto Queeny. The company's first office was located at 1812 South Second Street and employed three people. Since Monsanto was the only company in America producing saccharin, the business expanded quickly. Soon Queeny began producing vanilla and aspirin. John became chairman of the board in 1927 when his son Edgar ascended to the company's presidency. At that time, the company employed over 2000 people and had branches in the U.S. and England.

John and his wife Olga lived at 3453 Hawthorne Boulevard. Queeny purchased the old Southern Hotel in 1920 which was once owned by Robert Campbell. He was a member of many city organizations including the Missouri Historical Society and he directed the Lafayette-South Side Bank and Trust Company. Queeny was also known for his charity and educational philanthropy.

By early 1933, John's health

John Queeny's grave.

was declining due to a malignant tumor. He died on the afternoon of March 19 at 74 years of age. The official cause of death was of a carcinoma. His body was taken to Arthur Donnelly Mortuary on Lindell for visitation. A private family funeral was held before burial at Bellefontaine.

ALBERT LAMBERT

(December 6, 1875 - November 12, 1946)

Aviation pioneer, Albert Lambert, started his career working in his father's drug business, Lambert Pharmaceutical Company. During his time there, he developed an avid interest in aviation and believed it would dramatically change modern transportation. He formed the Aero Club of St. Louis and later became its president. The club promoted the sport of ballooning by staging races and air shows. In 1907, Albert was elected to the City Council.

So taken with airplanes, Lambert eventually took up flying himself. His first instructor was Orville Wright. In 1911, he flew at an exhibition at Fairgrounds Park and he established an air mail route within the city. During World War I, Major Lambert trained pilots. He was discharged in 1919 and one year later he began work developing an airfield in St. Louis, a field which he maintained at his own expense. In 1923, Lambert Field hosted an international air race. Charles Lindbergh came to St. Louis to compete. Lindbergh stayed and became a pilot for an air mail route between St. Louis and Chicago operated by the Robertson Aircraft Company. Lambert was a financial backer of Lindbergh's *Spirit of St. Louis* and his transatlantic flight in 1927. The next year, as per an earlier agreement, Lambert sold his airfield to the City of St. Louis. He served the city as a member of the Police Board and became its president in 1937.

Albert and his wife Myrtle were married in 1899 and lived at 2 Hortense Place. Tragedy struck the Lambert family in 1929 when one of their three sons, George was killed in a plane crash. On

Albert Lambert.

Monday, November 11, 1946, Albert worked on his expansion plans for Lambert Field at his North Kingshighway office. He was in good health when he went to bed that evening. Early the next morning, Albert died in his sleep. The physician called to the house ascribed Lambert's death to heart disease. He was 70. Mayor Kaufmann said of the aviator, "In the passing of Major Albert Bond Lambert, St. Louis has lost a distinguished and valuable citizen. He was truly our leading pioneer in aviation. He believed in it, and seeing its great potential when most other men were scoffing, he lived to see many of his plans materialize."

Flags at Lambert Field were lowered to half-mast for one week. The funeral service was conducted in his home. Governor Lloyd Stark and Mayor Kaufmann attended the service. A large white cross with the "Lambert" name adorns the grave off of Woodbine Avenue.

WILLIAM DEE BECKER

(October 23, 1876 - August 1, 1943)

The August 2, 1943 issue of the *St. Louis Globe Democrat* reported:

> Mayor William Dee Becker and five other city and county leaders
> were among 10 persons killed yesterday afternoon when a wing
> broke from an army glider in which they were riding at Lambert-
> St. Louis Field and the craft plummeted 2000 feet to the field as
> 5000 horrified spectators watched. It was the worst air disaster in
> the history of St. Louis.

William Becker was born in East St. Louis, Illinois. His family
moved to the Missouri side of the river when he was 3. He attended Smith Academy and Washington University Preparatory
School. He went on to Harvard and returned home to study law at
St. Louis Law School, forerunner to Washington University Law
School. William was admitted to the bar and served as a judge on
the St. Louis Court of Appeals from 1917 to 1940.

William married Margaret Louise McIntosh in 1902. The couple
lived on Lindell Boulevard and later moved to an apartment at
5374 Delmar. In 1940, while still serving as a judge, Becker won
the election for mayor of St. Louis. As mayor, William was a
leading proponent of aviation. He wanted St. Louis to be the
center of flight in the coming decades. He pushed for the needed
expansion of Lambert Field and the development of a second
airport. His other priorities were to clean up blighted neighborhoods in the city and develop the riverfront. Sadly, he never had
enough time to meet all these goals.

On Sunday, August 1, 1943, thousands of spectators gathered at
Lambert Field for an air show. Around three o'clock in the afternoon, Mayor Becker and several city and county officials were
interviewed before their flight in an army glider. For most of the
officials, it was their first ride in a glider. Mayor Becker's wife told
the crowd, "I want to go up too. I'm pretty angry with the army

because it won't let me." The men then boarded the glider which had been designed by Robertson Aircraft Corporation in St. Louis. The glider, towed by a 150-foot nylon cable from a C-47 airplane, had made a successful test flight earlier in the day. The plane took off and circled the airfield twice to gain altitude. On the third pass, directly in front of the main body of spectators, the airplane released the glider at about 3000 feet. Almost immediately the right wing of the glider buckled and separated from the fuselage. The glider was sent spinning towards the earth. The occupants were

The crash of the glider that killed Becker and others.

equipped with parachutes but could not have saved themselves in the twisting descent. Within seconds, the glider hit the ground in a horrific crash. The glider's estimated speed at impact was 230 miles per hour. The time was 3:55 p.m.

Emergency crews rushed to the scene. When the dust cleared, wreckage was strewn about the field. The spectators were stunned, one observer told the Globe-Democrat, "Women all around me were screaming and fainting. I saw men with their eyes staring straight ahead as if they were hypnotized...Many covered their eyes or turned their heads as the crash came, as if hoping to thus avert the catastrophe."

A.P. Kaufmann, the president of the Board of Alderman, was sworn in as Mayor of St. Louis on August 2. He called for all flags to fly at half-mast until after the funerals of the flight's victims.

William Becker was the second mayor to die in office. Archbishop John Glennon paid tribute to the mayor and sympathized with the families. On August 2, Mayor Becker laid in state in the Lupton Funeral home on Delmar. Hundreds of citizens filed past his casket. In a bit of irony, Becker had visited a friend at Lupton on his way to the airport for the glider flight. In less than 24 hours, Becker himself was resting in the same chapel. August 3 was proclaimed a day of mourning in the city of St. Louis. When the mayor's funeral began at two o'clock, all business in the city was suspended for one minute.

The funeral took place at the Scottish Rite Cathedral on Lindell Boulevard. Twenty-five hundred people were in attendance; another thousand waited outside. Dignitaries included Governor Donnell and the three current judges on the Court of Appeals which Becker once served. The presiding reverend described Becker as "one of God's noblemen, a great human being, a man who loved people, a man who sought to help the poor and downtrodden."

William Dee Becker was laid to rest in a roadside grave on Wintergreen Avenue.

SARA TEASDALE

(August 8, 1884 - January 28, 1933)

Sara Teasdale was born in St. Louis in 1884. She attended Mary Institute and later Washington University but, despite her family's affluence, her childhood was an unhappy one. Sara was shy and spent much of her youth alone in her room writing poetry. Her style was simple, straightforward, and classical, usually written in the form of sonnets and quatrains.

She grew up with an obsessive fear of illness and dying. In one of her sonnets called "Fear," she wrote:

> The cold black fear is clutching me to-night
> As long ago when they would take the light
> And leave the little child who would have prayed,

Frozen and sleepless at the thought of death.

Her first book of poetry, "Sonnets to Duse and Other Poems" in 1907 established Sara as a major poet. The book was published by William Marion Reedy, the well known editor of the Mirror. In 1918, her book entitled "Love Songs" won the Columbia University Poetry Society prize, forerunner of the Pulitzer Prize for poetry.

In 1914, Sara married Ernst Filsinger, owner of a St. Louis shoe manufacturing company, at her family's home at 38 Kingsbury Place. A few years later, she and her husband moved to New York City where she had lived before the wedding. The marriage failed to undermine Sara's depression and the couple divorced in 1929 without any children.

Sara's feelings for St. Louis were very mixed. She once called it a "howling wilderness." But shortly after returning to St. Louis for her marriage, she exclaimed, "...St. Louis seems really a good sort of place."

In 1932, while doing research work in London, Sara came down with pneumonia. The illness exacerbated her depression and Sara's health declined steadily. After her return to New York in September she was unable and perhaps unwilling to shake the effects of the pneumonia. The bedridden poet was cared for by her sister Mamie and friend Margaret Conklin. Sara spent her time reading her favorite authors and writing to friends. In one such letter to a poet friend she wrote, "The illness seemed to me a becoming time to make my final exit. But apparently that is to be delayed, and I am not too glad."

Mamie knew her sister was becoming dangerously depressed. Sara was taking sleeping pills at an alarming rate and

Sara Teasdale.

hired Rita Brown, a nurse, to be with her constantly. By December, she convinced herself that her blood vessels were ready to rupture and a stroke was immediate. Her doctor made no such claim. Before the year was out Sara went to Winter Park, Florida to stay with a friend. For two weeks, she lay alone in a darkened room waiting for death to take her.

By mid-January Sara was back in New York. On the twenty-seventh, a blood vessel broke in her hand. She was convinced that the stroke that she had been long predicting would now occur and gave Mamie the power of attorney for her estate in case a stroke debilitated her. The doctor agreed with the family that a psychiatrist should be called in. Margaret Conklin spent the evening of the January 28 with Sara. They listened to Beethoven's Fifth Symphony.

In the early morning hours of Sunday the twenty-ninth, Sara drew a bath, lay in the warm water, and closed her eyes. She had taken a heavy dose of sleeping pills while Rita Brown was sleeping. Not finding Sara in bed, nurse Brown searched the apartment and discovered the body in the bathroom.

The newspaper quickly reported the death as accidental and not suicide. On January 30, the same day that Adolf Hitler became Chancellor of Germany, the *St. Louis Post-Dispatch* ran the headline, "Accidental Death, Autopsy Report on Sara Teasdale." The final coroner's report, however, showed signs of morphine and phenobarbital in her system. This report was never made public.

On Wednesday, February 1, funeral services were conducted at Grace Episcopal Church in New York City. Her body was cremated and the ashes buried in Bellefontaine Cemetery. Mamie did not honor Sara's wish that her ashes be scattered at sea so "that there may remain neither trace nor remembrance." A small, simple monument marks her final resting place.

Margaret Conklin edited the final version of Sara's last book, "Strange Victory." The volume was published in October 1933.

THE LEMP FAMILY

Johann Adam Lemp was born in 1798 in Eschwege, Germany.

In 1838, he immigrated to St. Louis and established A. Lemp & Company, a family grocery at the corner of Sixth and Morgan. Adam expanded his business and began manufacturing vinegar and brewing beer. In the mid 1850's, the influx of Southern Germans to St. Louis increased Lemp's beer sales. The beer sales eventually proved so profitable that Lemp quit the grocery business and concentrated solely on brewing. In 1840, the family opened the Western Brewery. The brewery was located at 37 South Second Street at Walnut, near the current location of the Gateway Arch.

Adam and his wife Justine had one child, William, who was born in Germany on February 21, 1836, two years before the Lemps moved to St. Louis. William was educated at St. Louis University. And upon his graduation, he joined his father at Western Brewery. Later, William opened his own brewery with Wilhelm Stumpf. In 1861, he enlisted in the Union army and soon after married Julia Feickert. The couple had nine children.

William's father, Adam, died on August 28, 1862 one year after his son's marriage. Adam was buried at Bellefontaine near the Charless family lot. Upon his father's death, William returned to Western Brewery, where he developed an ability to foresee developing trends. In 1864, William undertook a major expansion of the brewery and he built a new plant at what is now DeMenil Place and Cherokee. The plant was located directly over a maze of natural caves which were used to refrigerate the beer and lager. By 1875, William Lemp was the largest brewer in St. Louis, producing 42,000 barrels a year. William was also popular among the citizens of St. Louis. He was on the board of several organizations including the St. Louis World's Fair

William Lemp.

Committee, though he did not live long enough to see the Fair.

On November 1, 1892 the Lemp business was incorporated as the William J. Lemp Brewing Company. William Jr. was named vice-president and his brother, Louis, was made superintendent. By the end of the century, the brewery was producing 500,000 barrels a year with sales of $3,500,000 and employed over one thousand people. The Lemp's most popular brand was *Falstaff*.

William Jr. was born in St. Louis on August 13, 1867. He attended Washington University and the United States Brewers Academy in New York. He was well-known in the city for his flamboyant lifestyle. In 1899, he married Lillian Handlan and had one child, William III. The couple lived at 3343 South 13th Street.

William also had three daughters: Anna, Elsa, and Hilda. In 1897, Hilda married Gustav Pabst, son of his friend and Milwaukee brewer Frederick Pabst.

William's brother, Louis, was born on January 11, 1870. He learned the brewing trade from some of the best master brewers in Germany. He was involved in several political and civic organizations in St. Louis and was also a successful equestrian and breeder. In 1906, he sold his interest in the brewery and moved to New York City to work with horses permanently. He and his wife Agnes had one daughter Louise. He passed away on October 7, 1931 in his New York apartment. Years later, Louise had her parent's ashes placed in the Lemp mausoleum at Bellefontaine.

The original heir apparent to the Lemp brewery was William's son, Frederick. He was born on November 20, 1873 and attended both Washington University and the U.S. Brewers Academy. He was the most ambitious and hard working member of the Lemp children. In the summer of 1901, Frederick was ill and left St. Louis to recover his health in Pasadena, California. Frederick died on December 12, 1901; he was only 28 years old. His parents were devastated by the loss of their young son and, in 1902, William erected a magnificent mausoleum costing $60,000 to honor Frederick. It is the largest mausoleum in Bellefontaine, located directly across Prospect Avenue from the

Wainwright Tomb.

William was dealt another blow in January 1904 when another Frederick, his closest friend, Frederick Pabst, also died. Soon after, William's physical and mental health declined and he paid little attention to his brewery. On February 13, 1904, William's depression grew unbearable. When he awoke in the morning, he was not feeling well. After breakfast, he returned to his bedroom and shot himself in the head with a revolver. An anxious servant, who found the bedroom door locked, went to the brewery to find William Jr. and Edwin. William's sons broke the door down and found their father lying on the bed, the gun in his right hand. Three doctors arrived to examine William but they could do nothing. He died as his wife, Julia, returned home. No suicide note was found. His estate and brewery were worth an estimated $16 million at the time of his death.

The funeral took place the next day in the mansion's south parlor two months before the opening of the World's Fair. The brewery was closed for the day and employees came to pay their respects before the private service was held. Adolphus Busch, a longtime friend of William, was an honorary pallbearer.

After the service, a cortege of 40 carriages proceeded to the cemetery. His grief stricken wife and two daughters, Elsa and Hilda, did not go to the cemetery. His crypt was not sealed so that Anna and Louis, who were out of the country, could see their father one final time.

In 1911, the Lemp mansion was converted into new offices for the brewery. William Jr. took over the brewery after the Fair closed in November 1904. He and his wife, Lillian were involved in a very public divorce in February 1909. And for a time, the city was abuzz with news of the trial which took place at the Old Courthouse. A year later, William moved to Alswel, a country estate in Webster Groves overlooking the Meramec River. He remarried a woman named Ellie Limberg in May 1915.

Elsa Lemp was the youngest of William Sr. and Julia's children. She was born February 8, 1883. In 1910, she married Thomas

Wright, the president of a St. Louis Metal Company. They were divorced in 1919, but remarried the next year. The couple lived at 13 Hortense Place.

Elsa often suffered from acute indigestion and nausea; the illness aroused bouts of depression. On the morning of March 19, 1920, Elsa Lemp Wright shot herself in the chest near the heart. Her husband Thomas came into the bedroom and found her lying in bed, just as her father before, with a revolver in her hand. Her eyes were open, she tried to speak but was unable. Elsa died moments later leaving no explanation for the tragic suicide. William Jr. and Edwin came to the house, as did Samuel Fordyce, a family friend. Upon arriving, William Jr. was quoted as saying, "This is the Lemp family for you." On March 23, a short service took place at the house and Elsa was placed in the Bellefontaine mausoleum.

Prohibition

The passing of the 18th Amendment in January, 1920 had devastating effects on the Lemp family business. Prohibition forced brewers around the country to produce new products in order to survive. Like many brewers, the Lemps produced a "near beer." However, the product was not profitable and when the family did not attempt to develop other new products, William Jr. decided to close the plant and liquidate the assets. He sold the *Falstaff* trademark to Joseph Griesedieck for $25,000. And in June 1922, the Lemp Brewery was auctioned off to the highest bidder.

William was despondent over the brewery's closing. He felt responsible for the collapse of the business his grandfather, Adam, had started more than 80 years before.

On December 29, 1922, at nine in the morning, William sat in his office at the mansion. He told his secretary Henry Vahlkamp that he was not feeling well. A short time later, William pulled a revolver from his desk drawer and shot himself in the chest. Vahlkamp and other employees rushed in and found William on the floor by his desk. He was still alive. They summoned a doctor but it was too late. William III fell to his knees beside his father and cried. His wife Ellie was notified at their apartment in the

Chase Hotel. The funeral took place at two o'clock on New Year's Eve in the offices at the mansion and William was placed in the mausoleum above his sister Elsa.

William Jr.'s brother, Charles, also worked for the brewery but later went into banking and finance. He was a recluse who never married. In 1929, he moved back into the mansion where he would live the remainder of his life. At age 77, with his health declining due to arthritis and his mental health unstable, Charles shot himself in his bedroom. He was the fourth Lemp to commit suicide and third to die in the mansion. He was the only Lemp to leave a suicide note. He wrote, "In case I am found dead blame it on no one but me." No funeral ceremony was conducted nor was the death announced.

After Charles death, the Lemp Mansion became a boarding house. And in 1977, a restaurant opened in the mansion.

Edwin Lemp was the last surviving member of William's children. In 1911, he moved to *Cragwold*, his estate in Kirkwood. Two years later he left the family business and retired at the age of 33. Edwin was 90 when he died on November 30, 1970. He never spoke of the family tragedies. He is buried in the Lemp's Bellefontaine mausoleum.

William Jr.'s son, William III, attempted to revive the brewery after Prohibition was repealed. He took over Central Brewers in East St. Louis, Illinois and in 1939 changed the name to William J. Lemp Brewing Company. The brewery had financial troubles from the outset and eventually declared bankruptcy. William III died on March 12, 1943; he was only 42. He also was buried at Bellefontaine.

JAMES McDONNELL

(April 9, 1899 - August 22, 1980)

James McDonnell was born in Denver and raised in Little Rock, Arkansas. His father ran a successful general store near their home. After high school, James attended Princeton University and it was there, as a freshman, that the young man took his first airplane ride. Years later he said, "It was the first time I went up in an airplane, and I liked it. It confirmed the interest I felt I had in aviation."

World War I broke out while James was still an undergraduate and he postponed his studies to join the army. After the war, James returned to Princeton, earned his degree and went on to earn a master's from M.I.T. where he studied the physical mechanics of airplanes and flight. James then joined the U.S. Army Air Corps Flying School in San Antonio. During his time there, he was among the first U.S. soldiers to parachute from a plane.

When McDonnell returned to civilian life, he entered an industry that played to his passion and began working for several aircraft companies. In 1939, while still working as an aeronautical engineer in Baltimore, James moved to St. Louis to lay the foundations for his own aircraft manufacturing company. St. Louis offered everything he needed to launch a successful business: an established airfield and experienced aircraft workers. In July, the McDonnell Aircraft Corporation rented a second floor office in a building near Lambert Field. The young company staffed only two employees and, despite its small size, James oversaw every aspect of his business. His company had no sales or earnings during the first year but eventually James' thoroughness would pay off.

When the United States entered World War II, the demand for military aircraft exploded and James McDonnell was primed to fill the void. He employed over 5,000 people to produce aircraft components, primarily for the Douglas Aircraft Company. In 1942, McDonnell received his own government contact and was commissioned to build the FH-1 Phantom, the first carrier-based jet fighter. He later built the Whirlaway, the first twin-engined helicopter. When the war finally drew to a close, McDonnell had cemented his company's position at the forefront of aircraft manufacturing.

With the advent of space flight in 1959, McDonnell won a NASA contract to build the Mercury; the capsule in which astronaut John Glenn orbited the earth. His company later built the larger, Gemini spacecraft. In 1967, McDonnell Aircraft merged with the Douglas Aircraft Company. James was named chairman and chief executive officer of the new company, McDonnell Douglas. One year later, the company started producing the DC-10, wide-body jet.

In 1972, McDonnell's nephew, Sanford McDonnell, was named the company's chief executive officer while McDonnell stayed on as chairman of the board. Over the years, the McDonnell Foundation made tremendous contributions to Washington University, St. Louis Country Day School and the McDonnell Planetarium.

In August 1980, James suffered a stroke and on Friday the 22nd he died in his home; he was 81. Flags at McDonnell Douglas were lowered to half-mast. His company, which had opened with two workers, employed over 83,000 St. Louisans at the time of his death.

McDonnell's funeral was held at Washington University's Graham Chapel. The service was attended by McDonnell Douglas officials and other business and political leaders such as August Busch III and Senator John Danforth. Chancellor of Washington University William Danforth gave the eulogy. Music was performed by the St. Louis Symphony Brass Ensemble. The McDonnell family lot in Bellefontaine gently slopes toward the road with a row of shrubs on either side of the garden bench monument.

THE SPINK FAMILY

For more than 100 years, the *Sporting News* has been a publishing mainstay in St. Louis. The paper was established by Al Spink, a native of Quebec, who was born on August 26, 1853. In 1870, at the age of 17, Spink moved to St. Louis and began his journalism career as a reporter for the *New York Times* and the *New York Herald*. Later, Spink worked for the *St. Louis Post-Dispatch* and the *St. Louis Chronicle*.

In the early 1880's, he got involved in the St. Louis athletic scene. He helped establish the St. Louis Browns with Chris Von der Ahe and is credited with the naming of Sportsman's Park. After the team's success, Al went on to establish his paper, the *Sporting News* on March 17, 1886. The first issue of the eight-page publication sold for five cents. His brother Charles joined him as manager of the paper.

In 1894, Al sold his shares in the paper to Charles and, five years later, he moved to Chicago with his family. Al died in his Oak Park home on May 27, 1928 and was buried in Chicago's Woodlawn Cemetery.

Al Spink.

When baseball began enjoying an unprecedented popularity, Charles Spink devoted his entire publication to the game and his paper was dubbed the "Baseball Bible." The paper's income was supplemented by trade publications such as the *Sporting Goods Dealer* and *Toys and Novelties*. Given the success of his journal, Charles became good friends with several baseball notables, such as Ban Johnson, founder and president of the American League, and Charles Comiskey, one-time St. Louis Browns and later owner of the Chicago White Sox.

In April of 1914, Charles underwent surgery for acute intestinal trouble. He never regained consciousness. He died at age 51 in St. Luke's Hospital at 2:00 a.m. on April 22 leaving an estate estimated at one million dollars. Charles' service was held in his Lindell home. Pallbearers included Charles Comiskey and William Dee Becker. Charles was buried in the Spink mausoleum on the north side of Woodbine Avenue.

Spink family mausoleum.

Charles' son, John George Taylor Spink, born November 6, 1888, took over the *Sporting News* after his father died. Taylor, who was two when the paper was established, attended Central High School for a time but never graduated. At 18, he joined the paper as an office boy.

Taylor, though gentle, was a driven man. He worked long hours and ran his paper for 48 years, longer than both his father and uncle combined. True to his father's interests, Taylor continued to devote the paper exclusively to baseball. He was the official scorer for eleven World Series and, in 1919, he helped uncover the Black Sox scandal. He also published the *Official Baseball Guide* and the *Baseball Register.*

On December 7, 1962 , Taylor suffered a heart attack and died in his in Clayton home. He had suffered from emphysema for many years. August Busch Jr., who was among the baseball executives in attendance at his funeral, said, "Baseball and Taylor Spink were and are inseparable." Taylor was buried in the family mausoleum. Two months before his death, in October 1962, the Baseball Writers' Association established a writer's award in his name at the Hall of Fame.

Globe-Democrat columnist Bob Burnes wrote of him upon his

death:

> There is no particular category into which he fits. You could supply a dozen adjectives, some of them pleasant, some of them complimentary and some otherwise, and they wouldn't describe all the sides of this man who built his publication into a remarkably fine sounding board for baseball.

The fourth member of the Spink family to serve as editor and publisher of the *Sporting News* was Taylor's son, C.C. Johnson Spink. He was born in St. Louis on October 31, 1916 and named after both his grandfather Charles and Ban Johnson. He was schooled at St. Louis Country Day, Culver Military Academy, and Trinity College in Hartford, Connecticut. He served in the Coast Guard and as a war correspondent during World War II. In the 1960's, Johnson converted the *Sporting News'* format and began covering all sports. He served as publisher until January 1977 when he sold his interest to the Times-Mirror Corporation. Johnson Spink continued as a consultant until his retirement five years later.

Johnson died after a brief illness in 1992. He was survived by his wife Edith, the former mayor of Ladue. His funeral Mass was celebrated at the Church of St. Michael and St. George in Clayton. He was buried in the Spink Mausoleum in Bellefontaine.

OTHER NOTABLES AT BELLEFONTAINE

WILLIAM BIXBY (January 2, 1857 - October 29, 1931) was a native of Adrian, Michigan. At 16, he began working for a Texas railroad. When the Missouri Pacific Railroad bought out the Texas line, William moved to St. Louis to work as a purchasing agent for the Missouri Pacific. Later, he took a position at the American Car and Foundry Company where he rose rapidly and eventually served as chairman of the board. Bixby retired in

1905 at the age of 48. He later became president of the Laclede Gas Light Company.

William was a member of many civic organizations and often gave of his time and money. He was president of the Art Museum and the Missouri Historical Society, director of the Public Library, an original incorporator of the American Red Cross, and served on the board of St. Luke's Hospital. William had an avid interest in art, he made significant contributions to the Art Museum. He also donated a large collection of rare books and manuscripts to the Historical Society.

Bixby died of a heart attack when he was 74. He was survived by four sons and two daughters. A simple funeral service was held in the living room of his Portland Place home on October 31, 1931. Nearly 500 family and friends congregated at his home. The Missouri Historical Society and the Art Museum were closed during the afternoon of the funeral. William Bixby joined his wife in the family mausoleum on Prospect Avenue.

WILLIAM BURROUGHS (January 28, 1855 - September 14, 1898) had a natural aptitude for mechanics and an inherent interest in the inner-workings of machines. Born in Auburn, New York, he spent much of his childhood in his father's machine shop. While working as a clerk for a bank, William developed an idea for a machine that would calculate numbers.

In 1881, he moved to St. Louis and began working at Hall & Brown Woodworking Company but he spent every free moment developing his machine. Finally in 1885, when he was 35, William had created a working model that could do simple mathematical calculations. William established the American Arithmometer Company with three partners and sold stock to finance the company's initial production. William continued to tinker with his invention and by 1891 he had created an adding machine that could print out calculations. Two years later he received his patent for the revolutionary device and started producing the machine. As word spread about the ease and usefulness of the adding machine, they began to make sales nationally.

In 1896, William received an honorary medal for his invention from the Franklin Institute in Pennsylvania. William retired from his business pursuits a year later. He died on Friday, September 15, 1898 in Citronelle, Alabama. He was only 43. William was survived by his wife and four children. His tall granite obelisk faces the road and is inscribed, "Erected by his associates as a tribute to his genius." It is located near Cypress Lake.

Seven years after his death, the American Arithmometer Company relocated to Detroit and in his honor was renamed the Burroughs Adding Machine Company.

FREDERICK DENT (October 6, 1787 - December 15, 1872) was the father-in-law of Ulysses S. Grant. The Cumberland, Maryland native was a soldier and a fur trader. He purchased his White Haven estate, later Grant's Farm, from Ann Lucas Hunt. Fred and his wife Ellen had eight children, the most prominent of which was his daughter Julia. Though Frederick was not pleased with his daughter's selection for a husband, Grant and Julia married at his city home at 4th and Cerre in August 1848. James Longstreet, later a Confederate General, was a member of the wedding party.

After Grant was elected president, Frederick spent a good amount of time at the White House. He died there after slipping into a coma in December 1872. The funeral was conducted in the Blue Room and President Grant accompanied the body back to St. Louis for burial. His wife Ellen, who had died and was buried in White Haven in 1857, was reinterred beside her husband at Bellefontaine. Their scroll-like monument states that Frederick "died at Executive Mansion Washington."

JOSEPH GRIESEDIECK (July 11, 1863 - July 14, 1938) was president of Falstaff Brewing Company. The native of Stromberg, Germany came to the States with his father Anton when he was 4. By the age of 15, Joseph was working for a malt house. He went to Philadelphia for a time to work at a brewery before returning to St. Louis and operating the National Brewery at 18th and Gratiot. Joseph later served as vice-president and general manager when his brewery merged with Independent

Breweries Company.

In 1912, Joseph formed the Griesedieck Bros. Brewing Company with his brother. The brewery was located at 18th and Shenandoah. Five years later, Joseph left the business to open the Griesedieck Beverage Company, a manufacturer of beer and soft drinks, and in 1921 became president of the Falstaff Brewing Company. He purchased the Falstaff trademark from William Lemp. During Prohibition, the company processed ham and bacon.

Griesedieck monument.

On July 11, 1938, Joseph was to celebrate his 75th birthday at his home when he fell in his bedroom and was taken to St. John's Hospital with a fractured hip. He died three days later due to complications from the injury. Joseph had been a brewer in St. Louis for nearly 50 years. On Saturday, a service was held at the Arthur Donnelly Mortuary on Lindell Boulevard before a funeral Mass at the St. Louis Cathedral. He is buried with his family on Woodbine in front of a tall circular monument, topped with an angel.

SAMUEL HAWKEN (October 26, 1792 - May 9, 1884) was the famous gunsmith who designed the Hawken Rifle with his brother Jacob (1786-1849) in their shop on Washington Avenue. Their invention, one of the most advanced rifles in its time, was used by hunters from the Alleghenies to the Rocky Mountains. Men like Kit Carson and Buffalo Bill Cody swore by it. Hawken also founded the Union Fire Company No. 2 and became one of the best volunteer fireman in the city.

Samuel was born in Hagerstown, Maryland and fought in the

Samuel Hawken's gravesite.

War of 1812. He first came to St. Louis in 1822. He died at his son-in-law's farm of "debility senile" at the age of 92. A large crowd attended his funeral on May 11 at the First Presbyterian Church. His famous rifle is etched into his granite grave marker, a monument erected by his grandsons.

PETER LINDELL (March 24, 1776 - October 26, 1861), a native of Worcester, Maryland, was a successful merchant who came to St. Louis in December 1811. Soon after his arrival, he was befriended by Manuel Lisa. Peter's three brothers, Robert, Jesse and John, followed him to St. Louis and assisted him at the family general store on Main Street. The store's extensive inventory of goods made the store a huge success. By the time the brothers retired from their business in 1824, they had amassed a sizeable fortune.

Under Peter's leadership, they got involved in real estate and made an even larger fortune. The brothers accumulated 40 blocks and another 1,200 acres outside the city limits. They also ran the Lindell Hotel on Washington Avenue. Lindell Boulevard, which once ran down the middle of his property, is named for him. He died suddenly and unexpectedly in 1861. He was a lifelong bachelor and his estimated worth at the time of his death was $6,000,000.

Peter Lindell.

The Lindell family lot is marked by a large obelisk.

VIRGINIA MINOR (March 27, 1824 - August 14, 1894) was a prominent leader in the women's suffrage movement in the mid to late 19th century. She was born in Goochland County, Virginia and received most of her education from home. She married her cousin, attorney Francis Minor, in 1843 and moved to St. Louis a year later. During the Civil War, Virginia volunteered at hospitals to care for the sick and wounded.

In 1866, their only child Francis died at the age of 14. That same year Virginia threw herself into suffragist movement and established the Woman Suffrage Association of Missouri. At the suffrage convention held in St. Louis in 1869, Virginia made an emotional and motivating speech which brought her national attention and propelled the suffragist cause around the country.

On October 15, 1872, Virginia attempted to register to vote but was turned away for not being a male citizen. She sued in St. Louis Circuit Court but lost the decision. The decision was later upheld on appeal at the Missouri Supreme Court. The case was presented to the United States Supreme Court by Virginia's husband, Francis. The judges agreed with the Missouri courts and denied Virginia and other women the right to vote. She continued unsuccessfully to push for the equal rights of women but in doing so laid the groundwork for the 20th Amendment.

Virginia died of atrophy and an abscessed liver on August 14, 1894. The funeral took place the next day at her residence, 8311 Lucas Avenue. According to her will, she gave $1,000 to Susan B. Anthony, of Rochester, N.Y., "in gratitude for the many thousands she has expended for woman." She also left $500 to each of her two nieces on the condition they remained unmarried. Virginia is buried with her husband and child on the west side of Vine Avenue.

BYRON NUGENT (July 31, 1842 - April 4, 1908) founded a small company, B. Nugent & Bro. Dry Goods Company, and turned it into one of the largest operations in the midwest. He was born in Marysburgh, Ontario and educated there before coming to the States in 1865. After spending time working at Lord & Thomas, now Lord & Taylor, in New York, he went to Chicago and was employed by a wholesale store. In 1869, Byron established his own small store in Mount Vernon, Illinois.

Byron married Julia Lake in January 1873 and two months later moved his business to St. Louis. His first dry goods store, B. Nugent, was located at Broadway and Franklin. A short time later, three of his brothers joined the business. In 1878, the store was moved across the street to a larger facility at 815 North Broadway. Eleven years later, B. Nugent & Bro. Dry Goods Company moved again to Broadway and Washington.

Byron Nugent.

Byron and his wife and two sons, Edwin and Julian, lived at 29 Westmoreland Place where he eventually died of a heart inflammation on April 4, 1908. He originally came down with Bright's disease in August 1907 while vacationing in Massachusetts. He recovered when he returned to St. Louis but again became ill in October. He was homebound from that day forward.

The funeral was con-

An advertisement for Nugent's store.

ducted in the main hall of his home on April 7. Fellow merchandiser Charles Stix of Stix, Baer and Fuller was in attendance.

He was buried in family mausoleum on Prospect Avenue.

II

Calvary Cemetery

Calvary Cemetery.

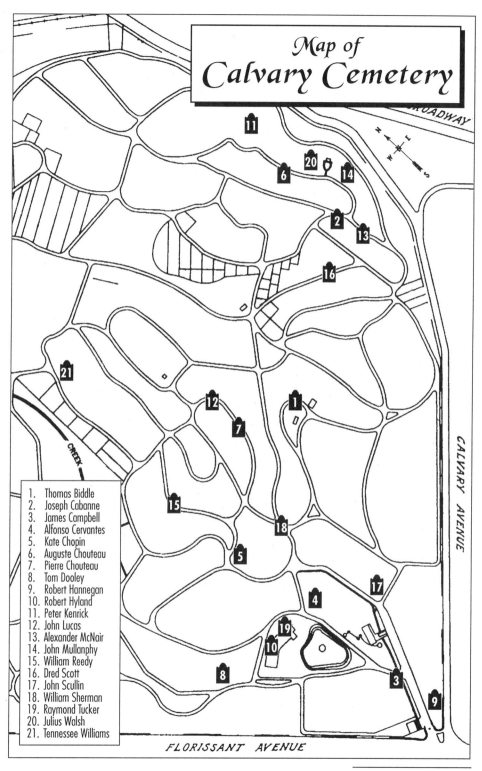

Map of
Calvary Cemetery

BROADWAY

CALVARY AVENUE

CREEK

1. Thomas Biddle
2. Joseph Cabanne
3. James Campbell
4. Alfonso Cervantes
5. Kate Chopin
6. Auguste Chouteau
7. Pierre Chouteau
8. Tom Dooley
9. Robert Hannegan
10. Robert Hyland
11. Peter Kenrick
12. John Lucas
13. Alexander McNair
14. John Mullanphy
15. William Reedy
16. Dred Scott
17. John Scullin
18. William Sherman
19. Raymond Tucker
20. Julius Walsh
21. Tennessee Williams

FLORISSANT AVENUE

After the cholera outbreak in 1849, an official city ordinance required that all new cemeteries be located beyond the city limits. At the time, there was thought that such a measure might stay the rising number of cholera victims. Most of the city's cemeteries, including all of its Catholic cemeteries had been filled to capacity due to the epidemic. Archdiocese records showed that on one day alone, June 25, 1849, 99 of 126 total burials were attributed to cholera. St. Louis Catholics were in need of another, larger burial ground.

In 1853, Archbishop Peter Richard Kenrick purchased 323-acre "Old Orchard Farm" northwest of the city from Kentucky politician Henry Clay. Kenrick established his own farm on half of this acreage and dedicated the other half to the development of a new cemetery. As the cemetery grew, more acreage was added to its site. Part of this property had once been used as an ancient burial ground by Native Americans and soldiers from nearby Fort Bellefontaine were also interred there. After its purchase, these remains were collected and buried in a mass grave under a large crucifix. It is located at one of the highest points of the cemetery.

Kenrick lived in the mansion on the western grounds for many years. Calvary was established on the eastern portion of the property and its association, the Calvary Cemetery Association, was incorporated in March 1867. Archbishop Kenrick was the association's first president. Graves from many of the Catholic cemeteries in the city such as Rock Springs and Holy Trinity cemeteries were reinterred in Calvary. The cemetery now contains over 315,000 graves in its 477 acres.

Like Bellefontaine, the cemetery takes advantage of its wooded environment. The tree covered lawns offer spacious room for those who sleep there. The roads within the gates graciously conform to the contours of the rolling hills.

The mausoleum near the entrance was dedicated in June 1961. Calvary is located next to Bellefontaine Cemetery at 5239 West Florissant Avenue at Union Avenue. The cemetery is open daily. The office is open Monday - Friday, 8:30 a.m. to 4:30 p.m., Saturday 8:30 a.m. to 12:30 p.m. A free map and information regarding some of the prominent citizens is provided at the office.

THE CHOUTEAUS AND PIERRE LACLEDE

In December 1763, Pierre Laclede and Auguste Chouteau stood atop a bluff overlooking the Mississippi River. Laclede described the benefits of all the resources the site had of offer to the boy who stood beside him. There were trees for lumber, stone outcroppings for foundations, clean water to drink, and the bluffs provided a natural wall against the threat of flooding. It was the ideal place to build a fur trading post and they marked their spot on the hill where the Old Courthouse now stands.

The Chouteaus, the "Founding Family of St. Louis," were involved in every aspect of the development of their town. They developed the land, constructed homes and warehouses, introduced a steady fur-trade and served its people

Auguste Chouteau.

by representing St. Louis' political interests. They were to become the most powerful family in the region.

Pierre Laclede Liguest was born in 1724 to a prominent family in Bedous, France. When he settled in New Orleans in 1755, he dropped his surname, Liguest, for Laclede and established his first fur-trading company, Maxent, Laclede, and Company. By 1762, Laclede was trading exclusively with the Native Americans in the Missouri valley; he made hundreds of trip up and down the Mississippi trading his products.

Auguste Chouteau was born in New Orleans to Rene Auguste Chouteau and Marie Therese Bourgeois. The exact date of his birth is unclear, though most historians believe it to be either September 7, 1749 or September 26, 1750. A few years after his birth, Auguste's birth father abandoned the family and returned to France. His mother Marie later met Pierre Laclede and the couple had four children, the oldest Jean Pierre was born October 10, 1758 in New Orleans. As the Catholic Church did not recognize divorce nor remarriage, the couple's children were born with the name Chouteau rather than Laclede.

Chouteau house.

Pierre Laclede became a father figure for young Auguste. Auguste worked as a clerk in his stepfather's business and quickly learned all about the fur trading industry. In August 1763, Laclede took Auguste along on a fur trading expedition up the Mississippi River to the Missouri valley. In early November they arrived at Ste. Genevieve, the first town established west of the Mississippi. The traders lodged and stored their merchandise at nearby Fort de Chartres at the invitation of the commander, M. Neyon de Viliers. In December, Laclede headed north up the Mississippi to explore possible sites for the headquarters for his business. He went all the way up to the mouth of the Missouri River before settling on a location just south of the rivers' confluence. Laclede marked the area and returned to the fort heartened. He told the commander, "I have found a situation where I am going to form a settlement which might become hereafter one of the finest cities in America."

Laclede spent the following winter months developing a design for his village. He decided to name the new settlement after Louis IX, who was the patron saint of the current French monarch Louis XV. Its streets would to be laid out in a grid like those of New Orleans.

On February 14, 1764, as warmer, spring air began to settle over the region, Laclede and Chouteau, and a group of workmen landed at the predesignated sight. The next day, they began clearing the land. By early April, when Laclede returned to the site, Chouteau and his men had constructed several cabins. Laclede's large residence was located on Main Street between Market and Walnut. As St. Louis grew, Native Americans from surrounding regions

Pierre Chouteau's gravesite.

began to visit the town to trade furs.

Soon after, Pierre Laclede made his stepson a partner in his business. Auguste spent most of his time among the Osage Indians, with whom the Chouteaus held exclusive trading rights. The Osage knew Auguste as an ambitious but fair man. He developed a relationship with the Osage which continued for years and earned him a significant fortune.

Laclede's son Jean Pierre, Auguste's half-brother, worked for the family business as well. The two brothers were quite close and Auguste taught young Pierre all about the fur trade and the art of negotiating with the Native Americans.

The brothers were of very different character. Auguste was calm and mild mannered, often keeping his feelings to himself while Pierre was more outgoing and emotional than his brother. He was not, however, considered irrational and he was well respected for his fair judgement.

In June 1778, Pierre Laclede was returning to St. Louis after two years in New Orleans. He became ill as he made his way up the Mississippi River. He would never make it back to the city he founded fifteen years earlier. Pierre died on June 20 at a village called Post of Arkansas on the Arkansas River. He was 54. Laclede was buried in an unmarked grave along the river. Today, the exact location of his remains are unknown.

Auguste took over the business in St. Louis while Jean Pierre continued to negotiate with the Osage. With the help of favorable government treatment and grants, the Chouteaus monopolized the fur trading business in St. Louis. They prospered further as the population grew and word spread of their success. Exploring beyond fur trading, Auguste invested a number of new ventures, including real estate, dry good stores, and banking.

In July 1783, when Jean Pierre was 25, he married Pelagie Kiersereau. The couple had three sons and a daughter before Pelagie's unexpected death in 1793, she was only 26. Less than a year later, Pierre married 15-year-old Brigitte Saucier. Brigitte cared for Pierre's four children and later had five sons of her own.

Auguste married for the first time in August of 1786. By this time he was the wealthiest man in the village. His wife Marie

Therese Cerre was the daughter of a wealthy St. Louis merchant. She was 17 and Auguste was in his mid-thirties. They had nine children, five daughters and four sons; the first two daughters died before the age of 8.

In 1789, Auguste purchased his step father's old home on Main Street. A second story was added and the home was remodeled into a stately mansion. It was the most lavish house in St. Louis and became the gathering place for town's elite class. Jean Pierre and his wife lived in a mansion further down on Main Street.

In the early 1800's, St. Louis was still quite small. Its streets were narrow and unpaved and its population spoke French exclusively. Auguste was appointed Colonel to the militia in 1808 and both Auguste and Jean Pierre were elected to the city's Board of Trustees in 1809. Despite suffering from a debilitating case of arthritis, Auguste was named its chairman. They went on to serve in numerous capacities for the city and their commitment was unparalleled. In 1813, President James Madison appointed Auguste as a member of the Territorial Legislative Council which was established to govern the Missouri territory. Jean Pierre was made an Indian Agent.

On November 23, 1816, Auguste informed the *Missouri Gazette* that he was retiring from the fur trade. Jean Pierre also retired and their children ran the business. The brothers, however, continued to work on their real estate and banking interests. Auguste laid the groundwork for the Bank of St. Louis and established the Bank of Missouri in 1816. Prominent men such as John O'Fallon, Alexander McNair, and John B. C. Lucas placed their influence behind Auguste's new bank. Both Auguste and Jean Pierre ran for Mayor of St. Louis in the 1820's but both lost their respective elections.

A great celebration took place in 1825 when French Revolutionary War hero Marquis de Lafayette visited St. Louis. Auguste, Mayor William Carr Lane and Stephen Hempstead were appointed to arrange the visit. A formal reception was held at Jean Pierre Chouteau's mansion.

Auguste Chouteau died on February 24, 1829. He was worth $100,000 plus a vast amount of real estate holdings. That day the

Missouri Republican reported:

> DIED, in this city, this morning, the venerable Col. AUGUSTE
> CHOUTEAU, the Patriarch of St. Louis. At the advanced age of
> eighty years, he closed a life of singular usefulness, possessing, in
> every vicissitude, the esteem of his fellow citizens. His eulogy is
> written in the hearts of the numerous circle of friends whom he
> had attached to him by his philanthropy, his unpretending be-
> nevolence, and the amenity of his manners.

His funeral was 9:00 a.m. the next day, he was buried in the
Catholic Church Cemetery on Walnut Street. The epitaph on
Auguste Chouteau's tombstone read: "Auguste Chouteau born in
New Orleans September 26, 1750 sent by M.L. de Laclede he was
the first to arrive in this savage land and founded the town of St.
Louis February 13, 1764. His life has been a model of civic and
social virtues. He died February 24, 1829, and rests in this tomb."
When Calvary Cemetery opened its gates, Auguste's remains were
moved. His new grave marker read, "His life was a model without
a stain."

In 1921, Auguste's great-great grandson Henri Chouteau had a
new tombstone made. He removed the reference to Laclede and
changed the year of Auguste's birth to 1740. There is no evidence
that the year is accurate.

For the next several years, Jean Pierre continued his work for
the city. He relinquished his duties as he slowed with age. Jean
Pierre Chouteau died of the effects of the cholera epidemic on July
9, 1849, at the age of 91.

Both Chouteaus are buried in Calvary with their families.
Auguste's tablet monument is located near the Priests' Lot. The
inscription still inaccurately lists 1740 as the year of his birth. His
son Henry (1805-1855) is on one side, daughter Gabriel (1794-
1887) on the other. Henry was killed in the same crash at the
Gasconade Bridge that Wayman Crow was injured in and Kate
Chopin's father was killed in. The Pierre Chouteau family lot sits
high atop a hill. The circular lot is centered with a large cross. His
mother, Madame Marie Therese Chouteau, who died on August

14, 1814, is also buried in the lot.

JOHN MULLANPHY

(1758 - August 29, 1833)

One day after John Mullanphy's death, the *Missouri Republican* wrote, "In his death the orphan and afflicted have lost a most liberal benefactor and literature a firm supporter."

John Mullanphy was the first millionaire and the first true philanthropist in St. Louis. Born and educated in Enniskillen, Ireland, Mullanphy joined the Irish Brigade of the French Army at the age of 20. After the Fall of the Bastille, John returned to Ireland and married Elizabeth Browne. The couple would have fifteen children, though seven died in infancy. In 1792, John and Elizabeth came to America and settled in Philadelphia. After a few years in Philadelphia, the family moved to Baltimore and then on to Frankfort, Kentucky. In Frankfort, Mullanphy opened a bookstore which proved extremely profitable.

Mullanphy came to St. Louis in 1804, just months after Jefferson had purchased the Louisiana Territory. Mullanphy opened a bookstore close to his home on Second Street. Given his service in France with the Irish brigade, Mullanphy spoke fluent French, a skill which won over new friends and customers in the largely French town. For a time, Mullanphy served the city as a justice of the peace. In this role, he conducted the civil marriage of Missouri's first governor, Alexander McNair.

Mullanphy pursued a num-

John Mullanphy.

Mullanphy monument.

ber of business ventures. He purchased real estate in and around the St. Louis area and, during the War of 1812, he sold cotton in New Orleans. Mullanphy made a sizeable fortune selling cotton to England and other European countries during the war and it became the basis for his fortune.

Understanding the importance of a solid education, John sent his children to the best schools in New Orleans and Paris. The family left St. Louis and lived for a time in Natchez, Mississippi and Baltimore but they returned in 1819 to make St. Louis their permanent home.

Mullanphy donated mass amounts of his fortune to charities. He financed the first hospital west of the Mississippi, St. Louis Mullanphy Hospital, on 4th and Spruce streets. He donated property in Florissant to St. Ferdinand and, in 1827, he presented a tract of land at Broadway and Chouteau Avenue to the Sisters of the Sacred Heart. Mother Philippine Duchesne built a church and a convent on the site, and at Mullanphy's request, educated orphaned girls there.

John had seven daughters and a son live to adulthood. His daughter Ann married Major Thomas Biddle, the paymaster at Jefferson Barracks. In August 1831, her husband was killed in a duel on Bloody Island.

After the death of her husband, Ann Mullanphy Biddle dedicated her life to charitable pursuits. She was liberal with her wealth and donated sizeable amounts of money and property to various charities, including the property which became Kenrick seminary. Ann was buried at in a grand mausoleum in Calvary Cemetery in 1858.

On August 29, 1833, two years after the duel, John Mullanphy passed away in his home "after an illness of some days duration." He was surrounded by his surviving children. Mayor John Darby who was a close friend of Mullanphy eulogized, "Among the distinguished men who were engaged in laying the foundations of St. Louis and building up the city, no one was most prominent than John Mullanphy. He read much and had one of the finest libraries west of the Mississippi. He was most liberal in his gifts for charitable objects and purposes." Mullanphy Street is named in his honor.

John's only son, Bryan, was perhaps the most well-known member of the Mullanphy family. As the only male heir, he re-ceived a large portion of the Mullanphy estate upon the father's death. Bryan was born in Baltimore in 1809 and studied law in Europe. In St. Louis, he established his own practice and later served as an Alderman, a Circuit Court Judge, and Mayor of St. Louis from 1847 through 1848. Bryan, who never married, was described by contemporaries as an eccentric liberal with truly, impressive intellect. His philanthropy matched that of his father. He was the founder of the Traveler's Aid Society. Mullanphy do-nated vast amounts of his wealth to the poor and provided hous-ing for the homeless. In his will, he left a portion of his estate to the Mullanphy Emigrant Relief Fund, "to furnish relief to all poor emigrants and travellers coming to St. Louis on their way bonafide to settle in the West."

Bryan was only 42 when he passed away on June 15, 1851 at his boardinghouse in the Missouri Hotel. It appears that Mullanphy had grown more eccentric with age and some took these peculiarities as a sign of insanity. Upon his death, the June 16 *National Intelligencer* said of him:

> ...he discharged his duties with remarkable fidelity, firmness, and impartiality; but always with certain eccentricities, which led many to suppose even then, that his mind was partially unsound.

Since then, these eccentricities had increased to such a degree, as to produce a very general impression that he was insane.

Mullanphy Community School at Tower Grove Avenue is named for him. He was buried in the Mullanphy family lot with his parents, John and Elizabeth. The tall monument stands atop a hill overlooking North Broadway.

JOHN B.C. LUCAS

(August 14, 1758 - August 29, 1842)

John Baptiste Charles Lucas was born in the small town of Pont-Audemer in Normandy, France. He graduated from the University of Caen in 1782 with a degree in law and returned to his home-town to practice. Before emigrating to America in April 1784, John married Anne Sebin. The couple settled on a farm called Montpelier near Pittsburgh, Pennsylvania where John dedicated himself to learning America's legal history.

A small and eccentric man, Lucas was of sound constitution. He was a tireless worker. John's hard work paid off and in 1792 he was elected to the Pennsylvania House of Representatives. He served in the state house for the next six years. In March 1803, he succeeded his friend Albert Gallatin in the Congress. After two years, President Thomas Jefferson appointed him United States judge for the northern district of Louisiana and John retired from Congress. Lucas had been recommended for the position by Benjamin Franklin, who was then the ambassador to France. The presidential appointment brought Lucas to St. Louis.

Despite political success, Lucas' personal life was beset with tragedy. In 1804, his child Adrian drowned after falling through the ice on Loutre Lake. Then in 1811, John lost his wife Anne. Two years later, during the War of 1812, their son Robert was killed in battle and in September 1817, his son, Charles was killed by Thomas Hart Benton in a duel on Bloody Island. John wrote of his son's death, "Nothing there remains of my late son, Charles Lucas, but his reputation." His hatred for Benton would consume his life and he often degraded his enemy in public.

Only Lucas' son James and daughter Anne survived their parents. James became a well-known banker and capitalist in St. Louis; he died in 1873. Anne donated much of her time and money to educational and religious institutions. She

John B.C. Lucas.

and her husband owned the farmland, later purchased by Frederick Dent and is currently Grant's Farm. Anne married Theodore Hunt and after his death in 1832, she married his cousin, Wilson Price Hunt; hence, the street name Lucas and Hunt. Anne died on April 12, 1879; she was 82. All three are buried in a Gothic mausoleum built into a hillside overlooking the Mississippi River

John Lucas built a new stone house at Seventh and Market streets and he lived the remainder of his life there. His political prominence led to his nomination for the first Missouri seat in the U.S. Senate. He lost the election to his bitter rival, Thomas Hart Benton. Like many distinguished men of the time, John invested aggressively in real estate and he became one of the largest land owners in St. Louis.

John Lucas died on August 29, 1842, two weeks after his 84th birthday. A tall granite obelisk simply engraved "Lucas" stands at the center of the Lucas lot in Calvary.

ALEXANDER McNAIR

(May 5, 1775 - March 18, 1826)

Alexander McNair.

Alexander McNair, the first Governor of Missouri, was born in Dauphin County, Pennsylvania. His parents David and Ann had eight children. Alexander was a small child when his father and his brother, Robert, left home to fight the British in the Revolutionary War. His father later died from wounds he sustained during the battle of Trenton. Upon his father's death, Alexander inherited the family farm.

As a grown man, McNair attended the University of Pennsylvania. He fought as a lieutenant during the Whiskey Rebellion in 1794 and, ten years later, settled in St. Louis to serve as a U.S. commissary. McNair also served as a colonel during the War of 1812. In St. Louis, Alexander held a variety of public offices including Inspector-General of the territorial militia and U.S. Marshall for the territory. He also sat on the board of trustees for the incorporation of St. Louis with the Chouteaus.

Alexander made contacts with the prominent members of St. Louis society. While John Mullanphy was serving as a justice of the peace in 1805, Alexander married his wife Marguerite. The couple resided on Third Street. During the first election for the Governor of Missouri on August 28, 1820, Alexander received seventy-two percent of the vote over his opposition, William Clark. But shortly thereafter, his political triumph was marred by personal tragedy. Two of his children died of typhoid fever just two weeks after his victory.

McNair was inaugurated Governor during the first session of the legislature held on September 18 at the Missouri Hotel at Main and North streets. One year later, on August 10, President James

Monroe officially announced Missouri's entry in the Union as the 24th state. The capitol of Missouri was moved from St. Louis to St. Charles in 1821 and later to Jefferson City in 1826. When McNair left the governor's office in 1825, he worked as an Indian agent.

In early 1826, Alexander came down with influenza. On the morning of March 18, he died in his home. He was survived by his wife and eight children. The *National Intelligencer* made its official pronouncement on April 7, 1826:

McNair's grave.

> It has become our painful duty to announce the death of our late Governor, Alexander McNair, in doing which we cannot refrain from joining with our fellow citizens and the bereaved family in lamenting his loss.

Originally, McNair was buried in the old Military Graveyard in St. Louis. His remains were reinterred in Calvary when it first opened. His red granite monument was "erected by the Calvary Cemetery Association, August 10, 1921. The one hundredth anniversary of the admission of Missouri to the Union."

DRED SCOTT

(circa 1799 - September 17, 1858)

Dred Scott may be the most famous, national figure buried in

Dred Scott.

Calvary cemetery, perhaps even in the whole region. Born a slave in Southampton County, Virginia, Scott would push the issue of slavery to the forefront of 19th century American politics and in so doing change the course of history.

Dred Scott belonged to a Virginian by the name of Peter Blow. In 1830, Blow and his family moved to St. Louis and brought Scott with them. When Blow died two years later, Scott became the property of Blow's daughter. She eventually sold Scott for $500 to Dr. John Emerson, an army surgeon stationed at Jefferson Barracks.

Eventually, Dr. Emerson was transferred to Fort Armstrong in Rock Island, Illinois and then later to Fort Snelling in Minnesota. Slavery was prohibited in both of these states. In 1836 while in Minnesota, Dred married another of Emerson's slaves, a woman named Harriet. A daughter Eliza was born in 1838 when the couple was returning to Jefferson Barracks after Dr. Emerson had been transferred back to Missouri. Their second daughter, Lizzie, was born at the Barracks.

In 1843, Dr. Emerson died and he left the Scotts to his widow Irene. On the advice of Taylor and Henry Blow, the sons of Peter Blow, Scott decided to sue for his freedom. The Blows believed that Scott's years in non-slave states had earned him the legal right to freedom. Scott's first case was heard on June 30, 1847 at the Old Courthouse in St. Louis. The court decision went against Scott. A second trial was conducted at the Old Courthouse and this time the decision fell in Scott's favor. Irene Emerson appealed the case a second time and it went to the Missouri Supreme Court. In March 1852 the court again reversed the preceding judgement.

By then, Irene Emerson had moved to the East coast and remarried a Massachusetts physician, Calvin Chaffee. She transferred her ownership of the Scotts to her brother John Sanford. Scott and his attorney Roswell Field, father of author Eugene Field, sued again in federal court but lost. When they sought a second federal trial their case was denied. In a final attempt to gain his freedom, Scott appealed to the United States Supreme Court. Montgomery Blair, a leading Washington lawyer and brother of Francis Blair,

Scott's grave.

represented Scott. The *Dred Scott v. John Sanford* decision was reached on March 6, 1857. The nation's highest court ruled that Scott's birth as a slave negated his rights as a U.S. citizen and he therefore had no right to sue in a federal court. The court simultaneously declared the Missouri Compromise unconstitutional. Scott's case was dismissed and his freedom fight ended precisely where it had begun.

Shortly after the decision, John Sanford returned Scott to Taylor Blow, the son of his original owner Peter Blow. Taylor freed Scott from bondage on May 26, 1857. But Scott's freedom was short-lived; he died in St. Louis on September 17, 1858. The *Daily Missouri Democrat* reported, "This celebrated individual died at his residence in this city, on Friday evening last, after an illness of some weeks."

Dred Scott was buried at Wesleyan Cemetery at Grand and Laclede. When the cemetery closed, his remains were reinterred in Calvary. His roadside grave is marked with a standing monument and a flat marker which reads, "In memory of a simple man who wanted to be free."

PETER RICHARD KENRICK

(August 17, 1806 - March 4, 1896)

Peter Richard Kenrick grew up in Dublin, Ireland. At an early age, he was consumed by religion, a vocation undoubtedly inspired by his uncle Richard, a parish priest, and his elder brother Francis, a seminary student. Peter attended St. Patrick's College in Maynooth, Ireland and was ordained a priest on March 6, 1832. A year later, he came to Philadelphia, where his brother Francis had been made a bishop. Peter quickly made a name for himself.

Peter was an affable man, known for his persistence and hard work. Besides his official duties, he wrote three books on religion. Among those whom Kenrick impressed most was Bishop Joseph Rosati of St. Louis. The two met in Rome and Rosati offered Kenrick an appointment as coadjutor, or assistant bishop. Peter accepted and was consecrated a bishop on November 30, 1841. A month later, he came to St. Louis. At this time, the St. Louis diocese had only one Catholic church in a city of 20,000 people, many of whom were Catholic.

In September 1842, Bishop Rosati died in Rome. Upon his death, Kenrick was named Bishop of St. Louis. He had been in the city less than two years. When St. Louis became an archdiocese in January 1847, Peter Richard Kenrick was made the first Archbishop in St. Louis. His brother Francis celebrated the official ceremony on September 3, 1848.

Kenrick made tremendous strides in developing the St. Louis archdiocese. He invested in real estate and used rent monies to support Catholic charities. In 1853, he purchased a farm north of the city and a portion of that acreage was set aside to establish Calvary Cemetery.

Kenrick was well-respected in the city. His manner was simple, his speech slow, with a faint touch of an Irish brogue. In July 1863, his brother Francis, who he had so admired, died in Philadelphia. Kenrick was deeply moved by the loss.

The St. Louis Archdiocese celebrated the fiftieth anniversary of his consecration as bishop in November 1891. Clergy from around the country came to pay tribute. The archbishop's health began to decline soon after the anniversary. In 1893, Kenrick appointed Bishop John Kain as his coadjutor. And two years later, with Kenrick's health in question, Kain was appointed Archbishop of St. Louis. Kenrick was given the title Archbishop of Marcianapolis.

Though on the surface he appeared to be well, Kenrick's health continued to fail him. He was feeling tired and ill and he spent most of his time at the archiepiscopal residence on Lindell Boulevard. As had become the custom, Brother Herbert from the Alexian Brothers' Hospital was staying with the archbishop through the nights.

Doctor Elisha Gregory examined his patient on Wednesday morning, March 4, and said of the archbishop's condition, "The Archbishop had a little chill and has a severe cold, but there's no immediate danger of death."

About 12:30 p.m., Thomas Franklin, Kenrick's servant, brought a warm drink to the archbishop. Thomas sat by his side as the archbishop slept. An hour later, Peter awoke, again complaining of chills. Thomas suggested turning up the furnace. "Yes, Tom, I could stand a little more warmth," Peter answered. These were his last known words. The housemaid, Hattie Mullarkey, entered the bedroom after Thomas had left. The archbishop was laying still, his arms were crossed on his chest and he had a smile on his face. She spoke to him but received no reply. She collected Thomas and the two quietly stepped back into the room. Thomas felt a faint pulse but within minutes the pulse had disappeared. Archbishop Peter Richard Kenrick passed away at 1:55 p.m.

Though Kenrick had been ill for some time his death surprised many, including his doctor. Archbishop Kain returned from an appointment soon afterwards and was told of Kenrick's passing. News of the archbishop's death quickly spread throughout the city.

Kenrick's body lay in state in his residence. Members of the clergy and friends of the archbishop paid their respects during the afternoon and evening. The procession of priests and nuns continued until the archbishop was moved to the Old Cathedral on Sunday, March 8. The body arrived at the black-draped cathedral amid a huge crowd that had gathered. Mourners filed past the coffin until after midnight. The cherry wood coffin was covered in black cloth, the inside was lined in purple denoting Peter's position as archbishop.

The funeral was celebrated on Wednesday, March 11. Kenrick was dressed in a yellow robe and purple cassock, and his miter upon his head. The *Globe-Democrat* devoted an entire page to the funeral. The cathedral was filled beyond capacity. And Catholic and Protestant communities were well represented including young seminarians from Kenrick Seminary. Several bishops and archbishops from around the country participated in the Mass. Archbishop Ryan eulogized his friend, "We saw him, a stately lily in the garden of the Church, and we saw the lily droop, till the powerless stem could no longer keep elevated the golden chalice; and when the lily droops, the stem and lily feel; and we felt that the flower hath fallen."

 Peter Richard Kenrick was buried in the cemetery he had established 43 years earlier. He was laid to rest in front of a large crucifix in the Priests' Lot.

(Archbishop John Kain led the archdiocese for the next eight years. He was a man of great executive ability and honesty. In May 1903, Kain went to St. Agnes Sanitorium in Baltimore where he died on October 13, 1903; he was 62. Bishop coadjutor, John Glennon, was appointed administrator. Kain's body was returned to St. Louis for a funeral Mass at the Old Cathedral. He is buried in Calvary beside his predecessor. Thomas Franklin, who served both archbishops, is buried in front of his leaders.)

WILLIAM TECUMSEH SHERMAN

(February 8, 1820 - February 14, 1891)

William was the sixth child of eleven born to Charles and Mary Sherman in Lancaster, Ohio. William's father died when he was nine and Thomas Ewing, a family friend and later a prominent U.S. Senator, aided Mary by taking William into his home.

Sherman's foster father arranged for him to go to West Point where he graduated sixth in his class. It was at West Point that William first met Ulysses S. Grant, a man who would become a close friend, military superior, and future president. Like Grant, Sherman had an unsuccessful career in the early years following his graduation from West Point. He never saw action during his Mexican War assignment with the occupational army in California. His highlights, at the time, were meeting frontiersman Kit Carson and investigating the discovery of gold on John Sutter's sawmill, a discovery which instigated the great California Gold Rush of 1849. Sherman was stationed at Jefferson Barracks in 1850 and he leased a house on Chouteau Avenue near 12th Street.

William returned East and married Ellen Ewing, the daughter of his foster father Thomas Ewing. Ewing was, by this time, Secretary of the Interior for President Zachary Taylor. Among the guests at the wedding, were the president, his cabinet and prominent senators Daniel Webster, Henry Clay, and Thomas Hart Benton.

William pursued several professions during the following years. After resigning from the army, he became a banker for one of James Lucas' San Francisco banks and later one in New York City. When the banks failed in the financial panic of 1857, he became a lawyer. Though he never studied law, he was admitted to the bar in Kansas, and joined a firm with two of Thomas Ewing's sons. In 1859, William became the superintendent of a new military school in Louisiana.

By 1861, the seccessionist cry in the South grew louder and many southern states were prepared to break away from the Union. Though Sherman had an affinity for the South, he was a northern man at heart. When Louisiana seceded from the Union in January 1861, Sherman resigned his post at the military school and returned to St. Louis where he took over the presidency of the Fifth Street Railroad Company. This position would last but a short time.

Sherman's future was transformed on April 12, 1861 with the Confederate bombing of Fort Sumter. Sherman rejoined the army and was appointed a colonel in the infantry during his first major

W.T. Sherman.

battle, the battle of Bull Run. Months later he was promoted to brigadier general. Shortly thereafter, Sherman asked to be relieved from duty; he was physically and mentally exhausted and thought by some superiors to be insane. Brigadier General Don Carlos Buell replaced him.

When Sherman returned to active duty, he was feeling much sounder and his military judgement was sharp. A letter to his wife reflected his attitude toward battle, "I begin to regard the death and mangling of a couple thousand men as a small affair, a kind of morning dash—and it may be well that we become so hardened." By March 1862, he was promoted to major general. He took part in the bloody battle at Shiloh where he was wounded in the hand and had three horses shot out from under him. His armies went on to capture Vicksburg, Chattanooga, and Knoxville. During the battle at Chattanooga in 1863, Sherman's 9-year-old son Willie fell ill with typhoid fever and died on October 3 in a Memphis hotel. It was a terrific blow to the Sherman family. Sherman wrote a friend on October 4, 1863:

> "The child that bore my name, and in whose future I proposed with more confidence than I did in my own plan of life, now floats a mere corpse, seeking a grave in a distant land, with a weeping mother, brother, and sisters, clustered around him. For myself, I ask no sympathy. On, on I must go, to meet a soldier's fate, or live to see our country rise superior to all factions..."

In the spring of 1867, Willie's body was disinterred and buried in Calvary Cemetery.

March to the Sea

When Grant become commander of the Union Army, Sherman succeeded him as commander of the Military Division of the Mississippi. His 100,000 man army took Atlanta in September

1864. Sherman's men completely decimated the city and proceeded to cut a path through Georgia and the Carolinas in the
now famous "March to the Sea." During the march, Sherman
found out from a New York newspaper that his son Charles had
died. The six month old boy had never been seen by his father.
Charles was buried at Calvary beside his brother Willie.

When Grant entered the White House in 1869, Sherman became
commander in chief of the U.S. Army. During the next decade he
wrote his memoirs and gave speeches to various veterans groups. In
one famous speech in 1880 he said, "There is many a boy here
today who looks on war as all glory, but, boys, it is all hell."

He retired from the army in 1883 and came back to St. Louis to
live at 912 Garrison Avenue. When officials within the Republican
Party urged him to run for the presidency, Sherman declined. He
enjoyed his retirement and visited old acquaintances like Ulysses
Grant. Grant was dying of cancer and attempting to finish his own
memoirs when Sherman visited him for the last time. Grant died
on July 23, 1885; Sherman participated in the funeral in New
York City.

Less than a year after the funeral, Sherman and his family
moved from St. Louis to New York City. On November 28, 1888,
his wife Ellen died of heart disease. She was buried at Calvary
beside her two sons. Friends and family could hardly communi-
cate with the grieving general. For weeks his own health declined,
he lost weight and his asthma worsened.

In late 1890, he confided to a friend, "I feel it coming some-
times when I get home from an entertainment or banquet, especially these winter nights. I feel death reaching out for me, as it
were. I suppose I'll take cold some night and go to bed, never to
get up again." As he predicted, he came down with a severe cold
and sore throat on February 6, 1891.

His asthma and acute erysipelas, an inflammation of the skin,
contributed to his illness. William's personal physician, Dr.
Alexander, attended the ailing general.

By Saturday the 14th, he was unconscious, his breathing la-
bored. The erysipelas had caused his neck and hands to swell, the
inflammation was also choking off air to his lungs. Though

Sherman was in a severe condition he suffered no pain. Two other doctors were consulted and agreed with Dr. Alexander that there was no hope for recovery. His daughters Minnie, Lizzie, Ellie and Rachel were by his side, as was the general's brother, Senator John Sherman. Members of his adopted family, the Ewings, were also present. When the news spread of the general's impending death, West 71st Street in front of his residence was filled with onlookers.

At 1:50 in the afternoon he breathed a heavy sigh and his body quit. The only sign of the erysipelas was a slight swelling under the eyes. President Benjamin Harrison, who served under Sherman during the March to the Sea, sent a message to the family:

> "I loved and venerated General Sherman, and would stand very near to the more deeply afflicted members of the family in this hour of bereavement. It will be as if there were one dead in every loyal household in the land."

Tuesday, February 17, the body lay in state in the front parlor of

Sherman's funeral procession.

his home. Sherman was dressed in full military uniform. The coffin was draped with an American flag, the General's sword, scabbard, and hat rested atop the flag. Three military guards stood at attention.

At ten o'clock in the morning visitors were allowed to see the General. Hundreds of citizens went through the parlor. Dignitaries, military personnel, and friends paid their respects. The widows of Generals George Armstrong Custer and Winfield Hancock wept upon viewing Sherman. Thousands more passed by the coffin on Wednesday.

In tribute to the General all flags in New York City were at half-mast during the funeral on Thursday. Government offices were closed, the New York Stock Exchange closed at noon. Sherman's son Thomas, a Catholic priest, conducted the funeral service. About 150 people, including cabinet members and numerous Generals, attended the private service. Julia Dent, the widow of General Grant, was also in attendance. After the service, former presidents Grover Cleveland and Rutherford Hayes arrived for the procession. President Benjamin Harrison reached the house a short time later.

At 2:00 p.m., six lieutenants carried the casket on their shoulders to the awaiting caisson outside the residence. Among the honorary pallbearers was Confederate General Joseph Johnston who fought against Sherman during the Civil War and ultimately surrendered to Sherman at war's end; the two became friends after the war and Johnston's presence at the funeral was symbolic of the Union's resiliency. (Ironically, Johnston died of pneumonia one month later due to the cold weather at the funeral march.) Thousands of people lined the streets of the procession route, hundreds more watched from windows and rooftops. Sherman was then returned to St. Louis. Former president Hayes was among those who came to St. Louis with the family.

On February 21, hundreds of St. Louisans awaited the arrival of the General at Union Depot, among them Governor David Francis. The train arrived at 8:30 in the morning. The procession moved up Eleventh Street to Pine, then north on Grand Avenue to Florissant Avenue to the gates of Calvary Cemetery. It took two hours and fifty minutes. The streets were jammed with people. It was the largest funeral procession the city had ever seen.

At Calvary, an honor guard fired three rifle volleys and a bugler played "taps." William Tecumseh Sherman was laid to rest beside his wife Ellen and his two sons in a roadside grave.

KATE CHOPIN

(February 8, 1851 - August 22, 1904)

Kate Chopin's writing career lasted a short fourteen years but during that brief time she produced over a hundred short stories, poems, and novels. Her writing appeared in magazines and newspapers nationwide. Readers were gripped by her passionate tales, her fluent style and true characters. Kate's own character — an individualist who smoked Cuban cigars and wore the most fashionable clothing— was equally enthralling as the personalities that filled her stories.

Kate O'Flaherty was born in St. Louis in 1851, a year after the cholera epidemic had killed thousands, including a high number of children. The Great St. Louis Fire also had wreaked its havoc, destroying most buildings in the warehouse district, one of which housed a business run by Kate's father ,Thomas.

Thomas O'Flaherty came to America from Ireland. He opened a successful boat shop on the St. Louis levee and soon established himself among the city's elite. He went on to become one of the founders of the Pacific Railroad. He married into a successful family but his wife died five years into the marriage. Six months later he was married again to Eliza Faris, Kate's mother. The family settled into a new home on Eighth Street, between Gratiot and Chouteau.

Disaster struck the family on November 1, 1855 when Thomas O'Flaherty was one of thirty-one people killed in the Gasconade Bridge collapse. Little Katie was only four years old. Archbishop Peter Richard Kenrick, a longtime family friend, conducted the funeral service and Thomas was buried at Calvary Cemetery near

Kenrick and the Priests' Lot.

Kate attended the Sacred Heart Academy on Fifth and Market. She left school for two years after her father's death. She returned to her studies for a time but stopped again during the Civil War. Kate spent most of the war years writing. During the war, her half-brother George died of typhoid fever while serving as a Confederate soldier. And her brother Tom was killed in 1873 in a carriage accident. Both were buried next to their father in Calvary.

Kate Chopin.

She married New Orleans native, Oscar Chopin in 1870. The couple lived in Cloutierville, Louisiana and raised six children. The Creole culture inspired many of Kate's tales. When Oscar died in 1881, Kate returned to St. Louis with her children and bought a house at 3317 Morgan Street, now Delmar, between Jefferson and Grand. She remained in the city the rest of her life.

It was during this period, that Kate began her writing career in earnest. In 1890, her first novel, *At Fault*, was published. It was her book of short stories, *Bayou Folk*, that gained Kate her literary fame. Kate's most acclaimed book, *Awakenings*, was published in 1899. It was the story of a young married woman who falls in love and has an adulterous affair with another man. At the time, Kate was condemned and criticized for its "unseemly" subject matter. Only later did it win its much deserved critical acclaim.

By the turn of the century, Kate Chopin was one of St. Louis' most well known citizens. She was included in the first edition of *Who's Who in America*. Kate moved to a rented house at 4232 McPherson Avenue at the end of 1902. Five of her adult children were still at home. She made a will during a period of illness and she told her children, "I hope I will die first so that I will not lose any one of you."

The St. Louis World's Fair opened in April 1904. Kate lived only six blocks from the parkgrounds and visited the fair most every day. Saturday, August 20 was very hot and humid day. Kate returned home tired, by midnight she was suffering from a terrible headache and lost consciousness. She revived the next day to the sight of her children including her son, Dr. George Chopin. She complained about the pain in her head. Kate seemed to improve but on Sunday night she once again slipped into unconsciousness. At noon, Monday, August 22, Kate Chopin died in her bed. The *Post-Dispatch* attributed her death to "hemorrhage of the brain, seemingly the result of unaccustomed exercise and exertion."

William Marion Reedy, editor of *the Mirror* and one of Kate's publishers, wrote of his friend:

> St. Louis lost a woman of rare intellect and noble character when death removed, last Monday, Mrs. Kate Chopin. A host of friends today honor her memory and cherish the boon of her acquaintance. She was a remarkably talented woman, who knew how to be a genius without sacrificing the comradeship of her children. As a mother, wife, and friend she shone resplendent and her contributions to fiction, though few, showed that she possessed true literary genius.

The St. Louis World's Fair continued without Kate. The funeral Mass was conducted at the New Cathedral on Wednesday, August 24. Kate was buried beside her daughter-in-law in Calvary Cemetery, her six children are now buried there.

One of the last poems Kate wrote was entitled *To the Friend of My Youth: To Kitty.*:

It is not all of life
To cling together while the years glide past.
It is not all of love
To walk with clasped hands from first to last.
That mystic garland which the spring did twine
Of scented lilac and the new-blown rose,

Faster than chains will hold my soul to thine
Thro' joy, and grief, thro' life—unto its close.

ROBERT HANNEGAN

(June 30, 1903 - October 6, 1949)

Robert Hannegan was a prominent member of the Democratic Party in the 1930s and 1940s and the man credited with keeping Harry Truman in the White House. It took only eleven years for Robert to rise from local politics to the national scene, a rapid climb which testified to his drive and political acumen.

Robert was born in St. Louis and educated in public schools; he attended St. Louis University where he was admired as an excellent athlete. He received a law degree from the University in 1925 and married his childhood sweetheart, Irma Protzmann.

Robert established a law practice and entered into the local political scene. In 1933, he was named the Democratic committeeman in the 21st Ward, his support of Mayor Bernard Dickmann earned him the chairmanship of the Democratic City Central Committee. In 1940, Robert threw his support behind the renomination of Senator Harry Truman of Independence, Missouri. Truman won the election by the slight margin and publicly credited Hannegan for his victory.

For a time, Robert returned to his law practice until Truman persuaded him to accept the vacant position of Commissioner of Internal Revenue. In this role, Hannegan became intimate friends with President Franklin Roosevelt and other top political leaders. Ultimately, Hannegan was appointed chairman of the Democratic National Committee. In January 1944, he was instrumental in Roosevelt's reelection for a fourth term and Truman's nomination as vice-president.

In April 1945, just weeks after the death of President Roosevelt, Robert and his family moved to Washington D.C. He served as Postmaster General in President Truman's new cabinet and was one of the president's chief political advisors. Hannegan's poor health forced him to step down as Postmaster General and National Democratic Committee chairman in November 1947. A year earlier he underwent an operation for hypertension. Ignoring doctors orders for complete rest, Robert returned to St. Louis where he and Fred Saigh Jr. purchased a majority interest in the St. Louis Baseball Cardinals. Robert became president of the club.

To relieve his ill health, Robert traveled with the family to Europe in 1949. While in Rome, he had a private audience with Pope Pius XII; three years earlier he was made a Knight of St. Gregory, Grand Order of the Holy Cross by the Pope. Robert also spent time during the year as a backer of the proposed Cardinal Glennon Memorial Hospital with Archbishop Joseph Ritter.

Robert's health was declining by early 1949, high blood pressure was taking its toll. In January, he sold his interest in the St. Louis Cardinals. In one of his final public appearances, a week before he died, Robert hosted President Truman in St. Louis and attended a dinner with him in Kansas City. On the evening of October 5, he suffered a mild heart attack. Robert Hannegan died at age 46.

President Truman sent a telegram to Robert's widow. It said in part:

> Despite the handicap of long continued ill health, Bob was a prodigious worker, with executive and administrative ability of the highest order...Mrs. Truman and I are thinking of you and the children in this hour of sorrow and send out with our heartfelt sympathy a prayer that the God of all comfort will sustain you in a loss so overwhelming.

An estimated 4,000 people crowded the St. Louis Cathedral for the funeral the next day. City, state, and national political leaders were among the mourners. President Truman himself was unable to attend but members of his cabinet were present to pay their respects. Two justices of the Supreme Court, the Governor of Missouri, and Texas Senator, Lyndon Johnson, were at the ceremony. The funeral Mass was celebrated by Reverend Gerald

McMahon. In his eulogy, McMahon related a discussion he had with Hannegan after a meeting for the proposed Cardinal Glennon Hospital. "He said then that while physicians had talked encouragingly to him, he realized that he might die at any time. 'And I am ready in every way,' he added."

Robert was buried just inside the main gate to the right. A large engraved cross stands behind the Hannegan marker.

TENNESSEE WILLIAMS

(March 26, 1911 - February 25, 1983)

Thomas Lanier Williams was one of the greatest and most admired playwrights of his time. In 1918, at the age of seven, he moved to St. Louis with his family. They rented a tenement apartment at 4633 Westminster Place, which later served as the setting for *The Glass Menagerie*. Tennessee's two decades in St. Louis were perhaps the unhappiest of time of his life. Years later he would describe St. Louisans as "cold, smug, complacent, intolerant, stupid, provincial." William's difficult family life, closely associated with his time in St. Louis, may have contributed to his dim perception of the city.

Williams had an overbearing, hard-drinking father and the two were never able to form a close relationship. His mother, Edwina, suffered the brunt of her husband's harsh temperament. Williams also had an older sister and younger brother. He was dearly devoted to his sister Rose who spent much of her life in a St. Louis sanitarium suffering from schizophrenia. Rose died in September 1996 and was buried in Calvary.

Williams attended Soldan High School and later graduated from University City High School. He went on to college at the University of Missouri at Columbia but dropped out during the Depression to take a job at International Shoe Company in St. Louis where his father was a clothing salesman. After two unhappy years of work, he enrolled at Washington University but later transferred to the University of Iowa, where he earned a bachelor's degree in 1938. During this time, he spent countless hours at the typewriter punching out the tales that would one day make him famous.

Tennessee's major literary breakthrough came with the success of *The Glass Menagerie* in 1944. The main character of Amanda Wingfield was based his mother, Edwina. Three years later *A Streetcar named Desire* won him his first Pulitzer Prize. He received a second Pulitzer Prize for *Cat on a Hot Tin Roof*.

Williams' plays often reflected themes in his own life. In 1979 he wrote, "My greatest affliction…is perhaps the major theme of my writings, the affliction of loneliness that follows me like a shadow, a very ponderous shadow too heavy to drag after me all of my days and nights." He often spoke of death, his favorite obsession. As a child he suffered from diphtheria which affected his kidneys and paralyzed both legs for a time. His eyesight was damaged and remained poor the rest of his life. He was terrified at the threat of heart or respiratory problems, real or imagined. As an adult he was a hypochondriac addicted to drugs and alcohol. And in 1969, his brother, Dakin had him hospitalized in the psychiatric unit at Barnes Hospital for his addictions. Tennessee spent three months there. From that point on, Williams was estranged from his brother.

By mid-February 1983, he was back in New York at the Elysee Hotel after extensive traveling around the world. The hotel was his Manhattan home for fifteen years. He was in a state of total exhaustion and once again addicted to drugs. He repeatedly told friends that death was closing in on him. He ignored the advice of doctors to be hospitalized.

On the morning of February 25, Williams' body was discovered slumped at the side of his bed by his longtime friend, John Ucker. He was officially declared dead at 11:10 a.m. An empty prescription bottle lay near him, two pills were found beneath his body, other medications and emptied wine bottles were on the night table. The coroner ruled his death as accidental. The autopsy showed that Williams had choked to death on a plastic cap from one of the prescription bottles. The cap lodged in his throat, cutting off air to his lungs, suffocated him. Friends claimed he had often opened bottle tops with his teeth and had apparently swallowed one on the night of February 24.

By noon, a huge crowd gathered outside the Elysee. Radio and television announced his death to the nation. The February 25 *St. Louis Post-Dispatch* headline read, "Tennessee Williams Found Dead In Hotel."

On March 3, Williams lay in state at the Campbell Funeral Home in Manhattan. Three days later a funeral mass took place at the St.

The funeral of Tennessee Williams at St. Louis Cathedral.

Louis Cathedral, only a few short blocks from his first home. More than 1,000 people attended the hour and a half service, hundreds more gathered outside. The reverend who conducted the service said, "The tragedy of Tennessee seems to be that the revelatory sword of suffering that pierced his heart seemed to be so much more therapeutic to others than to himself. He would seem to have remained all his life among the walking wounded."

Williams was buried in the family plot at Calvary Cemetery near his mother Edwina. He had wished to be cremated and "given back to the sea from which life is said to have come." Instead, he was buried in the city he most hated.

On March 8, marquees at twenty Broadway theaters were darkened for one minute in his memory. His raised headstone has a quote from his story *Camino Real*:

"The violets in the mountains
have broken the rocks"

ALFONSO CERVANTES

(August 27, 1920 - June 23, 1983)

Alfonso was born to Augustine and Victoria Cervantes in their home at 3723 Juniata Street in St. Louis. He attended St. Pius Elementary School and St. Louis University High School. After graduation, he enrolled in evening classes at St. Louis University and held a number of menial jobs. In December 1941, one day after Pearl Harbor, he enlisted in the Merchant Marines.

After the war, Cervantes returned to St. Louis and started his own insurance company. He helped organize and later was named vice-president of the Resort Corporation of Missouri which developed the Lodge of the Four Seasons at the Lake of the Ozarks. In 1949, Alfonso had his first taste of politics as an alderman. He was elected president of the Board of Alderman ten years later. In 1965, Cervantes defeated incumbent Mayor Raymond Tucker in the Democratic primary. He easily won the mayoral election to become the thirty-ninth Mayor of St. Louis.

Cervantes served as mayor for eight years, 1965 to 1973. He was known for his flamboyance and energy. He said of himself in a 1968 interview, "I don't picture myself as an intellectual or a thinker. I picture myself as a dedicated worker with common sense. My accomplishments are a result of my enthusiasm."

Alfonso Cervantes.

Downtown St. Louis went through a revitalization during his two terms. Construction was booming, the Gateway Arch and Busch Stadium were completed and the St. Louis Convention Center secured financing. It was later named Cervantes Convention Center. He also established anti-crime and summer jobs programs for youths.

Cervantes ran for a third term but lost in the primary to John Poelker. After retiring from politics, he established an insurance business called Cervantes-Diversified and Associates. He ran for mayor one final time in 1977 and again was defeated in the primary, this time by James Conway. At the time of the election, Alfonso also was battling cancer.

He was admitted to Barnes Hospital on June 9, 1983 as his condition worsened. Two weeks later, on June 23, Alfonso Cervantes died at the age of 62. He was survived by his wife Carmen, their five sons, and a brother and two sisters.

On Saturday, June 25, a police escort led the procession from the funeral home to the St. Louis Cathedral. Reverend Lucius Cervantes, the surviving brother of Alfonso, gave the eulogy. "Al loved to win. Did he want to be No. 1? You bet your life he did, in the worst sort of way." Mayor Vince Schoemehl was among the city officials present. Archbishop John May and Reverend Paul Reinert, chancellor of St. Louis University, conducted the Mass.

He is buried near the mausoleum.

ROBERT HYLAND

(March 25, 1920 - March 5, 1992)

Robert Hyland was the disciplined, aggressive leader of KMOX Radio. Hyland began his radio career in sales at a station in Chicago. In 1951, he returned to St. Louis and started at KMOX, where he climbed to senior vice-president of CBS Radio and general manager of KMOX Radio. Hyland established the now familiar format of talk radio with his "At Your Service" call-in programs. He was a workaholic with a hands-on management style; it was said he often arrived at his office at 1:00 in the morning. Under his guidance, "The Voice of St. Louis" became one of the most imitated radio stations in the country. It was there that he assembled and developed some of the most talented broadcasters in the business: Jack Buck, Bob Costas, Jack Carney, Jim White, Harry Caray, and numerous others.

Robert was born and raised in St. Louis. The Hyland family

Robert Hyland.

lived on Lindell Boulevard across from Forest Park. His father, Robert Sr., a well-known surgeon, was a pioneer in sports medicine. Dr. Hyland was the surgeon for the St. Louis Cardinals and the St. Louis Browns for more than thirty years. Among his baseball patients were Ty Cobb, Babe Ruth, and Lou Gehrig.

In November 1950 he was admitted to St. John's Hospital suffering from a liver condition. Dr. Hyland died December 14 at the age of 64. His funeral took place at the St. Louis Cathedral with burial at Calvary.

Robert Jr. attended St. Louis University where he was captain of the baseball team. Upon graduation he was offered a contract by Branch Rickey to play for the Cardinals. At his mother's advice, Hyland rejected the offer.

Robert married Martha Claiborne in June 1941. The couple had two children. In 1958, Martha died and two years later Robert was wed to Patricia Sowle. They also had two children.

Hyland's philanthropy benefitted countless St. Louis charities. He founded the drug and alcohol treatment center at St. Anthony's Hospital and named it Hyland Center in honor of his father. He served in various capacities for the St. Louis Zoo, the St. Louis Symphony, and Municipal Theatre, among other city organizations. He received numerous honorary degrees and awards, including the 1988 St. Louis Man of the Year.

Late on the evening of Thursday, March 5, 1992, Robert Hyland died of cancer in his Creve Coeur home. He was 71. KMOX Radio dedicated the entire next day to memories of Hyland. Bob Costas said of him, "…he was one of the most impressive people I've ever met. And perhaps the most singular individual I've ever encountered. I've never known anyone else like him."

The St. Louis Cathedral hosted the funeral at eleven o'clock, March 9. Governor John Ashcroft and Archbishop John May were among the numerous dignitaries present at the ceremony. Monsignor John Ronquest, the pastor of the Old Cathedral where Hyland attended Mass every morning before work, celebrated the Mass with the assistance of thirteen priests. Jack Buck and Bob Costas were among the pallbearers.

Hyland was buried in the cemetery mausoleum, in the Our Lady of Consolation room, second floor.

TOM DOOLEY

(January 17, 1927 - January 18, 1961)

Tom Dooley was born in St. Louis to Thomas and Agnes Dooley. He attended Barat Hall and St. Louis University High School. In 1944, he completed one year of pre-med training at the University of Notre Dame before leaving to serve as a medical aid in the Navy. After the war, Tom returned to his studies at the Sorbonne in Paris and St. Louis University Medical School from which he graduated in 1953.

Tom rejoined the Navy and in May 1954 was assigned to a camp at Haiphong, Vietnam as medical officer. He helped develop the "Passage to Freedom," a program to evacuate refugees from Communist northern Vietnam to southern Vietnam. Tom was awarded the Legion of Merit in recognition of his work at Haiphong. He lost a significant amount of weight during this time and spent a short stint in a Japanese hospital to recuperate. While in the hospital he began writing a book of his experiences; *Deliver Us From Evil* became a best-seller. He later had two other best-sellers published. Twentieth Century Fox purchased the movie rights to all three books.

When Tom was discharged from the Navy in 1956, he decided to dedicate his life to aiding the people of Southeast Asia. With permission from the government of Laos and help from former Navy colleagues, he established a small hospital in Nam Tha near the Chinese border. He financed the hospital with the royalties from his first book. In 1957, he returned to the U.S. and with Dr. Peter Comanduras, a Washington D.C. medical professor, founded MEDICO, the Medical International Cooperation Organization. The non-profit business brought aid to areas that lacked medical facilities. He financed the organization with royalties from his second book *The Edge of Tomorrow* and funds generated from numerous speaking engagements. Within a year, MEDICO had established 17 programs in 12 countries. Tom's brother Malcolm was named executive director.

In June 1959, while doing work for MEDICO in Asia, Tom slipped in the jungle and injured his right side. A few months later, a malignant growth was found on his chest wall. He went to New York's Memorial Hospital for cancer surgery. The missionary doctor who had helped thousands of refugees was unable to help himself.

For a time, Tom went back on the lecture circuit to raise more funds for MEDICO and then returned to Laos. Tom entered a Hong Kong hospital in November 1960 suffering from fatigue and exhaustion, and a debilitating pain in his spine. He once again returned to the States in December and entered Memorial Hospital. Examinations showed that he had a recurrence of the cancer. By January his condition worsened. The doctors could do nothing but ease his pain. On his birthday, Tuesday, January 17, he was visited by Archbishop of New York Cardinal Francis Spellman. Early the next day, Tom died.

Outgoing President Dwight D. Eisenhower said of him, "There are few if any men who have equalled his exhibition of courage, self sacrifice, faith in his God and his readiness to serve his fellow man."

The body was returned to St. Louis on Friday, January 20. Visitation took place at Arthur Donnelly Funeral Home on Lindell Boulevard over the weekend. He was dressed in a dark suit with a Legion of Merit pin on his lapel, a rosary in his hands. On Sunday evening the body lay in state in All Souls Chapel at the St. Louis

Cathedral. Bishop Leo Byrne celebrated the funeral Mass on Monday at 9:30 a.m. Father George Gottwald gave the eulogy. He said of Dooley, "…he spurned material comfort and, with utter and complete selflessness, went to minister to the sick and needy and under-privileged in a far corner of the world because he was fully conscious that his ability as a physician was given him to serve God." Over 2,000 mourners from all over the world attended the ceremony, including representatives from the Laos government. Dr. Peter Comanduras, co-founder of MEDICO, and 25 other members of the organization were among those in attendance.

Dooley family grave site.

The medical missionary was buried with full military honors. An honor guard representing the five armed services escorted the cortege to the grave. Tom was laid to rest in Calvary beside his father and his brother near the mausoleum. He was buried with a medal of St. Christopher which had a poem by Robert Frost inscribed on the back:

> The woods are lovely, dark and deep,
> But I have promises to keep,
> And miles to go before I sleep.

The same words are inscribed on the large, flat stone that marks his grave. His numerous accomplishments and awards also are listed.

Joseph Cabanne.

JOSEPH C. CABANNE (October 16, 1846 - March 17, 1922) was born in St. Louis. His family were direct descendents of Madame Chouteau. On the advice of his uncle, Joseph got into the dairy business. He started with the Mont Cabanne Dairy located in what is now Forest Park when he was 21. In 1872, he established the St. Louis Dairy Company at 12th and Chestnut. The dairy prospered and moved in 1896 to a large facility on Pine Street. Cabanne innovations included the covered milk wagons, the first creamery in the city, first delivery of milk in bottles. He later introduced a milk filtering system. He sold St. Louis' first whole milk, at a lesser price than skimmed milk.

Joseph married Susan Mitchell in 1869 and the couple had seven children. He was an avid sportsman who participated in amateur boxing and played golf everyday at Triple A in Forest Park. Joseph was the first president of the Civic League and one of the founders of the Missouri Athletic Club.

By 1922, Joseph was living with his daughter and her husband at the Buckingham Hotel. In February he came down with pneumonia. He suffered for six weeks, unable to shake its ill effects. The normally healthy Cabanne became terribly depressed over his condition. On Thursday afternoon, March 16, 1922, he cut his throat with a razor. He was rushed to St. John's Hospital where he died the next day. Monday the 20th, his funeral was held at the St. Louis Cathedral. He and his wife are buried in a roadside lot, just to the right of Alexander McNair.

JAMES CAMPBELL (1848 - June 12, 1914) was one of St. Louis' wealthiest citizens when he died of pneumonia at *Indian Field*, his summer home in Greenwich, Connecticut.

The native of Ireland came to the United States with his family when he was still a small child. During the Civil War, at the age of 14, he served as a messenger at General John Fremont's headquarters. After the war, Campbell worked as a surveyor for the Atlantic & Pacific Railroad and began buying land ahead of the tracks. His first fortune was made when property values increased dramatically as the construction was coming to an end. Campbell multiplied his wealth in the bond market and invested in St. Louis' streetcar business. In 1909, he was appointed chairman of the board of the North American Company, parent company to United Railways and the Union Electric Company.

In the summer of 1914, Campbell had two minor operations for a sore on his neck. It was later discovered that he had blood poisoning as a result of the second operation and his health declined steadily. Five weeks later, he developed pneumonia. On Friday, June 12, James Campbell died in his Connecticut summer home. He was 66.

The next morning his body was returned to his home at 2 Westmoreland Place. The funeral was celebrated at the St. Louis Cathedral to a capacity crowd. John Scullin, a friend of the family, accompanied the widow and her daughter. At three o'clock, all streetcars run by the United Railway Company stopped for five minutes in honor of its chairman.

Campbell's mausoleum at Calvary was built in 1911; it is located near the main entrance. The inscription above the door reads, "The Family of James Campbell."

WILLIAM MARION REEDY (December 11, 1862 - July 28, 1920) one of the most notable literary figures of his generation, was the editor of the literary journal, *Reedy's Mirror*. Born in St. Louis and educated at Christian Brothers' Academy and St. Louis University, Reedy received his undergraduate degree in 1880. He began his writing career at the *Missouri Republican* and later worked for the *Globe-Democrat* where he wrote a weekly column called "Sunday in Forest Park." In 1893, William founded the *St. Louis Mirror*. Three years later the name was changed to Reedy's Mirror. William was an excellent orator, he gave humorous and intelligent speeches and had a wonderful gift for storytelling.

William was highly regarded in his efforts to giving young, unknown writers a voice. He encouraged and often published new literary talent from around the St. Louis area. Short-story writer Fannie Hurst, playwright Zoe Akins, and poet Sara Teasdale were among his discoveries. William married three times. Margaret Chambers became his third wife in 1909 and survived him; she died in December 1949.

William was suffering from heart disease when he traveled to San Francisco to cover the Democratic National Convention in 1920. He died suddenly and unexpectedly during that trip. His body was returned to St. Louis on Monday, August 2, and taken to his home at Berry and Manchester roads. At 2:30 p.m. on Wednesday, the funeral was celebrated in the auditorium of the St. Louis University Institute of Law.

Reedy is buried near the top of the hill. A red marble marker, tilted back above his grave, reads "Editor and Author."

JOHN SCULLIN (August 17, 1836 - May 28, 1920) was the Chairman of the Board of Scullin Steel Company. The native of St. Lawrence County, New York started his business career selling stoves for $20 month. From there, he went to work in the railroad business as a brakeman before establishing himself as a railroad contractor. His largest project was the construction of the Missouri, Kansas, and Texas Railroad in 1860. Three years later, he married Hannah Perry in Montreal. Scullin came to St. Louis in 1875 and constructed several streetcar lines. He later worked as a financier and founded the steel company.

On Saturday, May 22, 1920, Scullin became ill while attending a function at the Log Cabin Club in Ladue. The next day he was transported to St. Luke's Hospital diagnosed with uremic poisoning He died less than a week later, at 7:50 on Friday evening. The funeral was celebrated at St. Mary and St. Joseph Catholic Church on Monday, May 31. Ambassador David R. Francis was in attendance. Scullin's mausoleum is located near the Calvary entrance.

RAYMOND TUCKER (December 4, 1896 - November 23, 1970) A native St. Louisan, Raymond Tucker received degrees from both St. Louis University (1917) and Washington University (1920). He was a mechanical engineering professor at Washington University for 13 years before accepting a position as secretary to Mayor Bernard Dickmann in 1934. He continued to serve in the next administration, that of William Dee Becker, before returning to Washington University. In 1953, he won the Democratic primary and ultimately the election. He served the city for three terms until 1965. His revitalization program for the city began with the construction of the Gateway Arch and Busch Stadium. Tucker was instrumental in the passing of bond issues that brought about the Planetarium and the highway system, among others.

In June 1961, while still in the mayor's office, Tucker had his cancerous right lung removed at Barnes Hospital. He died of congestive heart failure November 23 in 1970.

Tucker's funeral was celebrated on Wednesday, November 27, 1970, at St. Mary and St. Joseph Catholic Church. Reverend Edward Feuerbacher of the parish and Auxiliary Bishop Joseph McNicholas presided over the ceremony in front of nearly 300 mourners, including Governor Warren Hearnes and Mayor Alfonso Cervantes. Cervantes said of his predecessor, "The community has suffered a serious loss in the death of Ray Tucker. His contributions to the community were twofold; as an educator, he prepared young men well in the field of engineering; as a public official, he became a strong administrator who started St. Louis on the way back."

Raymond Tucker is buried on the second floor in the St. Louis room of the mausoleum at Calvary. Tucker Boulevard in front of City Hall is named in his honor.

JULIUS WALSH (December 1, 1842 - March 21, 1923) served as president for numerous financial and rail companies in St. Louis. His father Edward was a prominent merchant and manufacturer. Julius left the city to attend St. Joseph's College in Kentucky and received his law degree from Columbia University in New York. Upon his father's death, Julius inherited four railroads and the directorship of the Bank of the State of Missouri.

In 1885, he established the Northern Central Line using horse cars and later converted to the cable car system. He went on to become one of the most prominent figures in streetcar development. He was a member and later president of the St. Louis Bridge Company which financed James Eads and his bridge across the Mississippi. In 1870, he married Josephine Dickson, daughter of Charles Dickson who was president of the bridge company. President Ulysses Grant, a friend of Walsh's, gave a dinner at the White House for Julius and his wife on their honeymoon. Among the significant positions Julius held were president and chairman of the Terminal Railroad, the Union Electric Light and Power Company, and the Mississippi Valley Trust Company. He served as president of numerous other companies and sat on the board of other institutions.

Walsh and his wife lived at 4510 Lindell Boulevard. They had seven children, four sons and three daughters. Their daughter Mary was killed near Tucson, Arizona in April 1916 when she and her husband were shot by police who mistook them for wanted bankrobbers. Julius was a friend of Henry Shaw and served on the board of the botanical garden for many years. He was also a director of the St. Louis World's Fair in 1904.

J.T. Walsh.

During the early part of March 1923, Julius was severely ill and bedridden with a diseased heart. He died on March 21. Saturday morning at 9:30 a short service was conducted at the home before removal of the body to the St. Louis Cathedral. Offices of the Terminal Railroad stopped work for two minutes in honor of their former chairman, other companies in which he owned showed similar respect. Archbishop Glennon celebrated the high Mass at the cathedral. Company officers served as pallbearers. The Walsh family is buried a short distance from the Mullanphys.

Bloody Island and a Disastrous Year

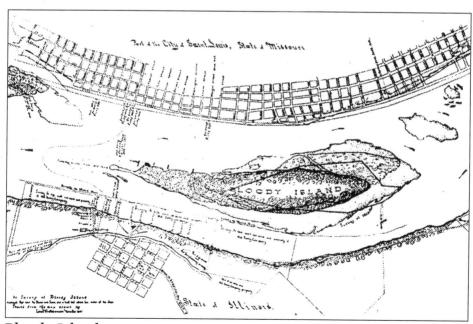

Bloody Island.

BLOODY ISLAND

Sandbar islands first appeared in the Mississippi River around the turn of the 18th century. These sandbars, built up gradually over the centuries by the rivers' shifting currents, caused navigational problems all along the Mississippi. As they rose, the current formed a new channel on the Illinois side and the river spread. By 1840, the river stretched 1 1/2 miles wide.

Duncan's Island, one of the largest sandbars along the St. Louis riverfront, was located on the Missouri side of the river, south of the city, between Market and Arsenal streets. In 1830, a St. Louisan by the name of Bob Duncan successfully raised a crop of corn on the island's sandy soil and thereafter the bar was referred to as Duncan's Island. Another significant sandbar, and the larger of the two, was called Bloody Island. This sandbar had a far more infamous history than Duncan's Island. It became the choice locale for many St. Louis duels.

For centuries, if a man's honor was disputed, he challenged his accuser to a duel. Duelling was an inauspicious part of civilized society, a way of settling disputes quickly. Many ended in the death of one or both of the participants. And though the acts were backwards and barbaric, they were fought with honor and respect.

The rules of a duel were agreed upon in advance; the methods were as varied as the participants. The challenged party in a duel was allowed to choose the location and the weapons. Each participant in a duel also was allowed a "second," or an assistant. The responsibilities of a second included, issuing the initial challenge, defining the terms, preparing the weapons, and standing in for a participant unable to perform his duty. The most common terms of a duel were the choice of weapons (pistols, swords, etc.) and the distance at which the duelist would stand. If a duelist fired a shot before the "fire" command was given, the second was permitted to shoot the man who had fired. Each man was also allowed to have a doctor or surgeon on hand.

In 1822, the Missouri Legislature passed a law to prohibit duels. In 1835, they passed another law making it a felony to partake in a duel even if no participant was harmed. Bloody Island, however, did not fall under Missouri nor Illinois jurisdiction. The state's hands effectively were tied as neither one could enforce its duelling prohibitions. Bloody Island became a virtual "free zone" and it is impossible to quantify the exact number of duels that took place beneath its trees.

One of the earliest duels on Bloody Island took place in 1810 between Doctor Bernard Farrar, the first American doctor to practice west of the Mississippi, and a young lawyer named James Graham. Farrar, stationed at Fort Bellefontaine at the time, was asked to act as a second for his brother-in-law, Lieutenant John Campbell who had been accused by Graham of cheating in a card game. When Campbell failed to appear on the island for the duel, despite his own friendship with Graham, Farrar was required to step in.

Pistols in hand, the two men stepped off the established distance and fired at one another. Both men were wounded; Farrar's injury was minor, Graham's more serious. Farrar revived Graham and worked to stop the bleeding but Graham subsequently died of his wound.

Three of the most famous duels on the island took place between 1817 and 1831. And four of the six participants would die from their wounds. The first of these duels arose between Thomas Hart Benton and Charles Lucas, both prominent lawyers in St. Louis. Charles Lucas was born near Pittsburgh, Pennsylvania on September 25, 1792. He was the second son of Judge John

Lucas. He came to St. Louis with the family when he was 13 and later fought in the War of 1812. Charles graduated law school and practiced in St. Louis, he was highly regarded around the city as an excellent young lawyer. He would later be appointed United States attorney for the Missouri Territory.

In October of 1816, Benton and Lucas opposed one another in a trial. During the closing arguments of the case, Lucas accused Benton of misstating the evidence he had presented. In the end, the jury's verdict came down in favor of Lucas's client but this no means settled the troubles between Benton and Lucas. Benton had taken personal offense at the insinuations made in court. In defense of his professional integrity, Benton challenged Lucas to a duel. However, Lucas refused, stating that he did not wish to settle professional differences in a personal manner.

On Monday, August 4, 1817, Lucas and Benton once again confronted each other at a polling location on election day. Lucas informed to election officials that Benton had not paid his taxes and hence had no right to vote. Benton responded by saying, "Gentlemen, if you have any questions to ask, I am prepared to answer, but I do not propose to answer charges made by any puppy who may happen to run across my path." Lucas was enraged by Benton's tone and wrote him a formal letter to settle the dispute. Joshua Barton, Lucas's second, delivered the message. Benton was in a mournful state when he received the note. He had spent the previous night with his friend Edward Hempstead who died after a fall from a horse. He told Barton, "I accept but I must now go and bury a dead friend; that is my first duty. After that is discharged, I will fight, tonight, if possible; if not, tomorrow morning at daybreak. I accept your challenge, sir."

That evening, Lucas left a note for his father who was an ardent opponent against duelling. "Embarked as I am in a hazardous enterprise, the issue of which you will know before you see this, I am under the necessity of bidding you, my brothers, sister, friends, adieu."

At 6:00 a.m. the next morning, August 12, 1817, the two parties arrived at the island. With Benton, was his second, Colonel Luke Lawless and Doctor Bernard Farrar, who had previously taken part in a duel himself. Accompanying Lucas was Joshua Barton and Doctor Pryor Quarles. Barton and Lawless had met the day before to decide the terms. Benton and Lucas took their positions, both men were calm and seemed relaxed. They faced each other at thirty feet apart, pistols at their sides. When the "Fire" command was given, both men fired in unison. Lucas collapsed to the ground with a bloody wound to the neck, just left of the windpipe. Benton stood uninjured; only later did he notice a slight contusion below the right knee. Lucas said he was satisfied but Benton was not. He angrily requested Lucas to stand and continue or fight again another day but Lucas was losing a significant amount of blood and could not stand. He was placed in the boat where he fainted before reaching the Missouri shore.

Within a few weeks, Lucas recovered from his wound. He had not been well long when Benton challenged him again. In the early morning hours of September 26, the men once again were rowing toward the island. The conditions of the duel remained the same but the distance between the men was shortened to ten feet. At that distance, a fatality was certain.

It was a hot day. Benton removed his coat and washed his arms and neck with water. The same men were present with the addition of Colonel Eli Clemson in support of Lucas.

"Gentlemen, are you ready?" asked Colonel Clemson.

"Don't you see I am not ready?" Benton angrily responded. Lucas waited while Benton took his place. As they stood a mere ten feet apart, pistols gripped against the side of their leg, Clemson mistakenly counted one...two...three instead of calling "Fire." Surprised by the change in procedure, there was a momentary pause before both men shot. Again Lucas missed while Benton's bullet, as in the first duel, found its mark. Benton approached Lucas who had fallen to the ground. The bullet had passed through Lucas's left arm and into his chest.

"Charles, it is an unfortunate affair! It is very unfortunate!" Benton told Lucas.

"Colonel, you have murdered me and I never can forgive you!" Lucas responded. He quickly added, "Yes, Colonel Benton, I am a persecuted man. You have persecuted me, and now have murdered me, but I can forgive you--I do forgive you!" Lucas held out his hand for Benton to take. Benton gripped the hand and said, "Your friends are with you." Benton turned away and moments later Charles Lucas died. He had celebrated his 25th birthday one day earlier.

Thomas Hart Benton regretted the incident for the rest of his life. He rarely spoke of the duel except on few occasions to close friends. Lucas's body was taken to his home. He is currently buried with the rest of his family at Calvary Cemetery. Joseph Charless, a strong critic of duelling, wrote in his *Missouri Gazette*:

> The infernal practice of duelling has taken off, this morning, one of the first characters in our country, CHARLES LUCAS, Esq., Attorney at Law. His death has left a blank in society not easily filled up. Tale bearers this is thy work! Innocent blood lies at thy doors!

The next Bloody Island duel took place in 1820 when Joshua Barton, who served as Charles Lucas's second, challenged Thomas Hempstead, brother of Edward. Barton was elected to the Missouri Legislature and later resigned that position to become Secretary of State and U.S. District Attorney for Missouri. Edward Bates, his law partner, agreed to serve as Barton's second.

Hempstead, born in 1791, was U.S. Military Storekeeper for St. Louis and Paymaster of the Missouri Militia. Ironically, his second was Thomas Hart Benton. The two duelists fired upon one another; both missed. Satisfied with a draw, the men reconciled and left the island.

In 1823, however, Joshua was back on the island. This duel arose as a result of an article he had written in the *Missouri Republican*. The article supported the charges made by Barton's brother, U.S. Senator David Barton, against General William Rector. According to Barton, Rector had abused his position as U.S. Surveyor General and awarded a large number of contracts to family and friends. Thomas Rector, William's brother, called Joshua on this charge. At six o'clock in the evening, June 30, Barton faced Rector. Details of the duel are not well-known. The end result, however, was clear: Joshua Barton was killed, while Thomas Rector remained unharmed. As the tale is told, the Rector family had a victory party later that same day. William Rector, however, would lose his appointment when President James Monroe reconsidered his selection.

Another duel, equally infamous as the Lucas-Benton affair and just as deadly, took place on Bloody Island in 1831. According to Charles Dickens in his *American Notes*, it was this duel that gave the island its name, Bloody Island. The players were Thomas Biddle and Spencer Pettus. Major Thomas Biddle was a Philadelphia native born on November 21, 1790. He came to St. Louis in August 1820 to serve as paymaster at Jefferson Barracks and later as a director of the St. Louis branch of the United States Bank. He had married John Mullanphy's daughter, Ann, in September 1823.

Born in 1802, Spencer Pettus had come to St. Louis in 1824 from Culpepper County, Virginia. Pettus, a lawyer by profession, was made Secretary of State under Missouri Governor John Miller just one short year after his arrival in St. Louis. In 1828, he defeated Bates for the U.S. House. At the time, Pettus was running for the Senate seat vacated by Thomas Hart Benton.

In July 1831, Pettus wrote an article in Benton's *Missouri Enquirer* criticizing Thomas and his brother, Nicholas Biddle, the president of the United States Bank. Pettus favored President Andrew Jackson's federalism and advocated abandoning the U.S. Bank altogether. Thomas, offended by such public criticism, wrote scathing articles of his own; in one article he compared Pettus to "a bowl of skim milk." But this did not quell his anger. On an early July morning, days before the election, Biddle went to the City Hotel at Third and Vine streets where Pettus was staying. Biddle instructed a servant to tell Pettus to show himself but Pettus responded that he did not wish to be disturbed. Biddle went upstairs and found Pettus sleeping in the hall in an attempt to escape the heat and mosquitoes in the rooms. Biddle, brandishing a horse whip, startled Pettus from his sleep with several sharp blows. A fight ensued and the two men wrestled. The commotion attracted the attention of everyone in the hotel and a brawl ensued as people attempted to pull the pair apart. Thomas Hart Benton, who lived in the same block, was awakened by the noise. Biddle was arrested for assault with intent to kill, but was later released. Beaten and bloodied, Pettus told his friend Benton of his intention to duel Biddle.

In early August, Pettus won the U.S. Senate election. In this victory, however, he had not forgotten Biddle's cowardice. Captain Martin Thomas, Pettus's second, delivered the challenge. Biddle's second, Major Benjamin O'Fallon, brother of John O'Fallon, gave a positive reply. At 5:30 p.m., Friday, August 26, they would settle their differences once and for all. A large crowd had gathered on the Missouri shore, many hung from windows and stood on rooftops to gain a better view. As the challenger, Biddle, who was near-sighted, opted to stand only five feet apart. At the command, each turned and fired; both men collapsed to the ground severely wounded. The weapons had fired almost simultaneously and everyone on shore heard only one shot. Witnesses said that Biddle and Pettus had stood so close that the barrels of their guns were nearly touching. According to the August 30, *Missouri Republican*:

Major Biddle was shot thro' the abdomen, the ball lodging within. Mr. Pettus was shot through the side, just below the chest, the ball passing entirely through the body.

Dr. Hardage Lane, Biddle's surgeon, went to his patient. "I feel very much hurt, Dr. Lane," Biddle told him. Lane examined the wound, he could stop the bleeding but nothing more.

The crowd awaited as both men were brought back to the Missouri shore by their seconds. Pettus was taken to Major Joshua Brant's house at Fourth and Washington where he died Saturday afternoon. He was 29. Thomas Hart Benton was by his side the entire time. A large segment of the population paid respects at the Sunday afternoon funeral. He was buried in one of the city cemeteries with no monument to mark his grave. He was later reinterred in Calvary Cemetery. Thomas Biddle died on Monday morning, August 29. His funeral took place the next day under a torrential rainstorm with burial in the Catholic Cemetery on Franklin Avenue. He and his wife Ann Mullanphy Biddle are buried in a large tomb in Calvary. When Biddle's remains were moved to Calvary on September 18, 1858, the undertaker found the bullet that killed him among the bones.

Though most 19th century duels were fought with pistols, some were fought with other weapons. In 1845, two men named Kibbe and Heisterhagen resolved their dispute with swords. The duel ended when Heisterhagen wounded Kibbe

Biddle mausoleum at Calvary.

in the face. Both parties were satisfied and the affair was settled. Yet another duel involved President Abraham Lincoln. In 1840, while still a Springfield lawyer, Lincoln was challenged by a man named James Shields. A very critical article had been written about Shields and he accused Lincoln of being the author. The two met, not on Bloody Island, but on the Missouri shores of the Mississippi across from Alton, Illinois. Cavalry sabers were the weapon of choice. Just before they were to clash, Lincoln explained that he had not written the article and Shields was satisfied. The duel was canceled and the two became friends.

By the 1830's, city officials sought to eliminate Bloody Island not only as a result of the duels, but more because of the navigational dangers the sandbar posed. The combination of Bloody Island and Duncan's Island, just to the south, made it increasingly difficult for ships to maneuver; the open water that did exist was becoming too shallow and ships were running aground. As most of St. Louis' economy depended on the river, the river had to stay navigable. To solve the problem, Mayor John Darby sought help from the federal government. In 1835, General Charles Gratiot Jr. who was commander of the Army Corps of Engineers at the time, appointed Lieutenant Robert E. Lee and Second Lieutenant Montgomery Miegs to expand the harbor. (In May 1864, Miegs established the military cemetery in Arlington, Virginia on grounds of

Arlington House, the estate owned by Robert E. Lee. He was buried in Arlington when he died in 1892.) Miegs and Lee first arrived in St. Louis in 1837 to examine the situation. Lee returned to Arlington House in Washington D.C. and developed a plan to put a system of underwater dikes in place that would shift the current toward the Missouri side of the river. The first dike on the southern tip of the island directed water at Duncan's Island. Another dike was to extend from the northern point of Bloody Island to the Illinois shore. Lee's plan was adopted from earlier proposals by Gratiot and the "Father of the Mississippi," Henry Shreve.

Lee and his family lived at Council Hall (owned by William Clark and inhabited by Dr. William Beaumont) when he returned to St. Louis in May 1838. The southern dike was constructed of rocks, stones and sand. The dike increased the depth of the river and eliminated a portion of Duncan's Island.

Only a small portion of the second dike was built that summer. In December, Lee was informed that Charles Gratiot, a strong proponent of the project, had been dismissed from the Corps of Engineers. Lee would have trouble securing financial assets from Gratiot's successor for the completion of the work.

In July 1939, Lee completed work on the second dike. By the next year, the depth of the river had increased significantly allowing the largest ships to again safely navigate the waters. By 1856, Bloody Island had merged with the Illinois shore. Later, it would become the end of a railroad line and a troop location during the Civil War.

Though the island had been eliminated, duels still occurred in St. Louis. In order to stop the practice, delegates at the Missouri Constitutional Convention in 1865 wrote a new section into the Constitution. It stated that "no person shall hereafter fight a duel, act as a second, accept or carry a challenge or agree to go out of the state (for instance, to Bloody Island) to fight a duel, could hold any office in the state." As many duellists held government office, duelling disappeared.

1849: A Disastrous Year

Cholera first appeared in St. Louis in 1832. The highly contagious disease killed hundreds but quickly faded and finally disappeared before reemerging for a short time the next year.

But, in December 1848, cholera once again appeared among the foreign immigrants, mostly German, arriving in New Orleans by ship. As these immigrants moved up into the Ohio and Mississippi valleys to make their new homes, so spread the cholera. During the last week of 1848 and early 1849, several ships arrived in St. Louis with passengers and crew carrying the disease; some were dead on arrival. At the time, city officials did not recognize the seriousness of the disease. Immigrants stayed in city boardinghouses without medical examinations nor quarantines.

By January, the disease was slowly spreading. Thirty-six people died of cholera that month. In February, the toll was 21. The deaths in March and April jumped to 78 and 126, respectively. Though 261 people had died, the city still did nothing to curtail the disease; ships continued to disembark their infected passengers on the St. Louis riverfront from New Orleans. By the second week of May, an average of 26 people died per day. St. Louis Hospital was filled beyond its capacity.

In the spring, a flood devastated the riverfront. Another disaster was born on May 17, 1849. At about 10:00 in the evening, the steamship *White Cloud* arrived at the foot of Franklin Avenue joining 24 other steamships. Shortly after tying off the ship burst into flames. It quickly spread to the other ships.

A stiff wind spread the flames to the levee, igniting the crates of goods that were awaiting shipment. Volunteer fire departments were all that existed in the city at the time, one of the first to respond was the fire company #5 at Third and Olive. From the levee the fire raged out of control to warehouses between Locust and Vine; from there it spread south to a ten-block area of densely-packed stores and warehouses in the central business district. Buildings along Market Street were blown up with gunpowder in order to halt the flames.

By the time the fire was brought under control, over 400 build-

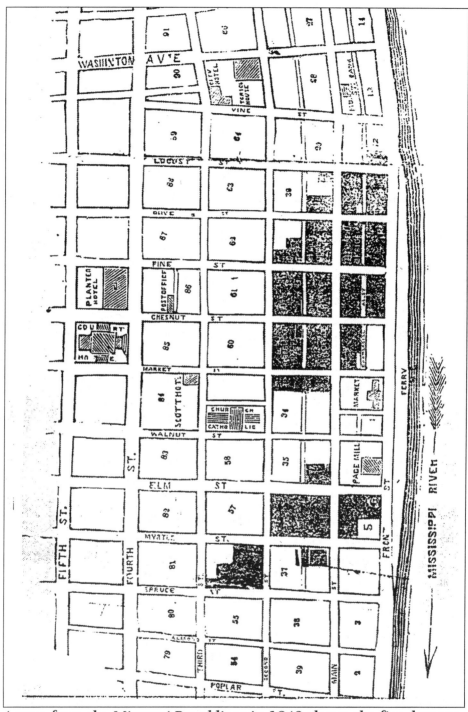

A map from the *Missouri Republican* in 1849 shows the fire damage in the shaded areas.

ings in a 15-block area had been destroyed. At sunrise the next morning, the citizens had their first look at the devastation. Stores, warehouses and homes were in ruins. The "Sublette & Campbell" store burned to the ground as did the house of Henry Blow. The estimated loss in property was $6.1 million.

It took years to reconstruct the city. Stricter building codes were put into place and structures were required to be rebuilt using brick, cast iron and other non-flammable materials. The fire resulted in the establishment of a full-time municipal fire department in 1856.

The fire did not put an end to the cholera epidemic. And a few short weeks after the Great Fire, the mortality rate ballooned to a high of over 86 deaths per day. Over 1,250 people died before the end of June. The June 19 issue of *The Missouri Republican* described the epidemic:

> The cholera is still sweeping off its scores of victims every day, and this at a time when the atmosphere is pure and elastic, and there appears to be no good reason for the prevalence of the mortality... Even while the purification is going on, many unfortunate persons must die, but still the effort to save others *should be made.*

Finally moved to action, the government passed an ordinance to establish the Committee of Public Health. In June, the committee set guidelines to prevent the spread and improve conditions. Schools were designated as hospitals, streets and alleys were thoroughly cleaned, people were instructed to boil their drinking water and only include meat in their diet. Vegetables were to be avoided unless thoroughly cooked; the sale of vegetables was forbidden in the city. And ponds around the city, including Chouteau's Pond, were drained. These measures did little to slow the disease. St. Louis lacked a sewer system at the time. Though the city did have a few drains which connected with the river, they were insufficient and pools of rain water and human waste often formed. Infected drinking water from the Mississippi River exacerbated the crisis.

Eventually, the committee established a quarantine station on Arsenal Island, just south of the city. Steamships were required to dock on the island and full examinations were made of each immigrant. Immigrants carrying the disease were forced to remain on the island until they recovered or died. None of the steps taken by the Committee of Public Health had any apparent effect on slowing or stopping the disease. July was the peak month, over 2,200 people died. Finally the death rate began to decline, and decline rapidly; only 54 people died in August, 13 in September. On August 1, the Committee of Public Health declared the end of the epidemic.

The final toll was about 4,280 cholera-related deaths or six percent of the population, nearly one-third were children under the age of six. It could be said that every family in St. Louis had at least one member die of the disease.

IV

Other St. Louis Resting Places

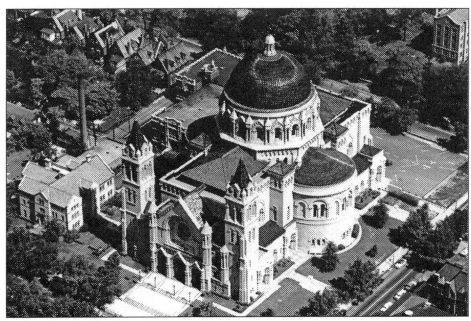

St. Louis Cathedral.

Rose Philippine Duchesne

(August 29, 1769 - November 18, 1852)

Mother Duchesne was canonized a saint on July 4, 1988. Pope John Paul II celebrated the Mass of canonization in Vatican City, Rome. The next day, St. Louis' Archbishop John May celebrated another Mass at the church of the Gesu in Rome.

Philippine was born to wealthy parents in Grenoble, France. Her father was a nationally known political figure and her mother came from a family of prominent textile manufacturers. The Duchesnes had twelve children and Rose Philippine, in a foreshadowing of what was to come, was baptized in the Church of St. Louis in France. She attended school at a French monastery where she was influenced by the religious order. Soon after, she accepted her vocation and, at the age of 18, she decided to become a nun.

The role of the Catholic Church had been examined sceptically and vilified throughout the Enlightenment and, during the most radical phase of the French Revolution, Catholicism was outlawed. During this turbulent period, Duchesne risked her life in order to help others. Afterwards, she joined the order she would be with for the rest of her life, the Society of the Sacred Heart. Through the Society, she started girl's schools in Grenoble and Paris.

For years she longed to come to America and work with the Native Americans. When Bishop Louis DuBourg of New Orleans asked the Society with help for his missions, Mother Barat, founder of Sacred Heart, gave her permission for Philippine and four other nuns to come to America. DuBourg promised the sisters a school and convent in America.

She arrived in New Orleans after a 73-day voyage during which her ship was stormed by pirates. The nuns then journeyed up the Mississippi to St. Louis, arriving August 21, 1818. Philippine was ill with scurvy upon her arrival. After a short recovery, the nuns proceeded to their new home in St. Charles. There they lived in a small and Spartan log cabin. In September, the first free school west of the Mississippi opened; a tuition-based academy opened weeks later. Among the first students were the relatives of Auguste Chouteau and Manuel Lisa. The income from the academy went to fund missionary work with the Native Americans.

Bishop DuBourg transferred the nuns to Florissant after one year in St. Charles. They built new schools and a novitiate for nuns to study. The school today is at One Rue St. Francois. Philippine's bedroom in the convent was a small closet under the stairs; she wished to be close to the chapel and not disturb others as she often prayed through the night. Mother Duchesne would ultimately supervise six schools in Missouri and Louisiana. In 1827, she opened the Academy of the Sacred Heart in St. Louis, and the city's first orphanage for girls. The academy merged with Villa Duchesne in 1968.

Rose Philippine Duchesne.

Philippine cherished what few relationships she had. Father Peter De Smet and the Jesuits, who came to St. Louis three years after the nuns, were benefactors of the Sacred Heart. Archbishop Peter Kenrick and Bishop Joseph

Rosati were also fond acquaintances.

In 1841, when Philippine was 72, she lived with the Potawatomi in Sugar Creek, Kansas. It was one of the most fulfilling aspects of her missionary work. She returned to the St. Charles convent a year later where she spent much of the time reading, sewing, and often in prayer. Mother Duchesne's eyesight began to fail in her eighty-first year. A visit from Father De Smet helped raise her spirits. Her body was weakening at an increasing rate, her mind racked with forgetfulness. She wrote her sister, "I have stopped calculating when I shall meet death. It will be when God wills. Old age has many sacrifices to make, and it can be a period of great value as one's purgatory. It will certainly be a less rigorous one than that of the next life."

Though Mother Duchesne was virtually bedridden by August 16, 1852, she continued to attend Mass in the chapel every morning. She wrote Father De Smet, "Your kindness toward me in the past gives me the assurance that I shall see that kindness continue to the end of my life. Yesterday I received the last sacraments, and I hope you will not forget me in your prayers. If you do me the favor of asking prayers for me, that will be a great charity." Her doctor prescribed medications but nothing improved her condition.

The morning of November 16, she was much too weak to leave bed, missing church services for the first time. Father Verhaegen, a Jesuit priest she had known for many years, came to hear her last confession and anoint her. In response to the invocation, she said in a barely audible tone, "I give you my heart, my soul, and my life—oh, yes—my life, generously." Mother Rose Philippine Duchesne died shortly after noon. She was 83.

She was placed in a wooden coffin and moved to the chapel. Father Verhaegen celebrated the funeral Mass at St. Charles Borromeo Church. She was buried in a cemetery near the church. Her original grave marker, a $2.50 piece of wood, said "very severe to herself and very kind to others."

Father Verhaegen recorded her burial:

"On the 20th of November, 1852, I, the undersigned, buried the

mortal remains of Madame Philippine Duchesne, professed religious of the Society of the Sacred Heart, aged 83 years."
[signed] P. J. Verhaegen, S. J.

Mother Duchesne now rests in the chapel at the Academy of the Sacred Heart in St. Charles. A small pink monument with the inscription, "Mother Duchesne" marks her final resting place.

BISHOP JOSEPH ROSATI

(January 30, 1789 - September 25, 1843)

Joseph Rosati was a native of Sora, Italy. He became a member of the Lazarist order and studied theology at their seminary in Rome. It was in Rome that Joseph first met Bishop DuBourg of New Orleans. Rosati had long wanted to come to America and when DuBourg extended him an invitation he quickly accepted.

Joseph arrived in Baltimore in July 1816 and from there moved to Louisville, Kentucky. By the time he landed in St. Louis on October 17, 1817, he had perfected his English. While still a young man, Rosati took charge of St. Mary's College. He founded and served as the first superior at a Lazarist college in Perry County, Missouri which opened in 1819. One year later, he was named Superior of the Lazarists in the United States.

Joseph served as an administrator of the diocese of New Orleans and in March 1824, he was appointed coadjutor to Bishop DuBourg. Three years later, he became the first bishop of the St. Louis diocese. As bishop, he supervised construction of the Old Cathedral and consecrated the holy building upon completion in October 1834. He assisted Father Peter De Smet and the Jesuits in founding St. Louis University and worked with Philippine Duchesne and the Sisters of the Sacred Heart. He also founded St. Louis Hospital and opened the first orphanage in the city.

In 1840, Bishop Rosati sailed to Europe for an appointment in Rome. He was assigned as a diplomatic liaison of the Vatican and went to Haiti to settle religious differences between the government of Haiti and the Roman Catholic Church. The Pope was well pleased with Rosati's success. In September 1843, Joseph was returning to St. Louis by way of France when he became ill in Paris. Physicians who attended to the bishop suggested he return to Rome to recover from the illness. Bishop Joseph Rosati returned to Rome but died on September 25; he was 59. He was buried in the chapel of the Vincentian House in Rome.

The St. Louis diocese received a letter from Rome. It read in part, "Here died Joseph Rosati, citizen of Sora, a Vincentian, a man of unusual virtue, the highest fervor and of singular modesty. He was a zealous propagator of the holy name throughout America."

On August 26, 1954, 111 years after Joseph Rosati's death, he returned to St. Louis for burial in the crypt at the St. Louis Cathedral. Father Clarence Corcoran, the professor of music at Kenrick Seminary, escorted the body. Clergy from around St. Louis were in attendance for the Mass; Archbishop Joseph Ritter celebrated the service. The archbishop said in his eulogy, "We may hope that through our prayers it may please God to raise the saintly Bishop Rosati along with his equally holy confreres and contemporary founders of the Catholic faith in this area, the Rev. Felix Andrels C.M. and Blessed Philippina Duchesne, to honors of the altar." Following the service, Rosati's remains were blessed and entombed in the crypt under the Chapel of All Souls. His body was placed in the crypt beneath that of Cardinal Glennon.

On May 23, 1971, Rosati's remains were moved once again, this time to the crypt beneath the Old Cathedral.

HENRY SHAW

(July 24, 1800 - August 25, 1889)

Henry Shaw worked for two years in a British hardware store. At age 19, he left Europe to settle in St. Louis. He arrived on May 4, 1819 and rented a house on Main Street. He started a small hardware store on the levee and ran the business alone for several years. By the time he was 40, after 21 years in America, Henry had amassed a fortune.

Henry Shaw.

Shaw sold the business and traveled Europe for the next ten years. During this period he was struck by the beauty of the botanical gardens throughout the continent. Upon returning to the States, he set aside a portion of his property in the southwest part of the city for the cultivation of plants and flowers. He built a house in the middle of his garden and a second residence downtown at what is now Seventh and Locust streets.

Henry dedicated the remainder of his life to his botanical garden and philanthropy activities. He established Tower Grove Park on his property near the garden and he donated the park to the city in 1868. Henry was simple and sensitive in his nature, always acting as a benefactor for those who spoke without a voice. He gave money to help support orphanages, churches, and hospitals. He never married in his 89 years.

As he grew older, Henry delegated his duties within the garden. In 1889, he spent the summer in Mackinac Island, Wisconsin to rest his body and gain his strength. The trip benefitted his spirits but his health declined soon after his return to St. Louis.

Henry spent his last weeks in his garden home reading Dickens and other favorite authors. Though his fever was mild, at times he would fall into a stupor, become inattentive and have difficulty speaking. His doctors believed he had contracted malaria. Nothing could be done for the philanthropist.

On August 25, 1889, Shaw passed away with three of his trusted employees beside him, including Superintendent of the Garden, James Gurney. As the night went on there were pauses and irregular gasps of breath. Then the great man whispered, "Seventy-nine." Those around him were surprised by the words. "No, eighty-nine," said Mrs. Edom, his housekeeper of 30 years. Henry looked at her but was unable to speak, he died moments later. That morning, the gates to the garden were wreathed in and the flags in Tower Grove Park were at half-mast. Governor David Francis sent the following telegram:

> Please express my sincere condolence to the relatives and devoted friends of Henry Shaw. In his taking off St. Louis loses a munificent benefactor, Missouri a distinguished citizen. May the memory of his life full of good acts and noble sentiments incite his fellow men to higher aims and better deeds."

Henry Shaw's body lay in state at the garden museum. The room was filled with fifteen foot palms. There were over 50 honorary pallbearers including Adolphus Busch, William Lemp, and James Yeatman. Christ Church Cathedral held the funeral on Saturday, August 31. Offices around the city closed early, hundreds of spectators crowded the streets and sidewalks around the cathedral long before the service began. Afterward the ceremony, a procession led the body back to the botanical gardens. Henry was placed in the mausoleum in front of his garden home; Shaw himself had the tomb built years earlier.

Shaw's grave at the Missouri Botanical Garden.

The mausoleum is an impressive mixture of Byzantine and Renaissance architecture. The octagonal structure has eight pillars of red granite supporting a double dome topped with a Latin cross. The sarcophagus is made of Italian marble. Upon its lid is a bas-relief carving of Henry Shaw asleep with his left hand on his chest, clutching a rose.

According to his will, much

of his estate was donated to several charitable and business institutions in St. Louis; among them Washington University, Missouri Historical Society, Good Samaritan Hospital, Little Sisters of the Poor, and his own Botanical Garden. Shaw Boulevard and Shaw Elementary School were named for him.

The 79-acre Missouri Botanical Garden is a leading research center for botanists studying plant life. It boasts the world's first geodesic dome greenhouse and the largest Japanese garden in North America.

FATHER PETER DE SMET

(January 30, 1801 - May 23, 1873)

Father De Smet emigrated to the United States at the age of twenty from his home in Termonde, Belgium. He was stationed in a Jesuit novitiate in Baltimore when he was transferred to Florissant, Missouri; also known at the time as St. Ferdinand, with a small population just over 400 residents. Here, De Smet and his fellow Jesuits cleared the land and built a new novitiate which became the Jesuit Province of Missouri, the center of activity for the Western states. The Sacred Heart nuns, who had established themselves three years earlier under Mother Superior, Philippine Duchesne, helped the Jesuits establish their novitiate.

On September 23, 1827, Peter John De Smet was ordained into the priesthood by Bishop Joseph Rosati. The following day, Father DeSmet celebrated his first mass. The next year, at the request of the Bishop, Peter and his Jesuits began the work of establishing a college in St. Louis. Peter himself helped with the construction by cutting stones and carrying bricks. The college, located at Ninth and Washington, opened in November 1829 with only 40 students but quickly expanded. The college was called St. Louis University. Peter was the University treasurer and a professor of English. He spent the next decade expanding Jesuit activities in both America and Europe.

Peter's most fulfilling work was as a missionary. He traveled extensively through the unexplored regions of the West and established missions for both white men and Native Americans. He was referred to by some as the apostle of the Rocky Mountains. The Native Americans trusted the holy man and affectionately referred to the good father as "Blackrobe." He was often a mediator for the Native Americans when conflicts arose with the white settlers who were moving Westward.

In 1849, the honor of Assistant Vice-Province of Missouri was bestowed on Father De Smet. Later, he was named Procurator General of Missouri. On November 18, 1852, Philippine Duchesne died in St. Charles. The two had become friends and often wrote and visited each other. He wrote of her years later, "I keep the memory of Mere Duchesne in the highest respect and veneration. Her praise has been and is on the lips, not only of her own Sisters in religion, but of all those who had the honor and the happiness of her acquaintance."

Throughout his travels Peter met people from all walks of life, from the rich to the poor, to the holy to the unrepentant. Among them was Abraham Lincoln whom he found to be sympathetic to his causes, including the Native Americans.

Father De Smet was back home in Belgium in February 1872. On the 12th he suffered an attack of nephrites, an acute inflammation of the kidney. His condition improved enough for him to sail back to America but the illness relieved him from his Jesuit duties. To occupy his time he began writing a history on the Jesuit Province in the Midwest. But his condition steadily worsened and by May he lost sight in his left eye. The following day, after saying Mass, he told a server, "This is the end. I shall never again ascend the altar." Peter re-

Father Peter De Smet's gravesite.

quested Last Sacraments on May 20, 1873 and he died on the 23rd

St. Louisans mourned his loss. He was praised as a gentle man with strong convictions. The *Missouri Republican* wrote of the priest:

> "In him the world loses one of the most intrepid pioneers of Christian civilization. If he did not accomplish all that he believed possible, he at least gave an example of what a profound conviction can do in the struggle against insurmountable obstacles."

St. Francis Xavier's Church hosted the May 24 funeral. The Archbishop of St. Louis, Richard Peter Kenrick, conducted the service. After the ceremony the Father was led back to Florissant for burial.

Father De Smet rests on the grounds of the Museum of Western Jesuit Missions, 700 Howdershell. The cemetery can be seen from the road; a large stone cross centers the small burial ground.

JOHN CARDINAL GLENNON

(June 14, 1862 - March 9, 1946)

Like the first Archbishop of St. Louis, Peter Richard Kenrick, John Joseph Glennon came from Ireland. He was born in the small town of Kinnegad. He attended the College of St. Finlan at Mullingar and later pursued his seminary studies at All Hallows in Dublin. Glennon came to America to serve at the diocese of Kansas City where he was ordained a priest on December 20, 1884. Less than two years later, he was elevated to bishop and became the coadjutor to Bishop Hogan of Kansas City. He served in that position for seven years.

In April 1903, Bishop Glennon was appointed coadjutor Archbishop of St. Louis. When Archbishop John Kain died in October, John Glennon became the third Archbishop in St. Louis. He was a comparatively young 41 years old at the time. Glennon was known for his simple, friendly manner and good humor. He also was a superb speaker. Glennon served as Archbishop through the Depression and two World Wars and he was able to inspire soldiers and their families through his words. On V-E Day, 1945, the archbishop gave an emotional speech at the Soldier's Memorial downtown.

Archbishop Glennon's greatest accomplishments were the building of the St. Louis Cathedral and Kenrick Seminary. In 1905, he announced his plans for building a new cathedral. Glennon visited cathedrals in Europe for inspiration and ideas. After careful consideration, he settled on a combination of Romanesque and Byzantine architecture. On October 18, 1908, the cornerstone was laid for a new cathedral on Lindell and, exactly six years later to the day, the cathedral was dedicated.

In 1915, Kenrick Seminary, which was previously located on Cass Avenue, moved to its current location near Webster Groves. Glennon built the seminary on 380 acres of land. In 1934, more than 40 bishops and archbishops from around the country took part in the week long festivities celebrating the anniversary of Glennon's ordination to the priesthood. He was archbishop of St. Louis for 42 years.

On February 9, 1946, Archbishop Glennon left St. Louis to be elevated to the Sacred College of Cardinals by Pope Pius XII. He was suffering from a slight case of bronchitis when he made his first stop in his native Ireland. The Prime Minister of Ireland Eamon de Valera met with the archbishop as did hundreds of family and friends. From Ireland, he stopped in Paris before reaching Rome on February 14. The next day Glennon had a private audience with the Pope. He came down with a cold shortly after arriving and felt weary during much of his stay. On February 18, John Glennon and thirty-two others were elevated to the status of Cardinal. He said of the occasion, "It is a wonderful thing to be thus remembered at a time of life when I really should be forgotten, to be given this great honor before I die." Two days later, in a public ceremony, he made his first appearance before the Pope and received his biretta. The next day at St. Peter's Basilica, Pope Pius bestowed the red galeros upon the Cardinals. Ceremonies ended on the 22nd and each Cardinal received a ring signifying his office. Glennon was the first Cardinal of St. Louis.

Cardinal Glennon left Rome on Monday, March 4 and returned to Dublin. He planned to return to St. Louis on March 8. He stayed in a stateroom at the official residence of the president, Sean O'Kelly. The extensive travel and ceremonies had taken much of his strength. Though he was tired and weak he attended a dinner in his honor given by the president. By Wednesday, he was bedridden with bronchitis, pneumonia and later developed uremia. He was also mentally confused. Pope Pius sent a message to his new Cardinal, saying in part, "...we hasten to assure you of our fervent, prayerful remembrances for an early recovery." By Thursday evening, Cardinal Glennon was in a semi-comatose state. When a Sister of Charity who was nursing him asked where he wanted to be buried, he smiled and responded, "Not in Ireland, not even in Kinnegad, but in St. Louis among the people I love so well and where I have spent my life and labors. In fact, sister, I have marked a little crypt for myself in the Chapel of Holy Souls in the St. Louis Cathedral. It is there I wish to go."

John Cardinal Glennon.

On March 8, his sisters, and several nephews and nieces were at his bedside. Members of the clergy were also present. During the evening he spoke what would be his last words, "I belong to St. Louis." At 8:51 the next morning, March 9, Cardinal John Glennon died peacefully. President O'Kelly made the official death announcement and ordered flags to fly at half-mast. Glennon's predecessor,

Archbishop Kenrick, died 50 years earlier, almost to the day.

Glennon was taken to a first floor room in the presidential residence where his body lay in state. Prime Minister de Valera was among the first dignitaries to pay respects to the Cardinal. The next day the body was moved to All Hallows College, where Glennon was a seminary student. His oak coffin rested on the catafalque in front of the cathedral altar. Here, townspeople viewed Glennon before the funeral service on Wednesday, March 13. Following the Mass, the coffin was taken to Rineanna Airport in Shannon to its return to St. Louis.

Mayor of St. Louis Aloys Kaufmann and Auxiliary Bishop George Donnelly met the plane when it arrived at Lambert Field on March 14. A two-mile procession took the Cardinal to his residence on Lindell Boulevard, arriving at 3:30. An estimated 3000 people were waiting outside the residence when the procession arrived. Cardinal Glennon was then returned to his Cathedral where thousands of St. Louisans filed past his open casket.

Over 70 bishops and archbishops attended Glennon's funeral. Governor Phil Donnelly, Postmaster General Robert Hannegan, and three newly appointed cardinals from Rome also were present. Bishop Christopher Byrne, who delivered the homily, concluded his sermon, "And so in obedience to God's will we take our leave of you, by saying: our heart will always love and admire you. They shall be filled and overflowing with gratitude for your kindness, your blessing, your zeal, and your example." After the service, the casket was taken to the crypt beneath the All Souls' Chapel for final burial.

THE BUSCH FAMILY

After the death of Adolphus Busch in 1913, August Busch Sr. took over the Anheuser-Busch breweries. While the Lemp's and other brewers collapsed during Prohibition, Anheuser-Busch shifted its focus and stayed profitable by producing yeast, corn, and syrups for the baking industry. When Prohibition finally ended in 1933, the company sent its first case of beer to President Franklin Roosevelt.

August Busch was born on December 29, 1865. He attended the Morgan Park Military Institute in Chicago and later the Kemper Military Academy in Boonville, Missouri. After studying brewing in Europe, he returned to Anheuser-Busch as a brewer's apprentice. August built Bevo Mill and an extravagant French Renaissance chateau dubbed the "Castle" on the Grant's farm property. He was quiet and retiring and he was seldom seen at society functions. He and his wife Alice had two sons and three daughters. His sons, Adolphus III and August Jr., would each run the brewery.

Adolphus III was born at his parent's home, Number Two Busch Place on February 10, 1891. He bore a strong resemblance to his father and likewise he was shy and preferred the home life. In June 1913, when he was 21, he married Florence Parker Lambert at Grant's Farm. The couple lived at Grandview Farm. The mansion burned to the ground in 1917 due to a short circuit but was later rebuilt. They had one child, a daughter Marie, in 1914. The couple divorced in July 1930 and two months later Adolphus married Catherine Bowen, a member of a wealthy political family in Texas.

August Busch Jr. was born in St. Louis on March 28, 1899. He lacked a proper education and never completed elementary school. His first job was with the Manufacturers Railway Company, a subsidiary of Anheuser-Busch. He later served as a sergeant in World War I. He became general superintendent with the brewery on January 1, 1924. August or Gussie, as he was affectionately known, quickly moved up the ranks during the Prohibition era. It was after the repeal of Prohibition that Gussie first used the horse-drawn beer wagon for brewery promotions. The Clydesdale hitch was born.

By September 1933, August Busch Sr. was suffering painfully from gout, chest pains, and dropsy. He rarely visited the brewery. On Sunday evening, February 10, 1934, he awoke several times during the night suffering from intense pain and had trouble breathing. On Monday morning, August picked up a pamphlet entitled An *Open Letter to Rev. Charles E. Coughlin* and on the back cover wrote simply, "Goodbye precious mama and adorable children." At eight o'clock, his chauffeur, Tony Feichtinger, came to the room as was his daily practice. Tony asked August if he wanted to listen to

The Busch family gravesite.

some music on the radio. August nodded his approval and Tony moved to the console. Then August pulled a .32-caliber revolver from the nightstand and shot himself in the left side of the chest below the heart. Family members rushed to the bedroom and August died fifteen minutes later.

August lay in state in the living room of his Castle. Over 10,000 mourners viewed the body and paid respects to the family. The funeral took place at the mansion on Friday, February 15. Members of the St. Louis Symphony played just as they had for Adolphus' funeral twenty years earlier. His body was removed from his home and taken by hearse the short distance up Gravois to Sunset Memorial Park, 10180 Gravois Road. He was buried on a hilltop facing Grant's Farm, where he could forever view his chateau in the distance. A simple grave marker denotes his final resting place.

After August Sr.'s death, Adolphus III took over the brewery with Gussie serving as first vice-president. When the United States entered World War II, Gussie joined the army and served as a colonel. And in 1946, his brother Adolphus died of cardiac failure on August 29, after spending eight days at Barnes Hospital. He had suffered from stomach cancer and other ailments for some time. He was buried beside his father in Sunset Memorial Park. Adolphus III ran the brewery for 12 years, the shortest run of a Busch family member.

Gussie was named president and chief executive officer. He was the fourth Busch to head the company. The red brick schoolhouse, where his father attended classes, became his office. Gussie had a rough, gravelly voice and demanded quality in every aspect of his business. He began a program of major expansion of the brewery, constructing new breweries in Tampa and Jacksonville, Florida. In 1953, he purchased the St. Louis Baseball Cardinals from Fred Saigh for less than $4 million and was later instrumental in the development of the Busch Gardens Theme Parks.

Gussie was married four times. His first marriage in 1918 to Marie Church ended with her death from pneumonia in 1930, she was only 33. They had two daughters and lived in a mansion on Lindell Boulevard, a gift from his father. He married for a second time in 1933 to Elizabeth Dozier. They divorced in 1952. From this marriage was born a daughter Elizabeth and a son, current chairman of Anheuser-Busch, August Busch III. Seven children were born from his third marriage to Gertrude Buholzer. His youngest daughter Christina, 8 years old, died in an automobile accident in December 1974; his son Andrew was injured but recovered. In February 1976, tragedy of another kind involved his son Peter who accidently shot and killed a friend at Grant's Farm. His third marriage ended in divorce in 1978. Margaret Snyder, Gussie's former secretary and later a vice-president and member of the board of Anheuser-Busch, became his fourth wife in March 1981. Gussie was 82 at the time of the wedding.

Gussie resigned his chief executive position at Anheuser-Busch in May 1975 and his chairmanship two years later. He was given the title honorary chairman of Anheuser-Busch and remained as chairman and president of the baseball Cardinals. In 1988, Forbes magazine ranked him 36 among richest Americans. Gussie was one of the most popular and well-liked citizens in St. Louis. His philanthropy included gifts to Washington University and the Busch Memorial Student Center at St. Louis University. He donated to political interests as well. In 1950, he hosted President Harry Truman at Grant's Farm, the two became close friends.

He suffered from arthritis for many years and walked with a cane near the end of his life. In August 1989, Gussie spent three weeks in St. Luke's Hospital suffering from pneumonia. When he insisted on going home to Grant's Farm, medical equipment and nurses were dispatched to care for him in his final days. Gussie slipped into unconsciousness and died of pneumonia and congestive heart failure on Friday, September 29 at 12:25 p.m. in the same room where his father had committed suicide. His ten surviving children were at his bedside. The stadium flag was at half-mast and a moment of silence was observed before the Cardinals-Cubs game that evening; the Cardinal players wore black armbands in mourning. President George Bush said of him, "He had been a legendary figure in American life for almost a century as a successful businessman, community leader and philanthropist." A private funeral service was conducted in the Castle on Sunday, October 1. Only the family and close friends, numbering about 120, were in attendance. At noon, a team of Clydesdales pulling a beer wagon escorted the funeral procession to the gates of Grant's Farm. The flag from the coffin was presented to his son August III. Gussie was laid to rest beside his daughter Christina in Sunset Memorial Park.

The members of the Busch family are buried in a semi-circle facing a monument that features a boy feeding a fawn. The base of the sculpture is a piece of red granite with the name "Busch" engraved in it. A row of hedges and shade trees conceal the area.

On October 3, the New Cathedral was filled for a memorial Mass. Governor John Ashcroft and celebrity Ed McMahon attended as did many baseball dignitaries including Red Schoendienst, former Yankee Joe DiMaggio, and several baseball owners. Archbishop John May and Reverend Reinert were among several clergy to conduct the service.

HENRY KIEL

(February 21, 1871 - November 26, 1942)

Henry Kiel was born in St. Louis and was the first man to serve in the mayor's office for three, four-year terms. He was regarded as the "father of the Municipal Opera" which opened during his administration. Henry attended Smith Academy and later worked as a bricklayer for his father's construction company. Eventually, Henry took over his father's business and was responsible for the construction of Soldan High School, the Post-Dispatch Building, and the Ambassador Theater, among others.

He entered politics as a ward committeeman and was appointed chairman of the Republican City Central Committee. In 1913, he was elected Mayor of St. Louis. During his administration the city charter and zoning laws were revised, the MacArthur Bridge was completed, construction on the Municipal Auditorium, later called the Kiel Auditorium, and the Civil Courts Building was started, and the St. Louis Zoo and the Municipal Opera were established. In 1931, after retiring from office, Henry was appointed president of the St. Louis Police Board.

Kiel was described as a thoughtful politician who would listen to all concerns before making a decision. The Salvation Army awarded his dedication to the less fortunate with the Distinguished Service Cross. He was the seventh person in the United States to receive the award.

Henry Kiel.

During the summer of 1941, Henry suffered a paralytic stroke. Eighteen months later, on the morning of November 26, 1942, while confined to his bed at 1625 Missouri Avenue, he became seriously ill. He slipped into a coma at eight o'clock that evening and died less than an hour later. He was 71.

The next day, the broad headline read, "FORMER MAYOR HENRY W. KIEL DIES." Scottish Rite Cathedral on Lindell held the funeral. Governor Forrest Donnell gave the eulogy and Mayor William Dee

Becker served as a pallbearer. (Becker died less than a year later in the glider crash.) Afterwards, a private service for the family was held at St. Mark's English Lutheran Church on Clayton Road.

Henry Kiel is buried on the second floor in the mausoleum at Oak Grove Cemetery, 7800 St. Charles Rock Road.

HOMER G. PHILLIPS

(April 1, 1880 - June 18, 1931)

At 7:45, on the Thursday morning of June 18, 1931, Homer G. Phillips, a 51 year old attorney, left his home at 1121 Aubert Avenue and walked to Delmar Boulevard to catch his daily streetcar for his office at 23 North Jefferson. Phillips purchased a newspaper and read it while awaiting his streetcar. Shortly before 8:00 a.m., two men approached Phillips on the corner. The three conversed for a few moments and one of the men struck Phillips in the face and pulled a pistol. After firing three times at a close range, the attackers fled. Phillips died instantly.

Homer Gilliam Phillips, born in Sedalia, Missouri, was the son of a Methodist minister. He was orphaned as an infant and raised by his aunt. Shortly after the World's Fair, he graduated from Howard University Law School in Washington D.C. and came to St. Louis to practice. Homer was an established attorney and civic leader at the time of his death. He was known for his eloquence and persuasive tactics in the courtroom. He ran unsuccessfully for mayor against Victor Miller and placed third as a candidate in the 1926 Republican primary for Congress. He was a leading proponent and rallied African-American support for the establishment of City Hospital No. 2.

In April 1930, Phillips settled the estate of George Fitzhugh for the McFarland family. Phillips fee for this service was $1,000 and he held back the McFarland's settlement moneys worth $2,200 until this fee was paid. The McFarland's, however, viewed the fee as excessive. They vowed to take legal or any other action necessary to avoid its payment.

On the morning of June 18, that vow became a reality. St. Louis police arrested Augustus Brooks and George McFarland for the murder of Phillips. Eyewitnesses identified the two men as the Phillips' attackers on Delmar. Moreover, both men had numerous prior arrests. George McFarland's father, John, was also arrested but later released. Phillips had represented John and his wife in the Fitzhugh case and the police believed he offered the logical motive for the shooting.

The funeral of the late attorney was conducted at St. Paul's Methodist Church at Leffingwell and Lawton avenues on Monday, June 22. Homer G. Phillips was laid to rest in St. Peter's Cemetery, 2101 Lucas and Hunt Road. The five-foot marble headstone for Phillips and his wife Ida (she died in 1934) reads:

Two American Patriots: Your lives exemplify a commitment to equality, justice and peace. Your legacy lives on among us.

In February 1932, George McFarland was tried for Phillips murder. Individuals testifying on his behalf placed him somewhere else at the time of the shooting. A jury agreed and found him innocent of the murder. When Augustus Brooks was tried in August of the same year, he too was not guilty. The murder is officially considered to be unsolved.

During Henry Kiel's administration, Phillips negotiated with the mayor for a health care facility on the city's north side. In 1932, a year after Phillip's murder, construction began on a new hospital. On February 22, 1937, Homer G. Phillips Hospital celebrated its grand opening. City officials closed the hospital in 1979.

JOSEPH CARDINAL RITTER

(July 20, 1892 - June 10, 1967)

In April 1967, Joseph Cardinal Ritter celebrated the 50th anniversary of his ordination into priesthood. In less than two months, he was dead of a heart attack. Mayor Alfonso Cervantes said of Ritter, "The wisdom and leadership of the cardinal, a true supporter of enlightened civic causes, has helped make our community a better place in which to worship our Almighty God."

Ritter was born in New Albany. He attended the St. Meinrad Preparatory Seminary and was ordained a priest in 1917. He served as assistant pastor of St. Patrick's Church in Indianapolis. When he was appointed auxiliary bishop, at the age of 41, he became one of the youngest bishops in the United States. One year later, in 1934, he became Bishop of Indianapolis. He was recognized in the archdiocese as an excellent administrator; he finished that city's cathedral and established the Catholic Youth Organization. In December 1944, when the city was elevated to an archdiocese, Ritter became the first archbishop of Indianapolis.

On October 8, 1946, the archbishop came to St. Louis. He succeeded the late John Cardinal Glennon as the fourth archbishop of St. Louis. Ritter was a small man, only 150 pounds, and he led a healthy life. He was soft-spoken and approachable. And

Archbishop Ritter (at far right) standing at Cardinal Glennon's tomb.

he never sought attention or publicity. He fought for racial justice and in 1947 integrated Catholic schools to that end. He also was responsible for the fund drive which sponsored the construction of the Cardinal Glennon Memorial Hospital and established the Archdiocesan Expansion Fund for the buildings of new churches and schools. On December 20, 1960, Ritter was ordained a cardinal by Pope John XXIII. He was a liberal member of the Vatican Ecumenical Council II who wanted to expand the churches philosophies.

On Monday, June 5, 1967, the 74-year-old cardinal suffered a heart attack. He was taken to DePaul Hospital where he rested comfortably until he suffered another attack. Cardinal Ritter died on Saturday at 5:47 a.m.

On Monday, June 12, his bronze casket was removed to the St. Louis Cathedral where it lay in state for two days. Thousands of St. Louisans viewed the Catholic leader and two thousand mourners filled the cathedral for his funeral. Four cardinals and more than 100 bishops from around the country attended.

Cardinal John Patrick Cody of Chicago celebrated the Mass; Bishop Charles Helmsing of Kansas City, a former St. Louisan and friend of Ritter, delivered the sermon. He said of his friend, "He habitually radiated the joy of the Resurrection, while he knew that he would have to suffer persecution for justice's sake, as we well remember his pioneering efforts for racial and social justice." The pallbearers were eight of Cardinal Ritter's close friends. The funeral was broadcast on KMOX radio.

Cardinal Ritter chose to be buried in the Priests' Lot at Calvary Cemetery rather than the crypt in the cathedral. Numerous members of the clergy attended the brief service held at the gravesite by Auxiliary Bishop Glennon Flavin. A large monument with a stone cross marked his final resting place. The inscription on the monument read, "Thou Art a Priest Forever."

On May 2, 1994, Archbishop Justin Rigali had Ritter's remains moved to the St. Louis Cathedral for burial in the crypt.

GEORGE SISLER

(March 24, 1893 - March 26, 1973)

The Hall of Famer, George Sisler, was the best player in St. Louis Browns history. Ty Cobb said of him, "Sisler could do everything. He could hit, run, and throw and he wasn't a bad pitcher, either." George was born in Manchester, Ohio. He studied mechanical engineering and played baseball at the University of Michigan for coach Branch Rickey. Rickey became manager of the St. Louis Browns and signed George to a contract upon graduation from Michigan in 1915. The young college kid was mild-mannered and affable and quickly became a fan favorite. He began his career on June 28, 1915; pitching in a 4 to 2 loss to Chicago. He continued to pitch and played first base in between starts. He moved to first base permanently within two years. In his second season, when he was 23 years old, he twice secured victory for the Browns by outpitching the great Walter Johnson. In 1939, the two would enter the Hall of Fame together.

George and his wife Kathleen had three sons and a daughter. His sons all played in the majors like their father. George Jr. played one year with the St. Louis Browns. Dick played outfield for the Cardinals and Philadelphia Phillies before managing the Cincinnati Reds. And Dave pitched for the Boston Red Sox, Detroit Tigers, and Washington Senators.

During World War I, Sisler left baseball and fought as a lieutenant in the same unit as Ty Cobb and Christy Matthewson. When he returned to the game, George became the best hitter for the Browns, finish-

Sisler's grave.

ing his career with 2,812 hits and a lifetime average of .340. He batted over .400 in 1920 and 1922. In the 1922 season, he had a 41-game hitting streak; the streak remained a record until Joe Dimaggio hit in 56 games in 1941. Sisler won his second batting title with a .420 average and was named American League Most Valuable Player for the season. But the Browns lost the pennant by one game and would never again come close.

During the off season, George came down with influenza which developed into a sinus condition. The illness impaired his vision and forced him to miss the entire 1923 season. He had successful surgery and returned in 1924 as the Browns player-manager. The team never again reached its earlier status and Sisler resigned as manager in 1927, though he played for the Browns one more year. The next season, with his talents declining, he was sent to the Washington Senators then to the Boston Braves. He officially retired in September 1930; he spent 13 of his 16 seasons with the Browns.

In June 1939, Sisler was among the first elected to the Baseball Hall of Fame in Cooperstown. He was inducted with 11 others including Babe Ruth, Ty Cobb, and Cy Young. After his playing days were over, Sisler became a scout for Branch Rickey and the Brooklyn Dodgers. He later worked as a scout for the Pittsburgh Pirates.

In March 1973, George celebrated his 80th birthday in St. Mary's Health Center. George Sisler died on March 26, two days after his birthday. He was buried at Oak Grove Cemetery. In 1993, his remains were moved to the churchyard behind Des Peres Presbyterian Church. The church, founded in 1833, is one of the oldest west of the Mississippi and is now a National Historic Site. It is located on Geyer Road between Clayton and Manchester roads.

JAMES "COOL PAPA" BELL

(May 17, 1903 - March 7, 1991)

James Bell was born deep in the south in Starkville, Mississippi. He came to St. Louis with his family when he was 16. Though he had a job in a packing house, James always loved playing baseball. He played semi-pro ball for the Compton Hill Cubs before starting his career in the Negro Leagues in 1922 with the St. Louis Stars. He went on to play with the Pittsburgh Crawfords, Homestead Grays, and the Kansas City Monarchs. James was a gentle, quiet man; he earned the nickname "Cool Papa" due to his calm demeanor under pressure.

Bell's best quality as a player was his speed. In 1939 alone, he stole 175 bases. His roommate Satchel Paige once said that Bell was so fast that he could turn out the light and be in bed before the room got dark.

Bell started his career as a pitcher and later moved to center field. He hit over .400 several times during his 29-year career. His color never allowed him and hundreds of other talented African American players to play in the major leagues. He once said of it, "So many people say I was born too early, but that's not true. They opened the doors too late."

Bell retired from baseball in 1950. Two years later, when he was 49, Bill Veeck offered Bell a chance to play for the St. Louis Browns but he turned down the offer due to his arthritic legs. Until he retired in 1973, Bell worked as a security guard for the city of St. Louis. The following year, "Cool Papa" became the fifth Negro League player to be elected to Baseball's Hall of Fame. In 1971, his roommate, Satchel Paige, was the first black player elected. In 1983, Dickson Street was renamed to James "Cool Papa" Bell.

In January 1991, Bell's wife of 62 years, Clara, died following a brief illness. James was devastated by his wife's death. His own health was declining by this time; he was blind in one eye. On February 27, he suffered a heart attack and was hospitalized at St. Louis University. At 5:00 p.m. on Thursday, March 7, "Cool Papa" died. He was 87.

About 200 people attended the Saturday funeral Mass at Central Baptist Church including Mayor Vince Schoemehl. Pallbearers included baseball great Lou Brock and one-time Cardinal third baseman Ken Reitz. Lester Lockett, a former Negro League player, gave the eulogy. "You were put to bed way too soon," said Lockett. "But the light, especially for those who knew you, will never go out."

James "Cool Papa" Bell is buried at St. Peter's Cemetery, 2101 Lucas and Hunt Road. His wife Clara is also buried at St. Peter's but in a different section. Not until 1994 did a headstone mark his grave but his current monument pays homage to his great feats on the playing field.

JOE MEDWICK

(November 24, 1911 - March 21, 1975)

In March 1975, Joe Medwick was in St. Petersburg, Florida for the St. Louis Cardinals spring training. He served as hitting instructor for the Cardinals' minor league teams. At about ten o'clock in the evening of March 20, Medwick walked into the Bayfront Medical Center complaining of chest pains. The Cardinal team physician, Dr. Stan London, was notified and diagnosed Medwick with a massive heart seizure. Within a few hours, one of the most legendary members of the Gashouse Gang was dead.

Medwick was born and raised in Carteret, New Jersey with two sisters and a brother; his parents were Hungarian immigrants. Little Joe grew up playing all sports. In high school, he was all-state in football, baseball, and basketball. He received numerous scholarships, including an offer to play football at Notre Dame. His first professional try-out was with a Yankee farm team. They felt he was too young and unexperienced and released him.

Joe came to the Cardinal organization in 1930 and played for their minor league team in Scottsdale, Pennsylvania. He was a powerful right-handed hitter with a compact and muscular build. He played under the name Mickey King to protect his eligibility in case he decided to play football at Notre Dame. Joe was moved up to play in the Texas League in Houston where he picked up the nickname "Ducky" from a female fan.

Medwick came into the major leagues in August 1932 at the age of 20. He was given the number 7 and played left field. He was a tough, fiery competitor and his outbursts were often directed toward his own teammates. Within a few seasons, he became the hitting star of the Cardinals. The Gashouse Gang was made up of a unique brand of characters. General manager Branch Rickey and player-manager Frankie Frisch collected a group of tough, hard-nosed individualists such as Dizzy and Paul Dean, Leo Durocher, and Pepper Martin.

In 1934, the Gashouse Gang defeated the Detroit Tigers to win the World Series. Medwick was the center of controversy during the seventh game when he made a hard slide into the Tigers third baseman Marv Owen. The two started fighting until umpires separated them. When Medwick went to his left field position in the bottom half of the inning, fans pelted him with fruit. Baseball Commissioner Kennesaw Mountain Landis, who watched from his field box, removed Medwick from the game for his own protection. The next three seasons were Medwick's most outstanding, concluding in 1937 with his earning the Triple Crown. He led the league in home runs, RBI's, batting average, and nine other categories. He was awarded Most Valuable Player for the season.

By 1940, his talents had diminished along with his popularity amongst the fans. In June, one week after he was traded to the Brooklyn Dodgers, the Cardinals faced the Dodgers in Ebbets Field. When Medwick came to bat in the first inning, Cardinal pitcher Bob Bowman hit him in the head with the first pitch. Joe spent time at a Brooklyn hospital with a concussion and blurred vision, within a week he returned to the lineup. He played with various teams over the next seven seasons with little success; he briefly returned to the Cardinals in 1947 as a pinch-hitter. He played 16 years in the major leagues and accumulated 2471 hits and over 200 home runs.

In retirement, Medwick coached in the minor leagues before opening an insurance business. He returned to coaching in 1966 as hitting instructor in the Cardinals minor league system. On January 23, 1968, Medwick was elected to the Baseball Hall of Fame. A year later, in April 1969, he had hip surgery at Deaconess Hospital and a second operation four years later at Barnes.

In March 1975, the evening before his heart attack, he attended a dinner given by the Florida Governor for baseball's Hall of Famers. At about 3:00 a.m., Friday, March 21, Joe Medwick died of a heart attack at Bayfront Medical Center. He was survived by his wife Isabelle, who he married in 1936, and his children Mike and Susan. The funeral took place at Michael Fitzgerald Mortuary on South Lindbergh.

Joe Medwick is buried in the churchyard of St. Lucas United Church of Christ, 11735 Denny Road. His headstone has the Cardinals insignia engraved on it; a flat marker in front of his headstone is a testament of his baseball exploits:

> Member of 1934 World Champion St. Louis Cardinals. National League's Most Valuable Player and Triple Crown Winner in 1937. Lifetime Batting Average .324. He was elected to Baseball's Hall of Fame. Cooperstown, New York, in 1968.

ROBERT BURNES

(July 14, 1914 - July 11, 1995)

The "Benchwarmer," as Robert Burnes and his sports column were dubbed, appeared in the *Globe-Democrat* from 1945 to 1986. Burnes first joined the paper in 1935, two months after graduating from college. He covered the St. Louis Browns and went on to become the paper's sports editor eight years later. During his 51 years at the *Globe*, he wrote over 15,000 articles. He premiered on KMOX radio in 1953 and became the first host of *Sports Open Line*. Bob was an accomplished banquet speaker and supporter of

Robert Burnes.

several charitable and civic organizations in the area. He also was a member of the board of the Herbert Hoover Boys Club for many years.

Bob Burnes was educated at CBC High School and St. Louis University. He married Adele Daut in the early 1940's, they had four daughters. His life had its tragedies. In 1959, his father was killed in a street robbery. An even more tragic event occurred on May 15, 1993 when his daughter Cathie, a sportswriter at the *Post-Dispatch*, died of a brain aneurysm. She was 41.

Burnes lived in St. Louis Hills for over 40 years. On Tuesday, July 11, 1995, three days before his 81st birthday, he died in his home after suffering a heart attack. The funeral service was conducted at St. Raphael The Archangel Catholic Church on the morning of July 15. Bob Burnes is buried at Resurrection Cemetery, 6901 Mackenzie Road.

In his 1984 farewell column, Burnes wrote·

"It had been fun; it had been the greatest experience of my life. If in some small way it has brightened a day, added a word of explanation, espoused a cause or exposed a fraud, I have had ample reward."

ARCHBISHOP JOHN MAY

(March 31, 1922 - March 24, 1994)

On Wednesday, March 30, 1994, the St. Louis Cathedral was filled beyond capacity for the funeral Mass of Archbishop John May. Deacons carried the plain oak coffin of the archbishop down the center aisle. A white pall was draped over the casket with the Book of Gospels placed on top. Archbishop Justin Rigali, who was installed as Archbishop of St. Louis two weeks earlier, celebrated the Mass. Cardinal Joseph Bernardin of Chicago gave the homily.

John May was born in the northern Chicago suburb of Evanston. He received his seminary training in the Chicago area. He was ordained a priest on May 3, 1947; he was 25 years old. May worked as a parish priest and a hospital chaplain before taking an administrative position with the Archdiocese of Chicago; he became a bishop in August 1967. By Vatican decree, May was installed as Archbishop of St. Louis on March 25, 1980, replacing the retiring archbishop, John Cardinal Carberry.

The archbishop was known for his generosity and simplicity; he declined the use of a chauffeur, choosing instead to drive his Chevrolet. John May was very literate and enjoyed classical music. He was considered a moderate among his peers; his diplomatic talents led to his appointment to the presidency of the National Conference of Catholic Bishops.

John May was diagnosed with cancer in the summer of 1992. On March 13, the archbishop slipped into a coma. He was residing at the Mary, Queen and Mother Center, a nursing facility in Shrewsbury. He died on Thursday, March 24, at 11:50 p.m. of brain cancer. On March 29, his body was taken to the St. Louis Cathedral where his

John L. May.

body lay in state. A wheelchair-bound Cardinal Carberry was among those paying respects.

The funeral Mass was conducted the next day, March 30. After the service, the coffin was taken to the eastern side of the cathedral and placed in a crypt below that of John Cardinal Glennon. The inscription of his crypt has his name and the dates of his birth and death.

DAN KELLY

(September 17, 1936 - February 10, 1989)

"He shoots…he scores!" became the trademark of Dan Kelly. It was a call he picked up as a kid listening to Toronto Maple Leafs broadcaster Foster Hewitt. Dan was born in Ottawa, Ontario. His father died when he was two. His elder brother Hal became the leader of the family and looked out for him and their sister Teresa. Hal went on to become a broadcaster for the Toronto Maple Leafs and Minnesota North Stars. Like most children in Canada, Dan lived and breathed hockey. He played center for St. Patrick's College High, a Junior B team in Ottawa.

Kelly's grave.

After high school, Kelly got a job as a apprentice engineer at a local radio station in Ottawa. From there he went to a station in Smith Falls, Ontario where he broadcasted hog prices; it was his first on-the-air position, he was 19. He worked as a country music disc jockey and sports director before doing play-by-play for the Canadian Football League. But his dream job came in 1968 when he hosted Hockey Night in Canada. He became a national figure in his homeland.

In 1967, the St. Louis Blues entered the National Hockey League. Jack Buck and Jay Randolph handled the broadcasting duties during the first season. Blues owner Sidney Salomon Jr. heard Kelly and wanted him as the voice of the Blues. With the help of Robert Hyland, general manager of KMOX Radio, Salomon was able to bring the young Canadian to St. Louis. Dan Kelly worked for the Blues for over 20 years; most of those years he shared the broadcast booth with Walter "Gus" Kyle (Kyle died in November 1996 after a long battle with cancer). Besides his hockey duties, Kelly did play-by-play for the St. Louis Baseball Cardinals and the University of Missouri football games. Dan and his wife Fran had six children; his son John is an NHL broadcaster.

In the summer of 1988, he began experiencing pain while playing golf. Upon examination a large malignant tumor was discovered in his back; it quickly spread to the lungs. He continued working while receiving radiation treatments. Kelly broadcasted his final Blues game on November 19 and was hospitalized at St. Luke's. Dan Kelly died on February 10, 1989, almost exactly one year after the death of another Blues icon, Barclay Plager. He was 52. Robert Hyland said of Kelly, "In my opinion, he was the greatest, or at least one of the two greatest, hockey broadcasters ever. But he could also do football, and there weren't many better than him. He prided himself in that. He was just one of the greats of all time." A month before his death, Kelly was given the Lester Patrick Award for his service to hockey and named to the broadcasters wing of the Hockey Hall of Fame. He received the award in St. Luke's Hospital.

More than 500 mourners from across the country and Canada attended the funeral at Ascension Church in Chesterfield. Gus Kyle was among them. Reverends John Ditenhafer and Joseph Pins celebrated the Mass. The pallbearers were Mike Shanahan, Jack Quinn, Joe Micheletti, Jack Buck, and former Blues coaches Red Berenson, Al Arbour, and Scotty Bowman. Among the honorary pallbearers representing the Blues were Brian Sutter, Bernie Federko, Bob Plager, and general manager Ron Caron.

Dan Kelly was buried Resurrection Cemetery, 6901 MacKenzie Road.

BARCLAY PLAGER

(March 26, 1941 - February 6, 1988)

Barclay Plager was born and raised in Kirkland Lake, Ontario. Like most kids in Canada, he grew up with hockey in his blood. When he played junior hockey in Peterborough, Ontario, Scotty Bowman was his coach. He was drafted by the New York Rangers but traded to St. Louis in November 1967 with another young player named Red Berenson. In 1967, the Blues were playing in their inaugural season in the National Hockey League.

"Barc the Spark", as he was nicknamed, quickly became one of the most popular players for the Blues. He was the Blues captain for three seasons and played in four All-Star Games. During his nine-year career, he suffered no less than 15 broken noses. In 1977, Plager became head coach of the Blues but resigned two years later due to poor health and was replaced by his friend Red Berenson. Barclay was hospitalized with a head trauma caused by an injury during his playing days. He returned to coach the Blues in 1982 and had his jersey retired on March 9 of that year. He was made an assistant coach when Harry Ornest purchased the team.

In November 1984, Barclay was suffering from severe headaches and seizures. He was diagnosed with inoperable brain cancer, doctors gave him less than a year. Radiation and chemotherapy treatments extended his life beyond the year; by the summer of 1986, the baseball-sized tumor shrank to half the size but conventional treatments could no longer improve his condition. Barclay began extensive hyperthermia treatments in which holes are drilled into the skull and probes are applied directly to the tumor. The treatments were successful in fighting the tumor but caused mild brain damage. Plager had to again learn how to walk and talk. By January 1987, Barclay was healthy enough to resume coaching with the Blues. He was again greatly weakened by hyperthermia treatments and lost weight and was later partially paralyzed. As his condition worsened, he was admitted to St. Luke's Hospital.

On Saturday afternoon, February 6, Barclay Plager died peacefully in St. Luke's Hospital. He was 46. Three days later, the NHL All-Star Game was played at the Arena; Barclay had previously been named an honorary Captain. A funeral Mass took place at 11:00 a.m., February 12 at St. Monica Catholic Church on Olive Boulevard. The day before, he lay in state at Kriegshauser Funeral Home. During the ceremony the Blues' theme song was played, "When the Saints Go Marching In." Among the thousand mourners were Barclay's former coach Scotty Bowman and several teammates and current players. Blues broadcaster Dan Kelly tearfully eulogized Plager. (Kelly himself would die of cancer exactly one year later.) Plager was laid to rest at Bellerive Heritage Gardens (formerly Hiram Cemetery), 740 North Mason Road. Barclay was survived by his wife Helen, four children, and his brothers, Bob and Billy Plager.

V

Notable St. Louisans
Buried Elsewhere

Eugene Field's grave at the Church of the Holy Comforter near Chicago.

EUGENE FIELD

(September 2, 1850 - November 4, 1895)

Poet and journalist, Eugene Field was born in St. Louis to Roswell and Frances Field. His father was an attorney; his most celebrated client was Dred Scott. The family lived at 634 South Broadway. After his mother passed away when he was seven, Eugene was sent to Amherst, Massachusetts to live with his Aunt Mary. He attended Williams College and Knox College before entering the University of Missouri at Columbia. His first job was with the *St. Louis Evening Journal* in 1872. He worked at several newspapers before arriving in Chicago in August 1883 to work on the editorial staff at the *Chicago Morning News*. He stayed with the paper until his death. His national daily column called "Sharps and Flats" was a straightforward, humorous look at society. Collections of his newspaper writings were published in book form.

Eugene Field built his literary reputation on his stories and poetry, especially those relating to children. He was called "the children's poet"; his most famous poems were <u>Little Boy Blue</u> and <u>Dutch Lullaby</u>. He was a charming man who enjoyed great popularity; he had a warm, engaging personality that helped him gain friends easily. As the *Globe-Democrat* described him, "He could entertain a crowd of twenty for hours at a time, and his wit was as spontaneous as his good humor was contagious."

In October 1873, Eugene married Julia Comstock who he met at the University of Missouri. The couple had seven children. Two of his children preceded him in death; his son Melvin died in 1890 in Hanover, England at the age of 14. The loss brought great pains to Eugene and his wife. "While our boy still lived, I battled constantly in spirit and I think that another week would have killed me," Eugene wrote his wife. "Now that all is over, I am content, wholly reconciled. I believe our boy is happy now. It is selfish to wish him back."

Eugene's last visit to St. Louis was a year before his death when he gave a lecture at the First Congregational Church on Delmar. In the autumn of 1893, Eugene became seriously ill with typhoid pneumonia. He fought the illness and was fully recovered by Thanksgiving.

During the fall of 1895, Field was feeling ill; his normal stomach troubles had reoccurred but was not life threatening. On Sunday, November 3, he canceled a speaking engagement in Kansas City and stayed at his home in Chicago. When he complained about his discomfort, his doctor, Frank Reilly, suggested a good night's rest would improve his condition. Eugene went to sleep late; his 14-year-old son Fred slept in the same room. Early in the morning, at 5:00, Eugene turned in his bed and groaned. Fred's attempts to awaken his father were unsuccessful. Doctor Reilly arrived at the house and pronounced Field dead of heart failure due to a blood clot.

Thousands mourned Field's sudden and unexpected death. On Wednesday, November 6, 1895, Eugene's funeral Mass was celebrated at Fourth Presbyterian Church in Chicago. Reverend Doctor Frank Bristol officiated the service. Six of his old newspaper associates served as pallbearers. He was buried in the private service at Graceland Cemetery on the near north side of Chicago.

On December 30, 1925, his remains were moved approximately 10 miles north to the Church of the Holy Comforter in Kenilworth, Illinois. The only item found among his remains was his wedding ring which had been given to him by his aunt Mary.

T. S. ELIOT

(September 26, 1888 - January 4, 1965)

April is the cruelest month, breeding
Lilacs out of the dead land, mixing
Memory and desire, stirring
Dull roots with spring rain.
Winter kept us warm, covering
Earth in forgetful snow, feeding
A little life with dried tubers.

Excerpt from The Waste Land, 1922

Thomas Stearns Eliot was born in St. Louis, the seventh son of Henry and Charlotte Eliot. His father was president of the St. Louis Hydraulic Press Brick Company. His grandfather was William Greenleaf Eliot, founder of Washington University. The family residence was at 2635 Locust Street. Eliot attended Smith Academy in St. Louis and Milton Academy in Massachusetts. He completed his undergraduate studies at Harvard in three years and obtained a Masters of Art in his fourth year. Among his fellow students at Harvard was writer John Reed. He also studied in Paris at the Sorbonne.

In 1917, Eliot established himself as a poet with the publication of *The Love Song of J. Alfred Prufrock*. Five years later his lengthy poem *The Waste Land* won him literary fame; the poem was edited by his friend and fellow poet, Ezra Pound. His writings also included several plays and essays. Eliot moved to London at the beginning of World War I and became a teacher at Highgate School and a year later was employed by Lloyd's Bank. He went to work as a editor and director for the publishing house Faber and Faber. Eliot lived in an apartment in Chelsea overlooking the river Thames; he became a British citizen in 1927. His literary expertise was awarded in 1948 when he was awarded the Nobel Prize for literature. A year later, King George VI conferred the Order of Merit on him.

Eliot was quiet in his demeanor, lacking the flamboyance and eccentricity of others in his business, he spent much of his leisure time reading books on philosophy and languages. He often suffered through bouts of bronchitis and his emphysema was exacerbated by his heavy smoking. In 1915, he married Vivian Wood. Though Vivian was sickly during much of the marriage, she died unexpectedly in 1922, the same year that The Waste Land was published. Eliot was shattered by her death. In 1957, he surprised everyone by marrying his secretary, Valerie Fletcher; she was 38 years his junior. In September, he came

T.S. Eliot.

down with influenza and a return of his bronchitis.

Eliot twice came back to St. Louis, 1953 and 1959. He spoke at Washington University during the first trip and at Mary Institute during the latter. He was awarded a Medal of Freedom by President Lyndon Johnson but didn't go to Washington to receive it.

Eliot's physical condition continued to weaken during the early 1960's; the bronchitis and emphysema were taking their toll on his body. In December 1962, he collapsed in his home and was rushed to the hospital in a comatose state. Though his condition was critical, he strengthened enough to return home five weeks later. He once again collapsed in October 1964; his left side was paralyzed and he was in a coma but Eliot surprised his doctors by regaining consciousness the next morning.

Thomas Stearns Eliot relapsed into a coma at the end of December and died on January 5, 1965 in his London apartment. He was 76. Ezra Pound said of his friends death, "I am deeply saddened and profoundly moved by the death of T. S. Eliot, a grand poet and my dear and brotherly friend." St. Stephen's Church in East Coker, England was the site of the funeral two days later. East Coker was where his ancestors had emigrated from in the 17th century. Eliot had memorialized the village in the second of his *Four Quarters* poem entitled *East Coker*. Only his family and a few close friends attended the short ten-minute service. His body was cremated per his request at the Golders Green Crematorium in northwest London. On April 17, his ashes were returned to St. Stephen's for burial in the church. On that same day it was announced that the first college of the newly established University of Kent would be named Eliot College in the poet's honor. His memorial in the church reads,

> "In my beginning is my end."
> of your charity
> pray for the repose
> of the soul of
> Thomas Stearns Eliot
> Poet
> 26th September 1888 - 4th January 1965
> "In my end is my beginning."

On February 4, a memorial service was held at Westminster Abbey. Ezra Pound, who had not been seen in public for many years, came to express his sympathy. A statement was received from the White House, "The President wishes to pay tribute to a poet and playwright who had a profound impact on his times and who achieved distinction on both sides of the Atlantic." Stage actor Alec Guinness read from Eliot's poems.

JOSEPHINE BAKER

(June 3, 1906 - April 12, 1975)

Josephine McDonald was born in the Female Hospital in St.

Louis. Her mother, Carrie was only 20 and unwed. Carrie was impoverished and worked as a laundress and lived on Gratiot Street. The next year she had a second child, Richard. She later married Arthur Martin and the couple moved to 1526 Gratiot where she had two more children. The family was extremely poor and the four children slept on a single mattress.

Josephine often played hooky from school; she much preferred dancing and the theatre. She spent much of her time watching musicals, movies, and vaudeville acts at the Booker T. Washington Theatre at 23rd and Market. What little education she had ended in December 1919, when at the age of 13, she married Willie Wells. Because of her age the marriage was not legal. Josephine married legally four times but she took her name from her second marriage to Billy Baker.

When Josephine was 16, she joined a traveling dance troupe based in Philadelphia. She made it to Broadway the very next year as a member of the chorus line of Shuffle Along. She also appeared at the Cotton Club in Harlem. In 1925, Josephine went to Paris to appear in La Revue Negre at the Theatre des Champs-Elysees. In Paris she performed in rather risque attire. Once she appeared on stage in a mere flamingo feather and later she danced in a skirt of bananas in Folies Bergere. The show made her a star across France; the queen of the music halls. She opened her own club where she danced into the hearts of Parisians. By 1930, she added singing to her dance routines and appeared in several French motion pictures. She returned to America in 1936 to appear in the Ziegfeld Follies on Broadway. She became a French citizen a year later.

In 1940, while the war raged in Europe, Josephine lived in a chateau called Les Milandes in southwestern France. She attempted to build a resort on the 300 acres but fell into debt and was forced to sell the estate at auction in 1969. During the war, she served as a volunteer for the Red Cross and was a member of the Resistance movement. She was awarded the Legion of Honor for her work.

In 1954, Josephine adopted her first child. She would take in eleven more children over the next four years. She called the children the "Rainbow Tribe" since they were born of different nationalities. In January 1958, while Josephine was on tour, her mother Carrie died in France and was buried in the cemetery at Les Milandes; Carrie came to live with her daughter in 1945.

Josephine Baker.

Josephine had faced discrimination much of her life and had bitter feelings toward the United States for the injustices heaped onto blacks. She once told a radio interviewer, "I was born in America and grew up in St. Louis. I was very young when I first went to Europe. I was 18 years old. But I had to go. I wanted to find freedom. I couldn't find it in St. Louis, of course. It was one of the worst cities in America for racial discrimination. I hear it has changed, but I have never been there since. I have very bad memories of that time." Josephine came to Washington D.C. in 1963 to take part in Martin Luther King's march on Washington.

After Josephine's Les Milandes estate was auctioned off, she purchased a villa at Roquebrune-Cap-Martin in the French Riviera with the help of Princess Grace and proceeded with her return to the stage.

In early April 1975, Josephine attended an opening-night party celebrating her 50th anniversary as a French entertainer. She had opened her new show "Josephine" at the Bobino Music Hall in Paris. Josephine had a habit of calling her friend Marie Spiers every morning. On Thursday morning, April 10, Marie didn't hear from Josephine. She called to find Josephine still sleeping by the afternoon. When Josephine's maid was unsuccessful in waking her, Marie called a doctor and came to her Paris apartment. Josephine was laying on her side with a hand to her head; newspapers with reviews of her show laid about the room. She was taken to Salpetriere Hospital in Paris suffering a cerebral hemorrhage. The press was told that Josephine was suffering from exhaustion.

Marie and Margaret, Josephine's sister, stayed with Josephine who never regained consciousness. Princess Grace, a close friend and financial supporter of Baker when she fell into debt, was present when a priest gave Josephine the last rites. At 5:30 on the morning of Saturday, April 12, Josephine passed away.

The nationally televised funeral took place on April 15 at Church of the Madeleine, the Paris cathedral where Napoleon had been crowded Emperor. The hearse carried Josephine's flag-draped coffin past the Bobino Music Hall on its way to the cathedral. Twenty thousand people crowded the streets outside the cathedral; photographers clamored for the perfect shot. Hundreds of policemen were on hand to control the crowds. French dignities from around the country attended the ceremonies. Princess Grace and actress Sophia Loren, who attended Josephine's opening night performance, paid their respects to the entertainer. Only two of Josephine's twelve children were there.

Josephine's body was taken to Monaco for a second funeral arranged by Princess Grace. Mourners viewed the body at the Athanee, a Monte Carlo funeral home before the April 19 funeral. Two thousand people attended the funeral at St. Charles Church. Josephine's coffin was taken to a Monaco cemetery overlooking the Mediterranean and placed on an altar supported by four columns.

The coffin was placed in the cemetery storage shed until a stone was selected for her tomb. Josephine Baker was finally laid to rest on October 2, 1975.

VINCENT PRICE

(May 27, 1911 - October 25, 1993)

The actor known by many for his ghoulish portrayals in horror movies was born the youngest of four children in his family's home at 3748 Washington Avenue. The family later moved to 6320 Forsyth Boulevard. Price's family tree can be traced back to Peregrine White who was born on the ship Mayflower in Plymouth harbor shortly before the first Thanksgiving. His grandfather was a chemist who made his fortune by inventing baking powder and later producing flavor extracts for bakers. His father, also named Vincent, ran the Pan Candy Company. His company merged with another manufacturer in 1902 to establish the National Candy Company at 4320 Gravois. His father was named president of the enterprise which made a fortune during the 1904 World's Fair.

His family's wealth allowed Vincent to attend the best schools. He went to St. Louis Country Day followed by a four year education at Yale where he received a Bachelor of Fine Arts degree in 1933. Vincent immediately went to New York and tried to get work in the theatre. When his attempt failed, he took a position as an apprentice teacher. A year later he enrolled at London University's graduate program.

In 1935, his dream of a career on the stage was finally realized when he played a role in Chicago at the Gate Theatre in London. His next role as Prince Albert in Victoria Regina landed him on Broadway playing opposite Helen Hayes. His first motion picture appearance was in Service de Luxe. Vincent joined the ranks of actors such as Bela Lugosi and Boris Karloff when he began appearing in low-budget horror films such as House of Wax in 1953. He once said of his ghoulish portrayals, "The best parts in movies are the heavies. The hero is usually someone who has really nothing to do. He comes out on top, but it's the heavy who has all the fun." He first appeared at the St. Louis Muny Opera in 1940 in The American Way.

Besides acting, Vincent was a avid art collector who had his own gallery. He gave art lectures on colleges campuses and wrote several books on fine art, the most popular of which was The Vincent Price Treasury of American Art in 1972. He also served as president of the art council for the University of California at Los Angeles. Vincent was an accomplished cook who wrote bestselling cookbooks with his second wife Mary.

Vincent wed actress Edith Barrett in 1938 and divorced a decade later. They had one son, Vincent. He married again, this time to Mary Grant, but this marriage also ended in divorce; their daughter Mary Victoria was named after Vincent's first Broadway show. In 1974, he was married a third time to actress Coral Browne who died in 1991.

By 1993, Vincent's 80-plus years were taking a toll. He was suffering from emphysema and arthritis by October. He died of lung cancer on Monday, October 25 at his home in Los Angeles. His remains were cremated.

BETTY GRABLE

(December 18, 1916 - July 2, 1973)

Ruth Elizabeth Grable appeared in over 40 films. Her $300,000 a year salary was the highest paid to any actress in the mid-1940's. During World War II, her famous bathing suit pose was the favorite pin-up for G. I.'s fighting around the world. The blue-eyed blond was born in South St. Louis to Conn and Lillian Grable. Lillian enrolled her four-year-old daughter in dancing classes and saxophone lessons. Within a few years, Betty was performing at the West End Lyric Theatre, appearing in vaudeville shows, and singing on radio shows. She attended Mary Institute.

In the summer of 1929, her mother brought her to Hollywood where she was cast in small parts on the Sam Goldwyn lot. Four years later, she danced in The Gay Divorcee. In 1941, producer Daryl Zanuck signed her to a contract and she appeared in the musical, Down Argentine Way. It was her first starring role and launched her career.

Betty married actor Jackie Coogan in November 1937, but the marriage ended in divorce two years later. She had a relationship with actor George Raft before marrying band leader and trumpeter Harry James in 1943. They were married for 22 years. The couple had two daughters, Vickie and Jessica, and lived on an estate and raised horses on two ranches.

Betty retired from the movies after her last picture "How to be Very Very Popular" in 1955. She attempted a comeback without much success. She seldom visited St. Louis. Her final appearance came in 1971 in the Muny Opera production of "This is Show Business," co-starring Don Ameche.

In the early 1970's she moved to Las Vegas and lived with Bob Remick.

Betty Grable.

The two had met while appearing in a show together. In April 1972, Betty presented an award at the Academy Awards. After the show, she had difficulty breathing and a pain in her chest. Tests run at St. John's Hospital in Santa Monica revealed inoperable lung cancer. Betty had been a heavy smoker all her life. She was hospitalized for four months and underwent chemotherapy and cobalt treatments. She wrote a friend about her condition, "I finally decided after all these years it might be a good idea to get a physical…Well, it's a good thing I did, cause my chest x-ray came back abnormal. Lucky me, just in time. Here I was with a big malignancy."

Betty recovered enough to appear in the stage show "Born Yesterday" in January 1973. After the show closed, she was suffering severe stomach pains and nausea. When abdominal surgery was performed at St. John's, a large tumor was removed, but by this time the cancer had spread through her body. She left the hospital and returned to Las Vegas. Her health continued to fail; she began losing weight and becoming too dependent on morphine. By early July, she was back in St. John's for her final stay.

Betty died at 5:15 p.m., July 3. She was 56. The funeral was celebrated at All Saints Episcopal Church in Beverly Hills. Six hundred mourners including her two ex-husbands, Jackie Coogan and Harry James, attended. Betty Grable is buried at Inglewood Cemetery in Inglewood, California. Other notables in Inglewood include singer Ella Fitzgerald, actor Cesar Romero, and ventriloquist Edgar Bergen.

Appendices

APPENDIX 1:

ST. LOUIS CHRONOLOGY

1763: December. St. Louis is founded by Pierre Laclede and Auguste Chouteau. In February Chouteau begins clearing ground for construction of the village.

1770: March. Boston Massacre occurs when British soldiers fire on a crowd. Five are killed.

1778: June. Pierre Laclede dies on his way back to St. Louis from New Orleans. He is buried in a unmarked grave on the Arkansas River.

1781: October. The Revolutionary War ends with British General Cornwallis' surrender to George Washington at Yorktown, Virginia.

1803: May. Thomas Jefferson purchases the Louisiana Territory from France for $15,000,000. The area doubles the size of the United States.

1804: May. Jefferson sends Lewis and Clark to explore the far western territories.

July. Aaron Burr fatally wounds Alexander Hamilton in a duel in New Jersey. Hamilton dies the next day.

1806: September. Lewis and Clark arrive in St. Louis after their two-year expedition.

1808: July. Joseph Charless publishes the first issue on the *Missouri Gazette.*

1811: December. Wealthy merchant Peter Lindell arrives in St. Louis and opens a general store. He goes on to accumulate vast amounts of real estate.

1812: November. Edward Hempstead is elected the first delegate in Congress from the Missouri Territory.

1813: June. William Clark is appointed governor of the Missouri Territory.

September. Thomas Hart Benton and his brother Jesse take part in a gun battle against General Andrew Jackson in Nashville.

1814: August. British forces burn the U.S. Capitol building and the White House during the War of 1812.

1816: December. The Bank of St. Louis, the city's first banking institution, opens.

1817: August. Edward Hempstead dies of a brain hemorrhage a week after he is thrown from his horse. He was 37.

September. Thomas Hart Benton and Charles Lucas fight a second duel on Bloody Island. Lucas is killed.

October. Joseph Rosati first arrives in St. Louis and later becomes bishop.

1818: August. Philippine Duchesne arrives in St. Louis from New Orleans.

September. Mother Duchesne opens the first free school west of the Mississippi.

1819: May. Henry Shaw arrives in St. Louis. In twenty years, he amasses a fortune in the hardware business.

1821: August. Missouri becomes the 24th State. It enters the Union as a slave state.

1822: June. Doctor William Beaumont treats stomach wound of Alexis St. Martin. He begins extensive study of the digestive system.

1823: April. William Carr Lane is elected first Mayor of St. Louis.

1826: July. Stephen Watts Kearny supervises construction of Jefferson Barracks.

1827: September. Jesuit missionary Peter De Smet is ordained into the priesthood.

1829: February. St. Louis pioneer Auguste Chouteau dies. He's buried at Catholic Church cemetery and later moved to Calvary.

November. The Jesuits open St. Louis University to 40 students.

1831: August. Thomas Biddle and William Pettus both die after receiving fatal wounds during their duel on Bloody Island.

1833: March. Stephen Watts Kearny is appointed lieutenant colonel of the First Dragoons, the first cavalry unit of the United States Army.

August. Philanthropist and businessman John Mullanphy dies at 73.

September. Doctor Beaumont's book *Experiences and Observations on the Gastric Juice and the Physiology of Digestion* is published.

1834: July. Doctor Beaumont first arrives in St. Louis. He is stationed at Jefferson Barracks.

Publisher Joseph Charless dies. He was 62 years old.

October. Bishop Joseph Rosati consecrates the Old Cathedral upon its completion.

1836: May. The cornerstone is laid for the New St. Louis Theater at Third and Olive. It is the first theater in the city, designed by Meriwether Lewis Clark, son of William Clark.

1838: June. Bloody Island becomes part of the Illinois shore by the work of the Corp of Engineers under lieutenant Robert E. Lee.

September. William Clark dies at the home of his son, Meriwether Lewis Clark. His funeral is the largest in St. Louis history at the time.

1841: April. Planters House opens. It's the most exclusive hotel in the city. Charles Dickens once stayed at the hotel while visiting St. Louis.

1842: August. Judge John B.C. Lucas dies two weeks after his 84th birthday.

1843: September. Bishop Rosati dies in Rome and is buried there.

1848: September. Peter Richard Kenrick becomes the first Archbishop of St. Louis.

October. Stephen Watts Kearny dies at the home of his friend Meriwether Lewis Clark. He is buried on the private estate of John O'Fallon. In 1861 his remains are moved to Bellefontaine Cemetery.

1849: March. Bellefontaine Cemetery is incorporated under the name "Rural Cemetery."

Francis Blair and L. Pickering have umbrella duel on Second Street.

May. The steamboat *White Cloud* burst into flames, igniting the Great St. Louis Fire. The cholera epidemic is also in full bloom.

July. Doctor Bernard Farrar dies of cholera. Pierre Chouteau also dies at age 91.

1851: March. Steamboat Captain Henry Miller Shreve dies in St. Louis. He is buried at Bellefontaine Cemetery.

June. Bryan Mullanphy is laid to rest in the family lot at Calvary. The former mayor of the St. Louis was 42.

1852: November. Mother Philippine Duchesne dies at Sacred Heart Academy in St. Charles. She is 83 years old.

1853: February. St. Louis Public High School, first high school west of the Mississippi, opens with 72 students.

April. Doctor Beaumont dies in his St. Louis home.

1855: November. The new Gasconade Bridge collapses on opening day. Thirty are killed including Thomas O'Flaherty, Kate Chopin's father.

1857: March. The United States Supreme Court decides against Dred Scott who is suing for his freedom. Two months later Scott is freed by his owner.

1858: April Thomas Hart Benton dies in Washington D.C. President Buchanan visited him the day before. His body is returned to St. Louis for burial.

1859: June. Joseph Charless' son, Joseph Jr., is shot by Joseph Thornton who Charless had testified against in a trial. He dies the next morning.

1860: November. Abraham Lincoln is elected 16th President of the United States.

1861: April. Confederate forces bomb Fort Sumter, igniting the Civil War.

August. James Eads receives contract to build ironclads for the Union forces. The first boat *St. Louis* is launched October 12.

October. Wealthy merchant and real estate owner, Peter Lindell, dies in St. Louis.

1862: April. The Battle of Shiloh, one of the bloodiest of the Civil War, takes place in Tennessee. Generals William Tecumseh Sherman and Don Carlos Buell lead Union forces.

August. Adam Lemp, patriarch of the brewing family, dies.

1863: January. Abraham Lincoln's Emancipation Proclamation takes effect.

1864: September. General William Tecumseh Sherman takes Atlanta. His army cuts a path through Georgia and the Carolinas in the march to the sea.

1865: February. The St. Louis Public Library is born.

April. General Robert E. Lee surrenders his Confederate forces to Ulysses S. Grant at Appomattox. Five days later Abraham Lincoln is assassinated by John Wilkes Booth at Ford's Theater.

December. John O'Fallon dies at 74. He's buried in the largest lot in Bellefontaine Cemetery.

The Southern Hotel opens at Walnut between 4th and 5th streets, fourteen people are killed in a fire that races through the hotel in 1877.

1867: March. The Calvary Cemetery Association is incorporated.

September. Former Governor, General Sterling Price dies at his home on 16th Street.

1869: March. Edward Bates dies in his Morgan Street home.

1872: December. Frederick Dent, father-in-law of Ulysses Grant, dies in the White House. The president occupies the body to St. Louis.

1873: May. Father Peter De Smet dies in St. Louis. Archbishop Richard Peter Kenrick conducts the funeral Mass.

September. Susan Blow opens the first public kindergarten in America at Des Peres School in Carondelet.

1874: June. Eads Bridge opens to the public. Wagons make first trip across followed by a large crowd of people. Kate Chopin is among the pedestrians.

July. Eads Bridge has official opening ceremony with parade and fireworks. General William Sherman hammers in the final railroad spike.

1875: June. Union Depot opens at 12th and Poplar Street.

July. Francis Blair dies in his home of a brain hemorrhage.

September. Henry Blow dies at 58 in Saratoga, New York. His body is returned to St. Louis for burial at Bellefontaine.

1878: December. Joseph Pulitzer purchases the bankrupt *St. Louis Dispatch* at an auction on the steps of the Old Courthouse.

1879: October. Wealthy fur trader Robert Campbell dies in his Lucas Place home.

1884: May. Samuel Hawken, maker of the Hawken Rifle, dies at 92.

1885: May. Civic leader and businessman Wayman Crow dies in St. Louis.

1886: March. Al Spink establishes the *Sporting News*.

October. Chris Von der Ahe's St. Louis Browns win the baseball championship against the Chicago White Stockings.

1887: January. Chancellor of Washington University, Reverend William Greenleaf Eliot, dies in Pass Christian, Mississippi.

March. Engineer James Eads dies in Nassau, Bahamas. He was 66.

1889: August. Philanthropist Henry Shaw dies in his garden home at the Botanical Garden. He's buried in the garden mausoleum.

1891: February. General Sherman dies in New York. The largest funeral in St. Louis history leads Sherman to Calvary Cemetery.

1892: November. William J. Lemp Brewing Company is incorporated.

1893: June. The Pacific Railroad, the first line west of the Mississippi River, makes its initial run.

1894: August. Women suffrage leader, Virginia Minor, dies at 70.

September. Union Station opens. The station is designed by Theodore Link.

1895: November. Poet Eugene Field dies of heart failure in his Chicago home.

1896: March. Archbishop Peter Richard Kenrick dies and is buried at Calvary, the cemetery he founded.

May. Tornado rips through Lafayette Park area. Eads Bridge is damaged, all city utilities are lost for a time. Death toll:

138.

1898: April. A fire breaks out and engulfs the grandstand at Sportsman's Park. One hundred spectators are injured.

September. William Burroughs, inventor of the adding machine, dies in Citronville, Alabama. He was 43.

November. Civil War General Don Carlos Buell dies in his country home in Rockport, Kentucky.

1901: July. Banker and civic leader James Yeatman dies.

1903: October. John Glennon becomes third Archbishop of St. Louis.

1904: February. Brewer William Lemp commits suicide in his bedroom at Lemp Mansion.

April. St. Louis World's Fair opens.

August. Novelist Kate Chopin dies of a brain hemorrhage in her home on McPherson Avenue.

1908: April. Wealthy merchant Byron Nugent dies in his home. He was 65.

October. Archbishop Glennon lays the cornerstone for the New Cathedral. It is dedicated six years later.

1911: November. Norman Jay Colman, first Secretary of the Agriculture, dies aboard a train. He was 84.

1912: April. The steamship *Titanic* strikes an iceberg in the Atlantic Ocean and sinks. The death toll is over 1500.

1913: June. St. Louis Browns owner Chris Van der Ahe dies in his St. Louis home.

October. Adolphus Busch dies at his estate in Germany. An estimated 100,000 St. Louisans line the streets of the procession route on the day of his funeral.

1914: April. *Sporting News* publisher Charles Spink dies in St. Luke's Hospital.

June. The body of millionaire James Campbell is returned to St. Louis after he dies of pneumonia at his Greenwich,

Connecticut summer home.

1916: March. Kindergarten teachers from around the country attend the funeral of education pioneer Susan Blow.

June. The Democratic National Convention is held at the Coliseum on Locust and Jefferson. Woman's suffrage is the important issue of the day.

1918: November. St. Louisans celebrate the end of World War I. The streets are alive with celebration.

1919: August. Multimillionaire Samuel Fordyce succumbs to pneumonia in Atlantic City, New Jersey.

October. The *St. Louis Republic*, owned by David Francis, publishes its final issue.

1920: January. Prohibition begins with the passing of the 18th Amendment.

March. Elsa Lemp Wright, daughter of William Lemp, kills herself.

May. Steel magnate John Scullin dies in St. Luke's Hospital after being diagnosed with uremic poisoning.

July. Editor William Marion Reedy succumbs to heart disease while covering the Democratic National Convention in San Francisco.

August. Congress ratifies the 19th Amendment to the Constitution giving women the right to vote.

1921: December. The founder and chairman of Brown Shoe Company, George Warren Brown, dies in Tucson, Arizona.

1922: March. Dairyman Joseph Cabanne died in St. John's Hospital after cutting his throat with a razor.

June. The defunct Lemp Brewery is auctioned off.

Radio station KSD goes on the air. It is the first station to broadcast St. Louis Symphony Orchestra and the Muny Opera.

December. William Lemp, Jr. shoots himself in the chest in his office at Lemp Mansion.

1923: March. Financial and railroad magnate Julius Walsh succumbs to heart disease.

1924: January. August "Gussie" Busch, Jr. starts his career at Anheuser-Busch as a superintendent.

1927: January. Former Mayor of St. Louis and Governor of Missouri David Francis dies. He was 76.

May. Charles Lindbergh flies *The Spirit of St. Louis* on the first solo flight across the Atlantic. The 3600 mile flight takes over 33 hours.

1928: February. Edward Mallinckrodt dies of pneumonia in his Westmoreland Place home.

1929: September. The St. Louis Arena is dedicated. It is built to house the National Dairy Show.

1931: June. Lawyer Homer G. Phillips is fatally shot by two assailants while waiting his bus on Delmar.

October. William Bixby is buried in his Bellefontaine mausoleum after dying of a heart attack. He was 74.

1933: January. Poet Sara Teasdale is found dead in her bathtub. Her death is ruled accidental.

April. Prohibition ends. St. Louis breweries are back in business. Anheuser- Busch sends its first case to President Franklin Roosevelt.

1934: February. August Busch commits suicide at his Grant's Farm estate. He's buried at nearby Sunset Memorial Park.

October. The Gashouse Gang's St. Louis Cardinals win World Series from the Detroit Tigers.

1938: July. Brewer Joseph Griesedieck dies in St. John's Hospital from complications of a fractured hip, three days after his 75th birthday.

1939: June. George Sisler is inducted into Baseball's Hall of Fame in Cooperstown.

1941: December. Forces of the Japanese empire attack Pearl Harbor in Hawaii. The next day the United States enters World

War II by declaring war on Japan.

1943: August. A glider carrying Mayor William Becker and nine others crashes at Lambert Field during an airshow.

1945: August. United States drops a atomic bomb on Hiroshima, Japan. Three days later a second bomb is dropped on Nagasaki. World War II ends.

1946: February. Archbishop Glennon is elevated to Cardinal, first in St. Louis.

March. John Cardinal Glennon dies in his homeland of Ireland. His body is transported back to St. Louis for burial in his New Cathedral.

August. Adolphus Busch III dies of cardiac failure at Barnes Hospital. Gussie Busch replaces him as head of Anheuser-Busch.

October. Joseph Ritter is appointed archbishop of St. Louis, replacing Cardinal Glennon.

November. Albert Lambert dies in his sleep at his St. Louis home.

1947: November. The streets of St. Louis are illuminated for the first time by the St. Louis Gas-Light Company.

Robert Hannegan steps down as Postmaster General and National Democratic Committee chairman due to poor health.

December. Tennessee Williams' play *A Streetcar Named Desire* opens on Broadway. The playwright wins his first Pulitzer Prize.

1949: May. Charles Lemp is the fourth member of the family to commit suicide, third at Lemp Mansion.

October. Robert Hannegan dies of a heart condition in his home on Lindell.

1954: August. The body of Joseph Rosati is returned to St. Louis for burial at the New Cathedral.

1959: February. Tornado tears through St. Louis, 21 killed, thousands of buildings damaged including the St. Louis Arena.

1960: December. Archbishop Joseph Ritter is elevated to cardinal.

1961: January. Missionary doctor Tom Dooley dies of cancer in New York, one day after his 34th birthday.

1962: December. J.G. Taylor Spink dies in his Clayton home. He's laid to rest in the family mausoleum at Bellefontaine.

1963: July. The Forest Park Highlands, St. Louis' most popular amusement park, goes up in flames. Forest Park Community College is now located on the site.

1965: October. The last piece of the Gateway Arch is installed. The project took four years to complete.

January. Poet T.S. Eliot dies in his London apartment.

1967: June. Cardinal Ritter dies in DePaul Hospital after suffering second heart attack.

1968: January. Joe Medwick is elected to Baseball's Hall of Fame.

1970: November. Mayor Raymond Tucker dies in Barnes Hospital of congestive heart failure, weeks short of his 74th birthday.

1973: March. Hall of Famer George Sisler dies two days after his 80th birthday.

July. Actress and pin-up girl Betty Grable dies of lung cancer in California.

1975: March. Gashouse Gang member Joe Medwick succumbs to a heart attack in St. Petersburg, Florida.

April. Entertainer Josephine Baker dies in Paris.

1980: March. John May is installed as Archbishop of St. Louis.

August. James McDonnell passes away from the effects of a stroke.

1983: February. The body of Tennessee William is found on the floor of his New York hotel room. He died from accidental choking on the cap of a prescription bottle.

June. Mayor Alfonso Cervantes dies of cancer in Barnes Hospital.

1988: February. St. Louis Blues defenseman and head coach Barclay Plager succumbs to cancer.

July. Rose Philippine Duchesne is canonized a saint in Vatican City, Rome.

1989: February. "Voice of the Blues" Dan Kelly dies at 52 years of age.

September. Gussie Busch dies in his Grant's Farm bedroom, the same room his father committed suicide in.

1991: March Negro League icon James "Cool Papa" Bell dies in St. Louis Hospital.

1992: March. Robert Hyland, general manager of KMOX dies of cancer.

C.C. Johnson Spink, succumbs after a brief illness. He is the fourth and final member of the family to run the *Sporting News*.

1993: October. Actor Vincent Price dies of lung cancer in the Los Angeles home.

1994: March. Hundreds attend the funeral of Archbishop John May at the St. Louis Cathedral.

1995: July. *Globe-Democrat* sports columnist Bob Burnes dies. He was 80.

APPENDIX 2:

ALPHABETICAL CHART OF BURIAL PLACES

NAME	BIRTH DATE	BIRTH PLACE	DEATH DATE	DEATH CEMETERY
Josephine Baker	June 3, 1906	St. Louis	Apr 12, 1975	Monte Carlo
Edward Bates	Sept 4, 1793	Goochland County, VA	Mar 25, 1869	Bellefontaine
William Beaumont	Nov 21, 1785	Lebanon, CT	Apr 25, 1853	Bellefontaine
William Dee Becker	Oct 23, 1876	East St. Louis, IL	Aug 1, 1943	Bellefontaine
Cool Papa Bell	May 17, 1903	Starkville, MS	Mar 7, 1991	St. Peters
Thomas Hart Benton	Mar 14, 1782	Hillsborough, NC	Apr 10, 1858	Bellefontaine
William Bixby	Jan 2, 1857	Adrian, MI	Oct 29, 1931	Bellefontaine
Frank Blair	Feb 19, 1821	Lexington, KY	July 9, 1875	Bellefontaine
Henry Blow	July 15, 1817	Southhampton Cny, VA.	Sept 11, 1875	Bellefontaine
Susan Blow	June 7, 1843	St. Louis	Mar 26, 1916	Bellefontaine
Robert Brookings	Jan 22, 1850	Cecil County, MD	Nov 15, 1932	Bellefontaine
Brown Brothers				Bellefontaine
Don Carlos Buell	Mar 23, 1818	Marietta, OH	Nov 19, 1898	Bellefontaine
Bob Burnes	July 14, 1914	St. Louis	July 11, 1995	Resurrection
William Burroughs	Jan 28, 1855	Auburn, NY	Sept 15, 1898	Bellefontaine
Adolphus Busch	July 10, 1839	Badschwalbach, Ger	Oct 10, 1913	Bellefontaine
August Busch	Mar 28, 1899	St. Louis	Sept 29, 1989	Sunset
J. Charles Cabanne	Oct 16, 1846	St. Louis	Mar 18, 1922	Calvary
James Campbell	1848	Ireland	June 12, 1914	Calvary
Robert Campbell	Feb 12, 1804	Tyrone, Ireland	Oct 16, 1879	Bellefontaine
Alfonso Cervantes	Aug 27, 1920	St. Louis	June 23, 1983	Calvary
Joseph Charless	July 16, 1772	Westmeath, Ireland	July 28, 1834	Bellefontaine
Kate Chopin	Feb 8, 1851	St. Louis	Aug 22, 1904	Calvary
Auguste Chouteau	Sept 7, 1749	New Orleans, LA	Feb 24, 1829	Calvary
Pierre Chouteau	Oct 10, 1758	New Orleans, LA	July 9, 1849	Calvary
William Clark	Aug 1, 1770	Caroline County, VA	Sept 1, 1838	Bellefontaine
Norman Jay Colman	May 16, 1827	Richfield Springs, NY	Nov 3, 1911	Bellefontaine
Wayman Crow	Mar 7, 1808	Hopkinsville, KY	May 10, 1885	Bellefontaine
Frederick Dent	Oct 6, 1787	Cumberland, MD	Dec 15, 1872	Bellefontaine
Desmet, Jean Pierre	Jan 30, 1801	Termonde, Belgium	May 23, 1873	St. Stanislaus Seminary
Thomas Dooley	Jan 17, 1927	St. Louis	Jan 18, 1961	Calvary
Philippine Duchesne	Aug 29, 1769	Grenoble, France	Nov 18, 1852	Academy of Sacred Heart
James Eads	May 23, 1820	Lawrenceburg, IN	Mar 8, 1887	Bellefontaine
T.S. Eliot	Sept 26, 1888	St. Louis	Jan 4, 1965	St. Michael's
William G. Eliot	Aug 5, 1811	New Bedford, MA	Jan 23, 1887	Bellefontaine
Barnard Farrar	July 4, 1785	Goochland Cny, VA	July 1, 1849	Bellefontaine
Eugene Field	Sept 9, 1850	St. Louis	Nov 4, 1895	Graceland, Chicago, IL
Samual Fordyce	Feb 7, 1840	Guernsey Cny, OH	Aug 3, 1919	Bellefontaine
David Francis	Oct 1, 1850	Richmond, Kentucky	Jan 15, 1927	Bellefontaine
John Glennon	June 14, 1862	Kinnegad, Ireland	Mar 9, 1946	St. Louis Cathedral
Betty Grable	Dec 18, 1916	St. Louis	July 2, 1973	Inglewood Park, CA
Joseph Griesedieck	July 11, 1863	Stromberg, Ger	July 14, 1938	Bellefontaine
Robert Hannegan	June 30, 1903	St. Louis	Oct 6, 1949	Calvary
Samuel Hawken	Oct 26, 1792	Hagerstown, MD	May 9, 1884	Bellefontaine
Edward Hempstead	June 3, 1780	New London, CT	Aug 10, 1817	Bellefontaine
Robert Hyland	Mar 25, 1920	St. Louis	Mar 5, 1992	Calvary

NAME	BIRTH DATE	BIRTH PLACE	DEATH DATE	DEATH CEMETERY
Stephen Watts Kearny	Aug 30, 1794	Newark, NJ	Oct 31, 1848	Bellefontaine
Dan Kelly	1936	Ottawa, Ontario	Feb 10, 1989	Resurrection
Peter Richard Kenrick	Aug 17, 1806	Dublin, Ireland	Mar 4, 1896	Calvary
Henry Kiel	Feb 21, 1871	St. Louis	Nov 26, 1942	Oak Grove
Pierre Laclede	Nov 22, 1724	Bedous, France	June 20, 1778	Unknown
Albert Lambert	Dec 6, 1875	St. Louis	Nov 12, 1946	Bellefontaine
William Carr Lane	Dec 1, 1789	Fayette Cnty, PA	Jan 6, 1863	Bellefontaine
Lemp Family				Bellefontaine
Peter Lindell	Mar 26, 1776	Maryland	Oct 26, 1861	Bellefontaine
Theodore Link	Mar 17, 1850	Zimpfen, Ger	Nov 12, 1923	Bellefontaine
Manuel Lisa	Sept 8, 1772	New Orleans	Aug 12, 1820	Bellefontaine
Lucas Family				Calvary
Edward Mallinkrodt	Jan 21, 1845	St. Louis	Feb 1, 1928	Bellefontaine
John May	Mar 31, 1922	Evanston, IL	Mar 24, 1994	St. Louis Cathedral
James McDonnell	Apr 9, 1899	Denver, CO	Aug 22, 1980	Bellefontaine
Alexander McNair	May 5, 1775	Juniata County, PA	Mar 18, 1826	Calvary
Joe Medwick	Nov 4, 1911	Carteret, NJ	Mar 21, 1975	St. Lucas
Virginia Minor	Mar 27, 1824	Goochland County, VA	Aug 14, 1894	Bellefontaine
John Mullanphy	1758	Enniskillen, Ireland	Aug 29, 1833	Calvary
Byron Nugent	July 31, 1842	Marysburgh, Ontario	Apr 4, 1908	Bellefontaine
John O'Fallon	Nov 17, 1791	Jefferson Cnty, KY	Dec 17, 1865	Bellefontaine
Homer G. Phillips	Apr 1, 1880	Sedalia, MO	June 22, 1931	St. Peter's
Barclay Plager	Mar 26, 1941	Kirkland Lake, Ontario	Feb 6, 1988	Bellerive Heritage Gdns.
Sterling Price	Sept 20, 1809	Prince Edward County, VA	Sept 29, 1867	Bellefontaine
Vincent Price	May 27, 1911	St. Louis	Oct 25, 1993	Remains Cremated
John Queeny	Aug 17, 1859	Chicago. IL	Mar 19, 1933	Bellefontaine
William Marion Reedy	Dec 11, 1862	St. Louis	July 28, 1920	Calvary
Joseph Ritter	July 20, 1892	New Albany, IN	June 10, 1967	St. Louis Cathedral
Joseph Rosati	Jan 30, 1789	Sora, Naples	Sept 25, 1842	St. Louis Cathedral
Dred Scott	circa 1795	Southampton Cnty, VA	Sept 17, 1858	Calvary
John Scullin	Aug 17, 1836	Lawrence County, NY	May 28, 1920	Calvary
Henry Shaw	July 24, 1800	England	Aug 25, 1889	Mo. Botanical Garden
William Sherman	Feb 8, 1820	Lancaster, OH	Feb 14, 1891	Calvary
Henry Miller Shreve	Oct 21, 1785	Burlington County, NJ	Mar 6, 1851	Bellefontaine
George Sisler	Mar 24, 1893	Manchester, OH	Mar 26, 1973	Des Peres Presbyterian
Spink Family				Bellefontaine
Sara Teasdale	Aug 8, 1884	St. Louis	Jan 28, 1933	Bellefontaine
Raymond Tucker	Dec 4, 1896	St. Louis	Nov 23, 1970	Calvary
Chris Von Der Ahe	Oct 7, 1851	Hille, Germany	June 5, 1913	Bellefontaine
Julius Walsh	Dec 1, 1842	St. Louis	Mar 21, 1923	Calvary
Tennessee Williams	Mar 26, 1911	Columbus, MS	Feb 25, 1983	Calvary
James Yeatman	Aug 27, 1818	Wartrace, TN	July 7, 1901	Bellefontaine

Appendix 3:

Bibliography

BOOKS

Ackroyd, Peter. T.S. Eliot. London: Hamish Hamilton, 1984.

Baker, Jean-Claude and Chase, Chris. Josephine: The Hungry Heart. New York: Random House, 1993.

Baldwin, Helen. Heritage of St. Louis. St. Louis: St. Louis Public Schools, 1964.

Bartley, Mary. St. Louis Lost. St. Louis: Virginia Publishing Company, 1994.

Borst, Bill. Baseball Through a Knothole: A St. Louis History. St. Louis: Krank Press, 1980.

Cain, Marvin R. Lincoln's Attorney General: Edward Bates of Missouri. Columbia, Mo.: University of Missouri Press, 1965.

Callan, Louise. Philippine Duchesne: Frontier Missionary of the Sacred Heart 1769-1852. Westminster, Md.: The Newman Press, 1957.

Chambers, William Nisbet. Old Bullion Benton: Senator From The New West. Boston & Toronto: Little, Brown, & Company, 1956.

Clarke, Dwight L. Stephen Watts Kearny: Soldier of the West. Norman: University of Oklahoma Press, 1961.

Darby, John F. Personal Recollections. St. Louis: G. I. Jones and Company, 1880.

Dennis, Charles H. Eugene Field's Creative Years. Garden City, New York: Doubleday, Page & Company, 1924.

Drake, William. Sara Teasdale: Woman and Poet. New York: Harper & Row Publishers, 1979.

Faherty, William Barnaby, S.J. Henry Shaw: His Life and Legacies. St. Louis: University of Missouri Press, 1987.

Foley, William E., and Rice, C. David. The First Chouteaus: River Barons of Early St. Louis. Urbana & Chicago: University of Illinois Press, 1983.

Freeman, Douglas Southall. R.E. Lee. New York: Charles Scribner's Sons, 1961.

Gill, McCune B. The St. Louis Story. Hopkinsville, Ky. & St. Louis: Historical Record Association, 1952.

Gould, E. W. Fifty Years of the Mississippi: Gould's History of River Navigation. St. Louis: Nixon-Jones Printing Company, 1889.

Hannon, Robert E. St. Louis: Its Neighborhoods and Neighbors, Landmarks, and Milestones. St. Louis: St. Louis Commerce and Growth Association, 1986.

Hernon, Peter and Ganey, Terry. Under the Influence: The Unauthorized Story of the Anheuser-Busch Dynasty. New York: Simon & Schuster, 1991.

Hood, Robert E. The Gashouse Gang. New York: William Morrow and Company, 1976.

Horsman, Reginald. Frontier Doctor: William Beaumont, America's First Great Medical Scientist. Columbia & London: University of Missouri Press, 1996.

How, Louis. James B. Eads. Freeport, NY.: Books for Libraries Press, 1900.

Hyde, William and Conard, Howard L. Encyclopedia of The History of St. Louis. New York: The Southern History Company, 1899.

Kaser, David. Joseph Charless: Printer in the Western Country. Philadephia: University of Pennsylvania Press, 1963.

Kirschten, Ernest. Catfish and Crystal. Garden City, New York: Doubleday & Company, Inc., 1960.

Koykka, Arthur S. Project Remember. Algonac, MI: Reference Publications, Inc., 1986.

Laveille, B., S.J. The Life of Father DeSmet, S.J. Chicago: Loyola University Press, 1981.

Leverich, Lyle. Tom: The Unknown Tennessee Williams. New York: Crown Publishers, 1995.

Lipsitz, George. The Sidewalks of St. Louis: Places, People, and Politics in an American City. Columbia & London: University of Missouri Press, 1991.

Loughlin, Caroline, and Anderson, Catherine. Forest Park. Columbia,

Mo.: University of Missouri Press, and The Junior League of St. Louis, 1986.

Magnan, William B. and Marcella C. The Streets of St. Louis. St. Louis: Virginia Publishing Company, 1994.

McCall, Edith. Conquering the Rivers. Baton Rouge: Louisiana State University Press, 1984.

Mead, William B. Even the Browns. Chicago: Contemporary Books, Inc., 1978.

Oglesby, Richard Edward. Manuel Lisa and the Opening of the Missouri Fur Trade. Norman: University of Oklahoma Press, 1963.

Primm, James Neal. Lion of the Valley: St. Louis, Missouri. Boulder, Co: Pruett Publishing Company, 1981.

Reavis, L.V. St. Louis: The Future Great City of the World. St. Louis: Gray, Baker, and Company, 1875.

Rose, Phyllis. Jazz Cleopatra: Josephine Baker in Her Time. New York: Doubleday & Company, Inc., 1989.

Ross, Ishbel. The General's Wife: The Life of Mrs. Ulysses S. Grant. New York: Dodd, Mead and Company, 1959.

Rothensteiner, Reverend John. History of The Archdiocese of St. Louis. St. Louis: Blackwell Wielandy Company, 1928.

Scharf, J. Thomas. History of St. Louis City and County. Philadephia: Louis H. Everts & Company, 1883.

Scott, Quinta, and Miller, Howard S. The Eads Bridge. Columbia & London: University of Missouri Press, 1979.

Shalhope, Robert E. Sterling Price: Portrait of a Southerner. Columbia, Mo.: University of Missouri Press, 1971.

Sherman, William Tecumseh. Memoirs of General W.T. Sherman. New York: The Library of America, 1990.

Stadler, Frances Hurd. St. Louis: Day by Day. St. Louis: The Patrice Press, 1989.

Steffen, Jerome O. William Clark: Jeffersonian Man on the Frontier. Norman, Ok.: University of Oklahoma Press, 1977.

Stevens, Walter B. St. Louis: The Fourth City 1764-1909. St. Louis & Chicago: S.J. Clarke Publishing Company, 1909.

Stiritz, Mary. St. Louis: Historic Churches and Synagogues. St. Louis: St. Louis Public Library & Landmarks Association of St. Louis, Inc., 1995.

Sunder, John E. Bill Sublette: Mountain Man. Norman: University of Oklahoma Press, 1959.

Toth, Emily. Kate Chopin. New York: Wiliam Morrow & Company, 1990.

Van Ravenswaay, Charles. St. Louis: An Informal History of The City and Its People, 1764-1865. St. Louis: Missouri History Society Press, 1991.

Walker, Stephen P. Lemp: The Haunting History. St. Louis: The Lemp Preservation Society, Inc., 1988.

Ward, Geoffrey C. and Burns, Ken. Baseball: An Illustrated History. New York: Alfred Knopf, 1994.

Warren, Doug. Betty Grable: The Reluctant Movie Queen. New York: St. Martin's Press, 1981.

Wheeler, Richard. We Knew William Tecumseh Sherman. New York: Thomas Y. Crowell Company, 1977.

Wiiliams, Tennessee. Tennessee Williams: Memoirs. New York: Doubleday & Company, Inc., 1972.

Winter, William C. The Civil War in St. Louis: A Guided Tour. St. Louis: Missouri Historical Society Press, 1994.

DICTIONARIES/ENCYCLOPEDIAS

Missouri Biographical Dictionary. New York: Somerset Publishing, Co., 1995.

Webster's American Biography. Springfield, Massachusetts: G & C Merriam Company Publishing, 1974.

PERIODICALS

Kaiser, Max Jr. "Historical Markers" St. Louis Magazine. October 1992: 14-19.

The St. Louis Catholic Historical Review. "Alexander McNair" Volume 1, July-October 1919, No. 4-5.

Van Ravenswaay, Charles. "Bloody Island: Honor and Violence in 19th Century St. Louis" Gateway Heritage. Spring 1990: 4-21.

ARCHIVES

Bassford Scrapbook, Missouri Historical Society, St. Louis.

Bellefontaine Cemetery Burial Records.

Charless, Joseph, Vertical File, Missouri Historical Society, St. Louis.

Lucas, John B.C., Vertical File, Missouri Historical Society, St. Louis.

Mullanphy, John, Vertical File, Missouri Historical Society, St. Louis.

Phillips, Homer G., Vertical File, Missouri Historical Society, St. Louis.

Stevens, W.B. Scrapbook #100, Missouri Historical Society, St. Louis.

NEWSPAPERS

Daily Missouri Democrat
September 20, 1858. Death of Dred Scott.

December 18, 1865. Death of Col. John O'Fallon.
December 19, 1965. Colonel John O'Fallon.
September 30, 1867. Death of General Sterling Price.
October 1, 1867. Funeral of General Sterling Price and his Daughter-in-Law.

The Missouri Gazette
March 10, 1887. Captain Eads Dead.
March 17, 1887. James B. Eads.

The Missouri Republican
February 24, 1829. Auguste Chouteau.
August 30, 1833. John Mullanphy.
September 3, 1838. Governor William Clark.
May 22, 1849. Immense Conflagration!
August 25, 1878. A Memoir of Charles Gratiot, Sr.
June 19, 1849. Cleansing The Streets.

The National Intelligencer
April 7, 1826. Alexander McNair.
June 16, 1851. Death of Judge Mullanphy.

New York Times
November 5, 1895. Death of Eugene Field.
October 7, 1949. Robert Hannegan Dies in Home at 46.
October 11, 1949. Hannegan's Rites Attended by 4,000.
January 5, 1965. Eliot T.S. Eliot, The Poet, is Dead in London at 76.
January 8, 1965. Eliot Cremated in London; BBC Planning a Tribute.
February 5, 1965. Eliot is Mourned in London Service.
April 18, 1965. T.S. Eliot's Ashes Interred at Church in East Coker.
July 4, 1973. Betty Grable, Movie Pin-Up of '40's, Dies.
April 13, 1975. Josephine Baker is Dead in Paris at 68.
April 16, 1975. Thousands Mob Funeral of Josephine Baker in Paris.
October 27, 1993. Vincent Price, Noted Actor of Dark Roles, Dies at 82.

St. Louis Globe-Democrat
October 17, 1879. Decease of Robert Campbell, A Public-Spirited Citizen.
October 20, 1879. The Remains of the Late Robert Campbell Laid to Rest.
May 11, 1884. Funeral Services.
May 11, 1885. Wayman Crow Passes Away in His 77th Year.

May 13, 1885. The Funerals of Wayman Crow and John W. Larimore.

January 24, 1887. Death of Dr. W.G. Eliot.

January 27, 1887. Dr. W.G. Eliot's Funeral.

February 15, 1891. General Sherman Closes His Eyes in Painless Death.

February 17, 1891. General Sherman's Remains.

February 18, 1891. The Dead Soldier.

February 19, 1891. The General Public Permitted to See General Sherman's . . Remains.

February 22, 1891. The Grave's Long Furlough.

November 5, 1895. Gene Field Dead.

March 5, 1896. Archbishop Kenrick Dead.

March 6, 1896. The Dead Prelate.

March 9, 1896. Body of Archbishop Kenrick Now at the Old Cathedral.

March 12, 1896. Kenrick Obsequies.

September 18, 1898. Death of Wm. S. Burroughs.

November 20, 1898. Gen. D.C. Buell Dead.

November 23, 1898. Gen. Buell's Remains Arrive.

July 10, 1901. Funeral of Mr. Yeatman.

February 14, 1904. Millionaire Brewer Lemp Kills Himself.

February 16, 1904. W.J. Lemp's Body is Laid in Mausoleum.

August 23, 1904. Mrs. Kate Chopin, the St. Louis Authoress, Dead.

April 5, 1908. Byron Nugent Will be Buried Tuesday.

April 8, 1908. Nugent Funeral is Held in Downpour.

November 4, 1911. N.J. Colman Rites by Masons Monday.

November 7, 1911. Hadley at Colman Rites.

May 11, 1913. Body of A.D. Brown to Arrive Monday.

May 14, 1913. World's Fair Directors Attend Brown Funeral.

June 6, 1913. Chris Von Der Ahe, Baseball Idol, Dies.

June 9, 1913. Old-Timers Help Bury Von Der Ahe.

April 23, 1914. Funeral For Charles C. Spink to be Held This Afternoon.

March 28, 1916. Miss Susan Blow's Funeral Will Be Held Here Tomorrow.

March 29, 1916. 80 Kindergarten Teachers to Attend Blow Funeral.

August 4, 1919. Samuel W. Fordyce, Multimillionaire, Dies in East.

August 7, 1919. Many of Two States at Fordyce Funeral.

March 21, 1920. Lemp Heiress Killed Self by Shooting.

May 29, 1920. John Scullin, Banker, 84 Years Old, Dies After Week's Illness.

June 1, 1920. Funeral Services for Scullin Held.

July 29, 1920. William Marion Reedy, Noted Editor, Dies Suddenly While . . Visiting San Francisco.

December 30, 1922. William J. Lemp's Suicide Recalls Similar Death of Father and . . Sister.

January 1, 1923. Simple Services Mark Funeral of W.J. Lemp.

March 22, 1923. Julius S. Walsh Will Be Buried Saturday.

November 13, 1923. Theodore C. Link, Well-Known Architect, to be Buried . . Tomorrow.

January 16, 1927. David R. Francis, Ex-Governor, Dies after Long Illness.

January 19, 1927. State and City Pay Tribute at Grave of David R. Francis.

February 2, 1928. Edward Mallinckrodt, Sr. Succumbs to Week's Illness of . . Pneumonia.

February 4, 1928. Last Rites for Mallinckrodt.

June 19, 1931. Three Negros Held in Probe Into Killing of Attorney Phillips.

June 21, 1931. Parents of Boy Held Critized Phillips.

October 30, 1931. William K. Bixby Funeral Service to be Held Tomorrow.

November 1, 1931. Eulogy is Omitted at Funeral Services for William K. Bixby.

November 16, 1932. Robert S. Brookings' Ashes to Be Brought Here After Funeral.

November 20, 1932. Simple Rites Held at Graham Chapel Over Brookings' Bier.

January 30, 1933. Sara Teasdale, St. Louis Poet, Is Found Dead in Bathtub in . . N.Y. Home.

March 20, 1933. John Francis Queeny, Philanthropist, Head of Monsanto, Dies.

July 15, 1938. Joseph Griesedieck Funeral Tomorrow, Died From Fall.

November 29, 1942. Brain Clot Fatal After Long Illness.

December 1, 1942. Hundreds Attend Kiel Funeral.

August 2, 1943. Mayor Becker, Five City Leaders Among 10 Killed in Glider . . Crash.

August 3, 1943. St. Louis to Stop Business Today to Honor Victims of Glider . . Crash Fatal to 10.

August 4, 1943. 2500 Attend Funeral for Mayor Becker.

November 13, 1946. A.B. Lambert Dies In Sleep; Burial Tomorrow.

November 15, 1946. Civic Leaders At Rites For Maj. Lambert.

May 10, 1949. Charles A. Lemp, Ex-Brewer, Kills Self as Did Three Others in . . Family.

January 19, 1961. Tom Dooley Dies of Cancer at 34.

January 24, 1961. Dr. Thomas Dooley Buried With Honors.

December 8, 1962. Head of Publishing Empire Was Lifelong Battler For Sports.

December 10, 1962. Last Rites Held for Taylor Spink.

June 13, 1967. Thousands File Past casket of Cardinal Ritter.

June 16, 1967. Cardinal Ritter Eulogized as Servant of God.

November 24, 1970. Ex-Mayor Raymond Tucker Dies.

July 4, 1973. Betty Grable, St. Louis Gift to Hollywood, Dies.

February 20, 1979. Crusade With a Legacy.

August 23, 1980. James S. McDonnell Dies; Giant of Aviation and Space.

September 1, 1980. Nearly 900 Attend McDonnell Memorial.

June 24, 1983. A. J. Cervantas Dies at 62; Flamboyant Symbol of a City.

St. Louis Post-Dispatch

September 17, 1875. Funeral of Mr. Blow.

October 17, 1879. Death of Robert Campbell.

May 11, 1885. Wayman Crow, J.W. Larimore and William Young Passed . . Away.

May 12, 1885. Wayman Crow.

January 27, 1887. Funeral of Rev. Dr. Eliot This Afternoon.

August 26, 1889. Scenes at the Death-Bed of the Venerable Henry Shaw.

August 27, 1889. Mr. Shaw's Mausoleum.

August 28, 1889. The Body of Henry Shaw placed in the Garden Museum.

November 22, 1898. Gen. Buell's Remains.

November 23, 1898. Burial of Gen. D.C. Buell.

July 9, 1901. James E. Yeatman's Remains Will Rest in Bellefontaine.

August 23, 1904. Death Comes to Mrs. Kate Chopin.

April 5, 1908. Byron Nugent Dies After Long Illness at Home.

November 3, 1911. Norman J. Colman Dies on a Train on His Way Home.

October 11, 1913. Adolphus Busch to be Buried Here; Left $40,000,000.

April 22, 1914. C.C. Spink, Rich Sportsman and Publisher, Dies.

June 13, 1914. Campbell's Body, Sent From East, to Arrive in St. Louis . . Sunday.

June 16, 1914. James Campbell Funeral Brief.

March 27, 1916. Miss Blow Who Put Kindergartens Here, Dies in East.

August 4, 1919. Reminiscences in The Busy Life of Samuel W. Fordyce.

August 6, 1919. Samuel Fordyce Funeral.

May 29, 1920. John Scullin Funeral at Church Monday Morning.

August 2, 1920. Reedy Funeral Wednesday.

August 4, 1920. F.W. Lehmann Speaks at Funeral of Reedy.

December 13, 1921. G.W. Brown, Head of Shoe Company, Dies in Arizona.

December 19, 1921. Brown Shoe Factories Closed For Funeral.

March 18, 1922. J.C. Cabanne Was Pioneer in Diary Business Here.

March 21, 1923. Julius S. Walsh, Banker, Dies at 80 of Heart Disease.

March 25, 1923. Julius S. Walsh Funeral Held.

November 12, 1923. Theodore C. Link, Designer of Union Station, Dies at 73.

February 1, 1928. Wealthy Head of Mallinckrodt Family Dies at 83.

May 28, 1928. Alfred I. Spink, Founder of The Sporting News, Dies.

June 18, 1931. Negro Attorney, Perjury Witness, Slain on Street.

January 30, 1933. Accidental Death Autopsy Report on Sara Teasdale.

March 20, 1933. John F. Queeny, Head of Monsanto Co., Dies.

July 14, 1938. Joseph Griesedieck Dies, Injured in Fall.

March 9, 1946. Archbishop Glennon Dies in Eire.

March 10, 1946. 4-Day Homage to Glennon in Ireland.

March 14, 1946. Glennon Plane Arrives; Mayor Heads Escort Party into City.

March 15, 1946. Thousands View Cardinal's Body at Cathedral; Rites Tomorrow.

March 16, 1946. Mourners Pack Cathedral, with Throng in Street at Glennon . . Rites.

November 12, 1946. Maj. A.B. Lambert Dies in His Sleep; Pioneer St. Louis . . Aviation Backer.

October 6, 1949. Robert E. Hannegan Dies at Home Here; Set Truman on Path to . . White House.

October 10, 1949. High Officials Attend Hannegan Funeral Services at Cathedral.

August 19, 1954. City's First Bishop to be Entombed Here.

January 5, 1965. St. Louis-Born T.S. Eliot Dies; Revolutionized English Poetry.

June 10, 1967. Cardinal Ritter Dies at 74 After Second Heart Attack.

November 24, 1970. Former Mayor Tucker Dies.

November 27, 1970. Simple Service at Parish Church For Former Mayor Tucker.

March 27, 1973. Greatest Brownie Dies at 80.

March 21, 1975. Cardinal Legend Medwick Dies.

January 28, 1980. Lynn Patrick Dies; Blues' First Coach.

February 25, 1983. Tennessee Williams Found dead In Hotel.

February 28, 1983. Tennessee Williams Will Be Buried Here.

March 6, 1983. Tennessee Williams Laid To Rest Here.

June 26, 1983. 2,000 Pay Tribute to Cervantas.

February 7, 1988. Death Ends Plager's Cancer Fight.

July 5, 1988. Joy, Song, Celebrate New Saint.

January 1, 1989. 1988 St. Louis Man of The Year: Robert Hyland.

February 11, 1989. Sportscaster Dan Kelly Dies at 52.

February 14, 1989. Kelly Called "Great Human Being".

September 30, 1989. Gussie Busch Dies at 90.

October 2, 1989. Gussie Busch Buried in Private Service.

October 4, 1989. Busch: Brewer Eulogized as Benevolent Leader.

March 8, 1991. Baseball's "Cool Papa" Bell Dies.

March 17, 1991. Belated Respect: Baseball Says Goodbye to "Cool Papa" Bell.

March 7, 1992. Region Remembers Robert Hyland as Community Leader.

March 10, 1992. Hyland Eulogized as Optimist.

March 27, 1992. C.C. Johnson Spink of the Sporting News Dies.

October 27, 1993. Actor's "Evil Eye" Belied Charm.

March 26, 1994. Archbishop May Dies of Cancer.

March 30, 1994. Mourners Honor Archbishop May.

March 31, 1994. Archdiocese Pays Its Final Respects to Archbishop May.

April 27, 1994. Final Tribute: Woman Works To Get Headstone For "Cool . . Papa".

July 12, 1995. "Benchwarmer" Bob Burnes Dies.

July 16, 1995. "Kind and Gentle" Burnes Remembered.

November 19, 1996. Colorful Hockey Announcer Gus Kyle Dies at 75.

The Sporting News
April 30, 1914. Charles Claude Spink.

December 22, 1962. Game, 'Bible' Mourn Death of Publisher.

February 20, 1989. For The Record, Obituaries.

Photography & Illustrations

Page 82. G. Brown. *History of St. Louis, The Fourth City.*

Page 82. Brown mausoleum. *Kevin Amsler.*

Page 83. Queeny's grave. *Kevin Amsler.*

Page 85. A. Lambert. *Jarvis Lambert.*

Page 87. Glider crash. *St. Louis Mercantile Library.*

Page 89. S. Teasdale. *Missouri Historical Society, St. Louis.*

Page 91. W. Lemp. *History of St. Louis, The Fourth City.*

Page 98. A. Spink. *History of St. Louis, The Fourth City.*

Page 99. Spink family mausoleum. *Kevin Amsler.*

Page 103. Griesedieck monument. *Kevin Amsler.*

Page 104. Hawken's grave. *Kevin Amsler.*

Page 104. P. Lindell. *History of St. Louis, The Fourth City.*

Page 106. B. Nugent. *History of St. Louis, The Fourth City.*

Page 106. Nugent ad. *St. Louis Post-Dispatch.*

Page 109. Calvary Cemetery. *Jeff Fister.*

Page 111. Calvary map. *Roger Kallerud.*

Page 113. A. Chouteau. *Encyclopedia of the History of St. Louis.*

Page 114. Chouteau house. *Missouri Historical Society, St. Louis.*

Page 115. P. Chouteau's grave. *Kevin Amsler.*

Page 119. J. Mullanphy. *Encyclopedia of the History of St. Louis.*

Page 120. Mullanphy's monument. *Jeff Fister.*

Page 123. J.B.C. Lucas. *History of St. Louis, The Fourth City.*

Page 124. A. McNair. *History of St. Louis, The Fourth City.*

Page 125. McNair's grave. *Jeff Fister.*

Page 126. D. Scott. *Missouri Historical Society, St. Louis.*

Page 127. Scott's grave. *Kevin Amsler.*

Page 132. W.T. Sherman. *History of St. Louis, The Fourth City.*

Page 134. Sherman funeral. *Missouri Historical Society, St. Louis. Boehl and Koenig, photographers.*

Page 137. K. Chopin. *Missouri Historical Society, St. Louis. J. J. Scholten, photographer.*

Page 143. T. Williams' funeral. *St. Louis Mercantile Library.*

Page 144. A. Cervantes. *Missouri Historical Society, St. Louis.*

Page 146. R. Hyland. *West End Word.*

Page 149. Dooley grave. *Jeff Fister.*

Page 150. J. Cabanne. *Encyclopedia of the History of St. Louis.*

Page 154. J. Walsh. *History of St. Louis, The Fourth City.*

Page 157. Bloody Island. *St. Louis: Its Neighborhoods & Neighbors.*

Page 165. Biddle mausoleum. *Kevin Amsler.*

Page 168. Fire damage map. *Missouri Republican.*

Page 171. St. Louis Cathedral. *Arteaga photos.*

Page 173. R.P. Duchesne. *Phillipine Duchesne, Frontier Missionary of the Sacred Heart.*

Page 177. H. Shaw. *West End Word.*

Page 178. Shaw's grave. *Kevin Amsler.*

Page 180. De Smet's grave. *Kevin Amsler.*

Page 183. J. Glennon. *St. Louis Cathedral archives.*

Page 186. Busch's grave. *Kevin Amsler.*

Page 189. H. Kiel. *Missouri Historical Society, St. Louis.*

Page 192. J. Ritter. *St. Louis Cathedral archives.*

Page 194. G. Sisler. *Kevin Amsler.*

Page 200. R. Burnes. *Southtown Word. Claire Ruzicka, photographer.*

Page 201. J. May. *West End Word.*

Page 202. Kelly's grave. *Kevin Amsler.*

Page 207. Field's grave. *Kevin Amsler.*

Page 211. T.S. Eliot. *The Austin American-Statesman.*

Page 214. J. Baker. *St. Louis Mercantile Library.*

Page 218. B. Grable. *St. Louis Mercantile Library.*

INDEX

E

F

G

H

I

ABOUT THE AUTHOR

Kevin Amsler has been writing freelance for several years. Most of his time has been dedicated to novel and screenplay writing. Two of his screenplays have won him honorable mentions in nationwide screenwriting contests. His travel article regarding a Civil War battlefield was published last summer.

Kevin was born and raised in South St. Louis County. He attended Vianney High School, Meramec Community College, and the University of Missouri-St. Louis.